FINLAND

RUSSIA

ESTONIA

LATVIA

LITHUANIA

BELARUS

UKRAINE

MOLDOVA

ROMANIA

SERBIA

MACEDONIA

GREECE

Aegean

BULGARIA

*Black
Sea*

TURKEY

GEORGIA

AZERBAIJAN

ARMENIA

CYPRUS

nean Sea

The
Economist

POCKET
EUROPE
IN FIGURES

THE ECONOMIST IN ASSOCIATION WITH
PROFILE BOOKS LTD

This fourth edition published in 2000 by Profile Books Ltd,
58A Hatton Garden, London EC1N 8LX

First published by The Economist Books Ltd 1997

Material researched and compiled by
Mark Doyle, Robert Eves, Andrew Gilbert, Conrad Heine,
Carol Howard, Stella Jones, David McKelvey,
Henrietta Nelder, Simon Wright

Typeset in Univers by MacGuru
info@macguru.org.uk

Printed by
LEGO S.p.a. – Vicenza – Italy

A CIP catalogue record for this book is available
from the British Library

ISBN 1 86197 240 7

Contents

CONTENTS

CONTENTS

Notes

In this fourth edition of *The Economist Pocket Europe in Figures* we present a detailed picture of Europe today: how its countries compare and how they have changed over recent decades. The contents list on the previous pages gives a full list of the hundreds of subjects covered in the 11 main sections. Some 48 countries are considered.

The research for this book was carried out in 2000 using the most up-to-date and most authoritative sources available. The sources used are listed at the end of the book.

The extent and quality of the statistics available varies from country to country. Every care has been taken to specify the broad definitions on which the data are based and to indicate cases where data quality or technical difficulties are such that interpretation of the figures is likely to be seriously affected. Nevertheless, figures from individual countries will often differ from standard international statistical definitions. Availability of data also varies, particularly for the transition economies.

Serbia and Montenegro make up the Federal Republic of Yugoslavia. Macedonia is officially known as the Former Yugoslav Republic of Macedonia. Data for Cyprus normally refer to Greek Cyprus only. Data for the European Union (EU) refer to its 15 members following enlargement of the Union on January 1 1995. The euro zone's 11 members are all of the EU15 except Denmark, Greece, Sweden and the United Kingdom.

The all-important factor in a book of this kind is to be able to make reliable comparisons between countries. Although this is never quite possible for the reasons stated above, the best route, which this book takes, is to compare data for the same year or period and to use actual, not estimated, figures wherever possible.

Most countries' national accounts are now compiled on a GDP basis so, for simplicity, the term GDP has been used interchangeably with GNP.

Statistics for principal exports and principal imports are normally based on customs statistics. These are generally compiled on different definitions to the visible exports and imports figures shown in the balance of payments sections.

Figures may not add exactly to totals, or percentages to 100, because of rounding or statistical adjustment. Sums of money have generally been converted to US dollars at the official exchange rate ruling at the time to which the figures refer.

Definitions of the statistics are given on the relevant page or in the glossary on pages 12–14, which also explains various other terms.

Glossary

Balance of payments The record of a country's transactions with the rest of the world. The current account of the balance of payments consists of visible trade (goods), invisible trade (income and expenditure for services such as banking, insurance, tourism and shipping, together with profits earned overseas and interest payments) and current transfers (remittances from those working abroad, payments to international organisations, famine relief). Imports include the cost of "carriage, insurance and freight" (cif) from the exporting country to the importing. The value of exports does not include these elements and is recorded "free on board" (fob). Balance of payments statistics are generally adjusted so that both exports and imports are shown fob; the cif element is included in invisibles.

Big Mac index As published by *The Economist* it is based on the theory of purchasing-power parity, the notion that a dollar should buy the same amount in all countries; in the long run, the exchange rate between two currencies should move towards the rate that would equalise the price of an identical basket of goods and services in each country. Our "basket" is a McDonald's Big Mac, which is produced "locally" in 110 countries.

Crude birth rate The number of live births per 1,000 population. The crude rate will automatically be high if a large proportion of the population is of child-bearing age.

Crude death rate The number of deaths in one year per 1,000 population. Also affected by the population's age structure.

Current prices These are in nominal terms and do not take into account the effect of inflation.

Enrolment Gross enrolment ratios may exceed 100% because some pupils are younger or older than the standard primary or secondary school age.

ECSC European Coal and Steel Community, established by the Treaty of Paris, signed April 18th 1951 and effective 1952.

Ecu European currency unit. An accounting measure used within the EU and composed of a weighted basket of the currencies of 12 EU members. Replaced by the euro on January 1st, 1999.

EEC European Economic Community, established by the Treaty of Rome, signed March 25th 1957, effective 1958. The European Atomic Energy Community (Euratom) came into effect at the same time.

EMU Economic and monetary union. Stages for implementation were proposed in the Delors report which followed the 1988 Hanover European Council meeting. The Maastricht treaty agreed in December 1991 laid out a timetable for progress towards EMU and the adoption of a single currency.

EC European Community. Merger of ECSC, EEC and Euratom signed April 8th 1965, effective 1967.

EU European Union. Following the treaty agreed at Maastricht in December 1991 the EC was formally incorporated into a new and broader European Union. Until 1995 it had 12 members: Belgium, Denmark, France, Germany, Greece, Ireland, Italy, Luxembourg, Netherlands, Portugal, Spain and the United Kingdom. From January 1st 1995 membership increased to 15 as Austria, Finland and Sweden joined the Union.

Euro Introduced on January 1st, 1999, replacing the ecu. The euro zone's 11 members are all of the EU 15 except Denmark, Greece, Sweden and the United Kingdom.

Fertility rate The average number of children born to a woman who completes her childbearing years.

Foreign direct investment The purchase of assets in another country by a company or individual plus reinvested earnings and intra-company loans.

G7 The Group of Seven. Members are Canada, France, Germany, Italy, Japan, the United Kingdom and the United States.

GDP Gross domestic product. It is the sum of all output produced by economic activity within that country. GNP (gross national product) includes net income from abroad eg. rent, profits. For simplicity, the term GDP has been used interchangeably with GNP.

Government Finance and tax data may refer to central government only or to general government which includes central state and local government and the social security sectors.

Infant mortality rate The annual number of deaths of infants under one year of age per 1,000 live births.

Inflation The annual rate at which prices are increasing or decreasing. The most common measure is the change in the consumer price index.

Internet host A domain name that has an Internet address associated with it (eg www.economist.com). This would be any computer system connected to the Internet.

Invisible trade Exports and imports of such items you cannot drop on your foot, that is, services such as shipping, insurance and banking plus profits, dividends and interest received by or from overseas residents.

Life expectancy The average length of time a newborn baby can expect to live.

Market capitalisation The value of a company or companies calculated by multiplying the number of issued shares by their market price at a given time.

Marginal tax rate The rate of tax paid on an extra unit of income.

Migration rate The number of people per 1,000 population emigrating (minus figure) or immigrating (plus figure) to the relevant country.

Money supply A measure of the "money" available to buy goods and services. Various definitions of money supply exist. The measures used here are based on definitions used by the IMF and may differ from measures used nationally. Narrow money consists of cash in circulation and demand deposits; broad money also includes savings and foreign currency deposits.

OECD Organisation for Economic Co-operation and Development. The "rich countries' club" established in 1961. Now has 29 members: Australia, Austria, Belgium, Canada, Czech Republic, Denmark, Finland, France, Germany, Greece, Hungary, Iceland, Ireland, Italy, Japan, Luxembourg, Mexico, Netherlands, New Zealand, Norway, Poland, Portugal, South Korea, Spain, Sweden, Switzerland, Turkey, United Kingdom, United States.

Population density The total number of inhabitants divided by the surface area.

Real terms Figures are adjusted to allow for inflation.

Reserves The stock of gold and foreign currency held by a country to finance any calls that may be made for the settlement of foreign debt. Also used to buy and sell foreign currency to control fluctuations.

Trade-weighted exchange rates This measures a currency's depreciation (figures below 100) or appreciation (figures over 100) from a base date against a trade-weighted basket of the country's main trading partners.

Visible trade Exports and imports of things you can drop on your foot such as bricks, brass and bombs.

Part I
LAND
AND THE
ENVIRONMENT

Land and land use

Biggest countries
Land area, sq km

1	Russia	17,075,400	26	Lithuania	65,200
2	Turkey	779,450	27	Latvia	64,589
3	Ukraine	603,700	28	Croatia	56,540
4	France	551,500	29	Bosnia	51,130
5	Spain	504,780	30	Slovakia	49,500
6	Sweden	449,960	31	Estonia	45,125
7	Germany	356,910	32	Denmark	43,070
8	Finland	338,130	33	Switzerland	41,290
9	Norway	323,900	34	Netherlands	37,330
10	Poland	312,680	35	Moldova	33,700
11	Italy	301,270	36	Belgium	33,100
12	United Kingdom	244,880	37	Armenia	29,000
13	Romania	237,500	38	Albania	28,750
14	Belarus	207,600	39	Macedonia	25,715
15	Greece	131,990	40	Slovenia	20,250
16	Bulgaria	110,910	41	Cyprus	9,251
17	Iceland	103,000	42	Luxembourg	2,586
18	Hungary	93,030	43	Andorra	468
19	Portugal	92,390	44	Malta	320
20	Serbia & Montenegro	88,361	45	Liechtenstein	160
21	Azerbaijan	86,600	46	San Marino	61
22	Austria	83,850	47	Monaco	2
23	Czech Republic	78,370	48	Vatican	0.44
24	Ireland	70,280			
25	Georgia	69,700		**Total Europe**	23,933,278

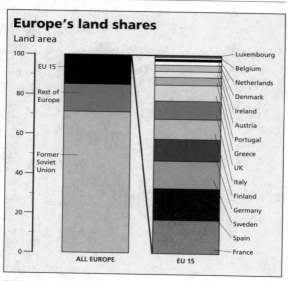

Europe's land shares
Land area

ALL EUROPE — EU 15, Rest of Europe, Former Soviet Union

EU 15 — Luxembourg, Belgium, Netherlands, Denmark, Ireland, Austria, Portugal, Greece, UK, Italy, Finland, Germany, Sweden, Spain, France

How agricultural?
Agricultural land as % of land area

1	Ireland	81		Belgium	45
2	Moldova	80		Luxembourg	45
3	Ukraine	73	26	Armenia	44
4	United Kingdom	71		Portugal	44
5	Greece	68	28	Croatia	43
6	Hungary	66		Slovenia	43
7	Denmark	65	30	Austria	42
	Romania	65	31	Albania	41
9	Liechtenstein	63		Malta	41
10	Poland	61	33	Latvia	40
11	Spain	60		Switzerland	40
12	Netherlands	59	35	Bosnia	39
13	Andorra	58		Germany	39
14	Italy	56	37	Georgia	38
15	Bulgaria	55	38	Estonia	34
	France	55	39	Iceland	23
17	Czech Republic	54	40	Cyprus	17
	Lithuania	54		San Marino	17
19	Turkey	52	42	Russia	12
20	Macedonia	51	43	Finland	8
	Slovakia	51		Sweden	8
22	Azerbaijan	48	45	Norway	3
23	Belarus	45			

How forested?
Forested area as % of land area

1	Finland	76		Romania	29
2	Sweden	68	24	France	27
3	Slovenia	51		Norway	27
4	Estonia	48	26	Turkey	26
5	Latvia	46	27	Italy	23
	Russia	46	28	Andorra	22
7	Slovakia	41	29	Belarus	21
8	Austria	39		Luxembourg	21
	Bosnia	39	31	Greece	20
	Macedonia	39	32	Hungary	19
11	Albania	38		Liechtenstein	19
	Croatia	38	34	Ukraine	18
13	Portugal	36	35	Armenia	15
14	Bulgaria	35	36	Cyprus	13
15	Belgium	34		Moldova	13
	Czech Republic	34	38	Azerbaijan	11
	Georgia	34	39	Denmark	10
18	Spain	32		Netherlands	10
	Switzerland	32		United Kingdom	10
20	Germany	31	42	Ireland	5
	Lithuania	31	43	Iceland	1
22	Poland	29			

Natural facts

National high points
Metres

1	Russia	Elbrus	5,642
2	Georgia	Mount Shkhara	5,203
3	Turkey	Mount Ararat	5,165
4	France	Mont Blanc	4,808
5	Italy	Monte Bianco	4,808
6	Switzerland	Dufourspitze	4,634
7	Azerbaijan	Bazar-Dyuzi	4,480
8	Armenia	Transcaucasia	4,090
9	Austria	Grossglockner	3,797
10	Spain	Pico de Teide	3,715
11	Germany	Zugspitze	2,962
12	Andorra	Pia de l'Estany	2,951
13	Bulgaria	Musala	2,925
14	Greece	Mount Olympus	2,917
15	Slovenia	Triglan	2,863
16	Albania	Korab	2,764
17	Macedonia	Korab	2,764
18	Serbia & Montenegro	Daravica	2,656
19	Slovakia	Gerlachovsky	2,655
20	Liechtenstein	Grauspitz	2,599
21	Romania	Negoiu	2,548
22	Poland	Mount Rysy	2,499
23	Norway	Glittertind	2,470
24	Bosnia	Maglic	2,396
25	Portugal	Ponta do Pico	2,351
26	Iceland	Hvannadalshnúkur	2,119
27	Sweden	Kebnekaise	2,111
28	Ukraine	Mount Goverla	2,061
29	Cyprus	Mount Olympus	1,951
30	Croatia	Troglav	1,913
31	Czech Republic	Sniezka	1,602
32	United Kingdom	Ben Nevis	1,342
33	Finland	Haltiatunturi	1,328
34	Ireland	Carrauntoohil	1,038
35	Hungary	Kékestetö	1,014
36	San Marino	Monte Titano	793
37	Belgium	Signal de Botranges	694
38	Luxembourg	Buurgplaatz	559
39	Moldova	Mount Balaneshty	429
40	Belarus	Dzyarzhynskaya	346
41	Netherlands	Vaalserberg	321
42	Estonia	Suur Munamagi	318
43	Latvia	Uidzeme	312
44	Lithuania	Jouzapine	294
45	Malta	Dingli Cliffs	253
46	Denmark	Yding Skovhoj	173

Highest mountains

Metres

1	Elbrus	Russia	5,642
2	Mount Shkhara	Georgia	5,203
3	Rustiveli	Russia	5,201
4	Dykh-Tau	Russia	5,198
5	Mount Ararat	Turkey	5,165
6	Kazbek	Russia	5,047
7	Mont Blanc	France/Italy	4,807
8	Klyuchevskaya	Russia	4,750
9	Ushba	Russia	4,710
10	Dufourspitze	Switzerland	4,634
11	Dom	Switzerland/Italy	4,545
12	Bazar-Dyuzi	Azerbaijan	4,480
13	Matterhorn	Italy/Switzerland	4,478
14	Dente Blanche	Switzerland/Italy	4,357
15	Nadelhorn	Switzerland/Italy	4,327

Longest rivers

Km

		Outflow	
1	Volga	Russia	3,530
2	Danube	Romania	2,860
3	Dnieper	Ukraine	2,200
4	Don	Russia	1,870
5	Northern Dvina	Russia	1,860
6	Pechora	Russia	1,810
7	Kama	Russia	1,800
8	Oka	Russia	1,500
9	Belaya	Russia	1,430
10	Kura	Azerbaijan	1,360
11	Dniester	Moldova	1,350
12	Rhine	Netherlands	1,320
13	Vyatka	Russia	1,310
14	Vistula	Poland	1,200
15	Elbe	Germany	1,160

Longest coastlines

Km

1	Russia	37,653	14	Germany	2,389
2	Norway	21,925	15	Portugal	1,793
3	Greece	13,676	16	Ireland	1,448
4	United Kingdom	12,429	17	Estonia	1,393
5	Turkey	7,200	18	Finland	1,126
6	Croatia	5,790	19	Cyprus	648
7	Italy	4,996	20	Latvia	531
8	Iceland	4,988	21	Poland	491
9	Spain	4,964	22	Netherlands	451
10	France	3,427	23	Albania	362
11	Denmark	3,379	24	Bulgaria	354
12	Sweden	3,218	25	Georgia	310
13	Ukraine	2,782	26	Romania	225

Saving nature

Protected areas
Number, 1997

1	Germany	518	19	Bulgaria	49
2	Sweden	241	20	Latvia	45
3	Spain	217	21	Czech Republic	44
4	Russia	210	22	Slovakia	41
5	Austria	176	23	Romania	39
6	Italy	169	24	Serbia & Montenegro	27
7	United Kingdom	148	25	Croatia	26
8	France	132	26	Albania	25
9	Finland	126		Ukraine	25
10	Norway	118	28	Greece	24
11	Denmark	112		Iceland	24
12	Switzerland	107		Portugal	24
13	Poland	106	31	Macedonia	16
14	Lithuania	79	32	Slovenia	14
15	Netherlands	75	33	Ireland	13
16	Belarus	57		Moldova	13
17	Hungary	54	35	Bosnia	5
18	Estonia	53	36	Belgium	4

Biosphere reserves
Number, 1997

1	Bulgaria	17	15	Belarus	2
2	Russia	16		Finland	2
3	Spain	14		Greece	2
4	Germany	13		Ireland	2
	United Kingdom	13	19	Croatia	1
6	France	8		Denmark	1
7	Poland	7		Estonia	1
8	Czech Republic	6		Netherlands	1
9	Hungary	5		Norway	1
10	Austria	4		Portugal	1
	Slovakia	4		Serbia & Montenegro	1
12	Italy	3		Sweden	1
	Romania	3		Switzerland	1
	Ukraine	3			

Protected wetlands
Number, 1997

1	United Kingdom	107	12	France	15
2	Italy	46	13	Finland	11
3	Ireland	45	14	Estonia	10
4	Denmark	38		Greece	10
	Spain	38		Portugal	10
6	Russia	35	17	Austria	9
7	Germany	31		Czech Republic	9
8	Sweden	30	19	Poland	8
9	Norway	23		Switzerland	8
10	Hungary	19	21	Slovakia	7
11	Netherlands	18	22	Belgium	6

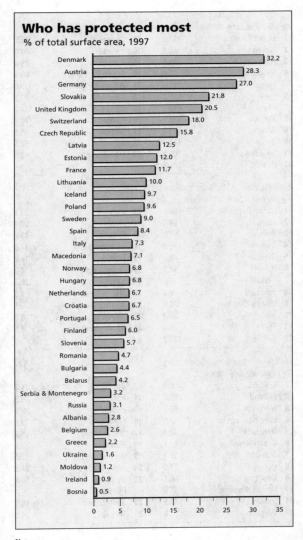

Who has protected most
% of total surface area, 1997

Denmark	32.2
Austria	28.3
Germany	27.0
Slovakia	21.8
United Kingdom	20.5
Switzerland	18.0
Czech Republic	15.8
Latvia	12.5
Estonia	12.0
France	11.7
Lithuania	10.0
Iceland	9.7
Poland	9.6
Sweden	9.0
Spain	8.4
Italy	7.3
Macedonia	7.1
Norway	6.8
Hungary	6.8
Netherlands	6.7
Croatia	6.7
Portugal	6.5
Finland	6.0
Slovenia	5.7
Romania	4.7
Bulgaria	4.4
Belarus	4.2
Serbia & Montenegro	3.2
Russia	3.1
Albania	2.8
Belgium	2.6
Greece	2.2
Ukraine	1.6
Moldova	1.2
Ireland	0.9
Bosnia	0.5

0   5   10   15   20   25   30   35

Notes
Protected areas are areas of at least 1,000 hectares that fall into the following categories: scientific or nature reserves; national parks; natural monuments or landscapes with some unique aspects; wildlife sanctuaries; other protected landscapes or seascapes.
Biosphere reserves are those internationally recognised supporting, self-sustaining and self-regulating ecological systems.

Air pollution

Carbon monoxide emissions
Kg per head, late-1990s

1	Luxembourg	194.8	13	Denmark	105.6
2	Norway	148.9	14	Ireland	91.0
3	Iceland	144.0	15	Finland	89.9
4	Belgium	141.4	16	Czech Republic	85.1
	France	141.4	17	United Kingdom	79.0
6	Italy	135.3	18	Germany	77.7
7	Portugal	133.1	19	Turkey	74.2
8	Greece	130.8	20	Hungary	70.9
9	Austria	123.2	21	Switzerland	65.5
10	Spain	111.5	22	Slovakia	62.5
11	Sweden	109.4	23	Netherlands	52.9
12	Russia	107.9			

Sulphur dioxides emissions
Kg per head, late-1990s

1	Czech Republic	68.0	13	Italy	23.1
2	Hungary	64.5	14	Denmark	20.7
3	Poland	61.3	15	Finland	19.5
4	Spain	49.1	16	Germany	17.9
5	Greece	48.2	17	France	16.2
6	Ireland	45.1	18	Luxembourg	14.3
7	Slovakia	37.5	19	Sweden	10.3
8	Portugal	36.2	20	Netherlands	8.0
9	United Kingdom	34.5	21	Austria	7.1
10	Iceland	32.3	22	Norway	6.9
11	Turkey	29.8	23	Switzerland	4.5
12	Belgium	23.7			

Nitrogen oxides emissions
Kg per head, late-1990s

1	Iceland	105.9	13	Spain	31.7
2	Finland	50.6	14	Italy	30.9
3	Norway	50.5	15	Poland	29.9
4	Luxembourg	47.5	16	France	29.1
5	Denmark	47.0	17	Netherlands	28.5
6	Czech Republic	41.1	18	Slovakia	23.1
7	Sweden	38.1	19	Germany	22.0
8	Portugal	37.6	20	Austria	21.2
9	Greece	35.1	21	Hungary	19.4
10	United Kingdom	35.0		Russia	19.4
11	Ireland	33.9	23	Switzerland	18.0
12	Belgium	32.9	24	Turkey	14.5

Emissions of volatile organic compounds
Kg per head, late-1990s

#	Country	Value	#	Country	Value
1	Norway	81.6	13	Spain	29.6
2	Austria	47.7	14	Ireland	28.7
3	Sweden	47.2	15	Denmark	28.3
4	Luxembourg	42.8	16	Switzerland	27.3
5	France	42.0	17	Czech Republic	26.4
	Greece	42.0	18	Russia	22.1
7	Italy	41.3	19	Germany	22.0
8	Iceland	36.3	20	Netherlands	21.4
9	United Kingdom	35.9	21	Poland	19.8
10	Finland	35.4	22	Slovakia	16.9
11	Portugal	34.7	23	Hungary	14.9
12	Belgium	29.8			

Emissions of carbon dioxide

	m tonnes, 1996			*Per head, tonnes, 1996*	
1	Russia	1,579.5	1	Norway	15.3
2	Germany	861.2	2	Czech Republic	12.3
3	United Kingdom	557.0	3	Finland	11.5
4	Italy	403.2	4	Estonia	11.2
5	Ukraine	397.3	5	Denmark	10.7
6	France	361.8		Russia	10.7
7	Poland	356.8	7	Germany	10.5
8	Spain	232.5	8	Belgium	10.4
9	Turkey	178.3	9	Netherlands	10.0
10	Netherlands	155.2	10	Ireland	9.6
11	Czech Republic	126.7	11	United Kingdom	9.5
12	Romania	119.3	12	Poland	9.2
13	Belgium	106.0	13	Ukraine	7.8
14	Greece	80.6	14	Greece	7.7
15	Norway	67.0	15	Austria	7.4
16	Belarus	61.7		Slovakia	7.4
17	Hungary	59.5	17	Italy	7.0
18	Austria	59.3	18	Bulgaria	6.6
19	Finland	59.2	19	Slovenia	6.5
20	Denmark	56.6	20	Macedonia	6.4
21	Bulgaria	55.3	21	Switzerland	6.3
22	Sweden	54.1	22	France	6.2
23	Portugal	47.9	23	Sweden	6.1
24	Switzerland	44.2	24	Belarus	6.0
25	Slovakia	39.6	25	Spain	5.9
26	Ireland	34.9	26	Hungary	5.8
27	Azerbaijan	30.0	27	Romania	5.3
28	Croatia	17.5	28	Portugal	4.8
29	Estonia	16.4	29	Azerbaijan	3.9
30	Lithuania	13.8		Croatia	3.9
31	Slovenia	13.0	31	Latvia	3.7
32	Macedonia	12.7		Lithuania	3.7
33	Moldova	12.1	33	Turkey	2.9
34	Latvia	9.3	34	Moldova	2.8

Waste and recycling

Total waste generation by sector

Agriculture, '000 tonnes, latest available

1	France	377,000	7	Norway	18,000
2	Spain	114,000	8	Netherlands	17,000
3	United Kingdom	80,000	9	Greece	7,780
4	Hungary	62,000	10	Czech Republic	5,460
5	Ireland	31,000	11	Slovakia	4,500
6	Finland	22,000			

Mining and quarrying, '000 tonnes, latest available

1	Poland	82,670	9	Czech Republic	5,000
2	France	75,000	10	Greece	3,900
3	United Kingdom	74,000	11	Ireland	2,200
4	Spain	70,000	12	Belgium	810
5	Sweden	47,000	13	Hungary	790
6	Germany	16,830	14	Slovakia	790
7	Finland	15,000	15	Portugal	470
8	Norway	7,600	16	Netherlands	330

Manufacturing, '000 tonnes, latest available

1	France	101,000	12	Netherlands	8,810
2	Germany	63,090	13	Slovakia	6,720
3	United Kingdom	56,000	14	Greece	6,680
4	Czech Republic	38,570	15	Ireland	3,780
5	Turkey	28,110	16	Norway	2,880
6	Italy	22,210	17	Denmark	2,740
7	Poland	22,200	18	Switzerland	1,500
8	Sweden	13,970	19	Luxembourg	1,440
9	Spain	13,830	20	Portugal	420
10	Belgium	13,730	21	Iceland	10
11	Finland	11,400			

Energy production, '000 tonnes, latest available

1	Germany	19,590	9	Netherlands	1,400
2	Poland	18,030	10	Finland	1,350
3	Czech Republic	17,060	11	Italy	1,330
4	United Kingdom	13,000	12	Belgium	1,140
5	Greece	9,300	13	Hungary	1,080
6	Turkey	8,680	14	Sweden	680
7	Slovakia	2,900	15	Portugal	390
8	Denmark	1,780	16	Ireland	350

Nuclear waste

Tonnes of heavy metal, 1998

1	France	1,165	6	Spain[a]	97
2	United Kingdom[a]	785	7	Finland	72
3	Germany	430	8	Switzerland	64
4	Sweden[a]	232	9	Hungary	53
5	Belgium	141	10	Czech Republic	45

a Provisional.

Municipal waste
Municipal, '000 tonnes, 1997

#	Country	Value	#	Country	Value
1	Russia	50,000	13	Austria	4,110
2	Germany	36,976	14	Greece	3,900
3	France	28,800	15	Portugal	3,800
4	United Kingdom	28,000	16	Czech Republic	3,200
5	Italy	26,605		Sweden	3,200
6	Turkey	20,253	18	Denmark	2,951
7	Spain	15,307	19	Norway	2,721
8	Poland	12,183	20	Finland	2,100
9	Netherlands	8,716	21	Ireland	2,032
10	Hungary	5,000	22	Slovakia	1,800
11	Belgium	4,852	23	Luxembourg	193
12	Switzerland	4,277	24	Iceland	150

Kg generated per person, 1997

#	Country	Value	#	Country	Value
1	Norway	630		Italy	460
2	Switzerland	600		Luxembourg	460
3	Denmark	560	15	Finland	410
	Iceland	560	16	Spain	390
	Ireland	560	17	Portugal	380
	Netherlands	560	18	Greece	370
7	Austria	510	19	Sweden	360
8	Hungary	500	20	Russia	340
9	Belgium	480		Slovakia	340
	France	480	22	Turkey	330
	United Kingdom	480	23	Poland	320
12	Germany	460	24	Czech Republic	310

Recovery rates
%, 1997

Paper and cardboard

#	Country	Value
1	Germany	70
2	Austria	69
3	Switzerland	63
4	Netherlands	62
	Sweden	62
6	Finland[a]	57
7	Denmark	50
8	Hungary[b]	49
9	Norway	44
10	Spain	42
11	France	41
12	Portugal	40
	United Kingdom	40
14	Turkey	36
15	Slovakia	34
16	Czech Republic	33
17	Italy	31

Glass

#	Country	Value
1	Switzerland	91
2	Austria	88
3	Netherlands	82
4	Germany	79
5	Norway	76
	Sweden	76
7	Belgium	75
	Iceland[c]	75
9	Denmark	70
10	Finland	62
11	France	52
12	Poland	44
13	Slovakia	40
14	Ireland	38
15	Spain	37
16	Italy	34

a 1995   b 1996   c 1992

Weather

Hot spots
Highest average temperatures[a], July, °C

1	Cyprus	Nicosia	37
2	Spain	Seville	36
3	Greece	Trikkala	35
4	Armenia	Erivan	34
5	Turkey	Izmir	33
6	Albania	Tirane	31
	Bulgaria	Plovdiv	31
	Georgia	Tbilisi	31
	Macedonia	Skopje	31
	Russia	Astrakhan	31
11	Italy	Palermo	30
	Romania	Bucharest	30
13	Croatia	Dubrovnik	29
	France	Marseille	29
	Malta	Valletta	29
16	Hungary	Budapest	28
	Portugal	Faro	28
	Serbia	Belgrade	28
	Ukraine	Simferopol	28

Cold spots
Lowest average temperatures[a], January, °C

1	Russia	Perm	-20
2	Finland	Inari	-18
	Turkey	Kars	-18
4	Norway	Spitzbergen[c]	-15
5	Sweden	Pitea[b]	-14
6	Estonia	Tallin[b]	-11
	Lithuania	Vilnius	-11
	Switzerland	Santis	-11
9	Spain	Madrid	-10
	Ukraine	Kiev	-10
	Latvia	Riga	-10
12	Armenia	Erivan	-9
	Austria	Klagenfurt	-9
14	Moldova	Kishinev	-8
15	Romania	Bucharest	-7
	Slovakia	Kosice	-7
	Poland	Przemysl	-7
18	Hungary	Debrecen	-6
19	Czech Republic	Brno	-5
	France	Embrun	-5
	Germany	Munich	-5

Most rain[a]

	Country	Place	mm rain	Month	Rainy days[c]
1	Switzerland	Santis[d]	302	Jul	18
2	Norway	Bergen	235	Oct	23
3	Albania	Tirane	211	Nov	16
4	Russia	Sochi	201	Jan	17
5	Croatia	Dubrovnik	198	nov	16
6	United Kingdom	Oban[d]	172	Dec	22
7	Ireland	Valentia[e]	168	Dec	21
	Portugal	Oporto	168	Dec	18
9	Spain	Santante	159	Dec	18
10	Slovenia	Ljubljano	151	Oct	14
11	Italy	Naples[e]	147	Nov	11
12	Germany	Munich	139	Jul	16
13	Austria	Innsbruck	134	Jul	19
14	Cyprus	Kyrenia	133	Dec	11
	France	Cherbourg	133	Nov	17
16	Greece	Trikkala	125	Dec	17
17	Monaco	Monte Carlo	123	Nov	7
18	Turkey	Izmir[e]	122	Dec	10
19	Romania	Bucher	121	Jun	12
20	Poland	Cracow	111	Jul	16

a Average. b February.
c Number of days with more than 1mm of rain.
d >0.25mm. e >1.0mm.

Part II

POPULATION

Population

From biggest to smallest
Population, m

1998			2025		
1	Russia	147.43	1	Russia	137.93
2	Germany	82.13	2	Turkey	87.87
3	Turkey	64.48	3	Germany	80.24
4	France	58.68	4	France	61.66
5	United Kingdom	58.65	5	United Kingdom	59.96
6	Italy	57.37	6	Italy	51.27
7	Ukraine	50.86	7	Ukraine	45.69
8	Spain	39.63	8	Poland	39.07
9	Poland	38.72	9	Spain	36.66
10	Romania	22.47	10	Romania	19.95
11	Netherlands	15.68	11	Netherlands	15.78
12	Serbia & Montenegro	10.64	12	Serbia & Montenegro	10.84
13	Greece	10.60	13	Belgium	9.92
14	Belarus	10.32	14	Greece	9.86
15	Czech Republic	10.28	15	Czech Republic	9.51
16	Belgium	10.14	16	Belarus	9.50
17	Hungary	10.12	17	Azerbaijan	9.40
18	Portugal	9.87	18	Portugal	9.35
19	Sweden	8.88	19	Sweden	9.10
20	Bulgaria	8.34	20	Hungary	8.90
21	Austria	8.14	21	Austria	8.19
22	Azerbaijan	7.67	22	Switzerland	7.59
23	Switzerland	7.30	23	Bulgaria	7.02
24	Slovakia	5.38	24	Slovakia	5.39
25	Denmark	5.27	25	Finland	5.25
26	Finland	5.15	26	Denmark	5.24
27	Georgia	5.06	27	Georgia	5.18
28	Croatia	4.48	28	Norway	4.82
29	Norway	4.42	29	Moldova	4.55
30	Moldova	4.38	30	Ireland	4.40
31	Lithuania	3.69	31	Bosnia	4.32
32	Ireland	3.68	32	Croatia	4.19
33	Bosnia	3.68	33	Armenia	3.95
34	Armenia	3.54	34	Albania	3.82
35	Albania	3.12	35	Lithuania	3.40
36	Latvia	2.42	36	Macedonia	2.26
37	Macedonia	2.00	37	Latvia	1.94
38	Slovenia	1.99	38	Slovenia	1.82
39	Estonia	1.43	39	Estonia	1.13
40	Cyprus	0.77	40	Cyprus	0.90
41	Luxembourg	0.42	41	Luxembourg	0.46
42	Malta	0.38	42	Malta	0.43
43	Iceland	0.28	43	Iceland	0.33
44	Liechtenstein	0.03			
	Monaco	0.03			
	San Marino	0.03			

Fastest growth
Annual average population growth, %

1990–98			1998–2005		
1	Turkey	1.87	1	Turkey	3.92
2	Cyprus	1.65	2	Cyprus	2.85
3	Luxembourg	1.35	3	Luxembourg	2.47
4	Malta	1.06	4	Iceland	2.13
5	Iceland	1.03	5	Malta	1.94
6	Azerbaijan	0.89	6	Azerbaijan	1.75
7	Switzerland	0.85	7	Ireland	1.49
8	Austria	0.71	8	Switzerland	1.47
9	Ireland	0.64	9	Macedonia	1.32
10	Netherlands	0.61	10	Austria	1.14
11	Macedonia	0.59	11	Norway	1.09
12	Norway	0.52	12	Netherlands	0.95
13	Slovenia	0.49	13	France	0.81
14	Greece	0.46	14	Sweden	0.74
	Sweden	0.46	15	Finland	0.66
16	Germany	0.44	16	Greece	0.60
17	France	0.43	17	Germany	0.54
18	Finland	0.42	18	Denmark	0.52
19	Denmark	0.32	19	Slovakia	0.47
20	Slovakia	0.29	20	Slovenia	0.42

Slowest growth
Annual average population growth, %

1990–98			1998–2005		
1	Bosnia	-1.84	1	Latvia	-2.41
2	Latvia	-1.21	2	Estonia	-2.22
3	Estonia	-1.13	3	Georgia	-1.28
4	Georgia	-0.92	4	Bulgaria	-1.20
5	Albania	-0.65	5	Romania	-0.78
6	Bulgaria	-0.55	6	Hungary	-0.73
7	Romania	-0.39	7	Ukraine	-0.65
8	Hungary	-0.30	8	Lithuania	-0.47
9	Ukraine	-0.25	9	Albania	-0.33
10	Lithuania	-0.14	10	Russia	-0.26
11	Croatia	-0.10	11	Belarus	-0.25
12	Russia	-0.07		Bosnia	-0.25
13	Armenia	-0.03	13	Croatia	-0.24
	Czech Republic	-0.03	14	Czech Republic	-0.19
15	Portugal	0.00	15	Italy	-0.06
16	Moldova	0.04	16	Portugal	-0.03
17	Belarus	0.07	17	Spain	0.06
18	Italy	0.08	18	Moldova	0.08
19	Spain	0.10	19	Armenia	0.13
20	United Kingdom	0.17	20	Poland	0.31

Population density

Most crowded countries
Population per sq km

	1955			1975	
1	Malta	994	1	Malta	963
2	Belgium	291	2	Netherlands	334
3	Netherlands	263	3	Belgium	321
4	United Kingdom	210	4	United Kingdom	230
5	Germany	197	5	Germany	221
6	Italy	161	6	Italy	184
7	Switzerland	121	7	Switzerland	154
8	Czech Republic	118	8	Luxembourg	140
	Luxembourg	118	9	Czech Republic	127
10	Hungary	106	10	Denmark	117
11	Denmark	103	11	Moldova	114
12	Portugal	93	12	Hungary	113
13	Poland	84	13	Poland	105
14	Austria	83	14	Portugal	98
15	France	79	15	Slovakia	97
16	Moldova	78	16	France	96
17	Slovakia	77	17	Armenia	95
18	Slovenia	76	18	Austria	90
19	Romania	74	19	Romania	89
20	Croatia	70	20	Slovenia	86

Most crowded EU regions
No. of people per sq km, 1997

1	Brussels	Brussels	5,898
2	Berlin	Germany	3,816
3	Hamburg	Germny	2,251
4	Bremen	Germany	1,652
5	Ile de France	France	922
6	Attiki	Greece	906
7	West-Nederland	Netherlands	839
8	Madrid	Spain	628
9	Nordrhein-Westfalen	Germany	526
10	North-West England	United Kingdom	487
11	Zuid-Nederland	Netherlands	486
12	Viaams Gewest	Belgium	437
13	Campania	Italy	426
14	Saarland	Germany	418
15	South-East England	United Kingdom	416
16	West-Midlands England	United Kingdom	410
17	Lombardia	Italy	376
18	Madeira	Portugal	332
	Oost-Nederland	Netherlands	332
20	Yorkshire and The Humber	United Kingdom	324

	1998[a]			*2025*	
1	Monaco	16,410	1	Malta	1,343
2	Malta	1,178	2	Netherlands	395
3	Netherlands	463	3	Belgium	337
4	Belgium	311	4	United Kingdom	244
5	United Kingdom	244	5	Germany	227
6	Germany	235	6	Switzerland	184
7	Liechtenstein	200	7	Luxembourg	180
8	Italy	196	8	Italy	172
9	Switzerland	180	9	Albania	149
10	Luxembourg	165	10	Moldova	144
11	Armenia	135	11	Armenia	140
12	Czech Republic	133	12	Denmark	124
13	Moldova	130		Poland	124
14	Poland	127	14	Czech Republic	122
15	Denmark	125	15	Azerbaijan	112
16	Albania	122		Slovakia	112
17	Slovakia	112	17	France	110
18	Hungary	110		Turkey	110
19	Portugal	109	19	Cyprus	103
20	France	107	20	Portugal	102

Least crowded EU regions
No. of people per sq km, 1997

1	Ovre Norrland	Sweden	3
2	Mellersta Norrland	Sweden	6
3	Norra Mellansverige	Sweden	13
4	Ahvenanmaa/Aaland	Finland	17
	Manner-Suomi	Finland	17
6	Smaland Med Oarna	Sweden	24
7	Centro	Spain	25
8	Ostra Mellansverige	Sweden	39
9	Kentriki Ellada	Greece	49
10	Noreste	Spain	57
11	Nisia Aigaiou, Kriti	Greece	58
12	Sud-Ouest	France	59
13	Vastsverige	Sweden	60
	Voreia Ellada	Greece	60
15	Scotland	United Kingdom	66
16	Sudosterreich	Austria	68
17	Sardegna	Italy	69
18	Bassin Parisien	France	72
19	Mecklenburg-Vorpommern	Germany	78
20	Sur	Spain	85

a Monaco not available for other years.

City living

Capital facts

Country	Capital city	Ranking	Population, '000
Albania	Tirana	39	279
Andorra	Andorra-La-Vella	45	25
Armenia	Yerevan	21	1,281
Austria	Vienna	12	2,068
Azerbaijan	Baku	14	1,918
Belarus	Minsk	16	1,758
Belgium	Brussels	26	1,121
Bosnia	Sarajevo	33	522
Bulgaria	Sofia	23	1,192
Croatia	Zagreb	27	1,047
Cyprus	Nicosia	40	193
Czech Republic	Prague	22	1,225
Denmark	Copenhagen	19	1,383
Estonia	Tallinn	36	397
Finland	Helsinki	24	1,150
France	Paris	1	9,608
Georgia	Tbilisi	20	1,309
Germany	Berlin	6	3,324
Greece	Athens	8	3,112
Hungary	Budapest	15	1,836
Iceland	Reykjavik	41	168
Ireland	Dublin	28	977
Italy	Rome	9	2,685
Latvia	Riga	30	783
Liechtenstein	Vaduz	46	7
Lithuania	Vilnius	32	579
Luxembourg	Luxembourg-Ville	43	79
Macedonia	Skopje	34	485
Malta	Valletta	42	102
Moldova	Kishinev	31	655
Monaco	Monaco	44	33
Netherlands	Amsterdam	25	1,137
Norway	Oslo	29	959
Poland	Warsaw	11	2,260
Portugal	Lisbon	5	3,754
Romania	Bucharest	13	2,054
Russia	Moscow	2	9,314
San Marino	San Marino	47	4
Serbia	Belgrade	18	1,482
Slovakia	Bratislava	35	460
Slovenia	Ljubljana	38	295
Spain	Madrid	4	4,070
Sweden	Stockholm	17	1,578
Switzerland	Berne	37	344
Turkey	Ankara	7	3,131
Ukraine	Kiev	10	2,663
United Kingdom	London	3	7,639
Vatican	Vatican City	48	1

Note: Estimates of city populations for 1999 taken from UN statistics for agglomerations.

Most urbanised countries
% of population living in urban areas

1985			2000	
1	Monaco	100	1 Monaco	100.0
	Vatican	100	Vatican	100.0
3	Andorra	96	3 Belgium	97.3
	Belgium	96	4 Andorra	93.0
5	Iceland	90	5 Iceland	92.5
6	Netherlands	89	6 Luxembourg	91.5
	United Kingdom	89	7 Malta	90.5
8	San Marino	87	8 United Kingdom	89.5
9	Malta	86	9 Netherlands	89.4
10	Denmark	84	San Marino	89.4
	Germany	84		

Least urbanised countries
% of population living in urban areas

1985			2000	
1	Liechtenstein	20	1 Liechtenstein	22.6
2	Portugal	31	2 Albania	41.6
3	Albania	35	3 Bosnia	43.0
4	Bosnia	38	4 Moldova	46.1
5	Moldova	44	5 Slovenia	50.4
6	Cyprus	49	6 Serbia & Montenegro	52.2
7	Serbia	50	7 Romania	56.2
	Slovenia	50	8 Cyprus	56.8
9	Romania	51	9 Azerbaijan	57.3
10	Croatia	52	10 Slovakia	57.4

City population growth

		Rate of growth, 1990–2000, %	Population, 2000, '000
1	Porto, Portugal	5.67	1,922
2	Bursa, Turkey	4.72	1,304
3	Lisbon, Portugal	4.63	3,826
4	Gaziantep, Turkey	4.57	930
5	Istanbul, Turkey	3.74	9,451
6	Oslo, Norway	3.69	978
7	Adana, Turkey	3.63	1,294
8	Izmir, Turkey	3.31	2,409
9	Helsinki, Finland	2.96	1,167
10	Ankara, Turkey	2.34	3,203
11	Zagreb, Croatia	2.24	1,060
12	Düsseldorf, Germany	1.83	3,238
13	Belgrade, Serbia	1.18	1,482
14	Tyneside, Britain	1.12	980
15	Baku, Azerbaijan	1.01	1,936
16	Liverpool, Britain	0.96	914
17	Minsk, Belarus	0.92	1,772
18	Amsterdam, Netherlands	0.83	1,144
19	Bielefeld, Germany	0.77	1,297
20	Nuremberg, Germany	0.75	1,192

Sex and age

Most male populations
No. of men per 100 women, 2000

1	Albania	104.6
2	Turkey	102.0
3	Iceland	101.1
4	Macedonia	99.8
5	Cyprus	99.7
6	Serbia & Montenegro	98.8
7	Ireland	98.6
8	Sweden	98.4
9	Norway	98.3
10	Malta	98.2
11	Netherlands	98.1
12	Bosnia	97.9
13	Denmark	97.8
	Switzerland	97.8
15	Austria	97.5
16	Greece	96.9
17	United Kingdom	96.5
18	Romania	96.4
19	Luxembourg	96.2
20	Azerbaijan	96.0
	Belgium	96.0
	Germany	96.0

Most female populations
No. of men per 100 women, 2000

1	Latvia	83.0
2	Ukraine	87.2
3	Russia	87.8
4	Belarus	88.5
5	Estonia	88.7
6	Lithuania	89.4
7	Hungary	91.5
8	Georgia	91.6
9	Moldova	91.8
10	Portugal	92.7
11	Croatia	93.6
12	Italy	94.3
13	Poland	94.5
	Slovenia	94.5
15	Armenia	94.6
	Bulgaria	94.6
17	Czech Republic	94.9
18	Slovakia	95.0
19	France	95.1
20	Finland	95.2

Oldest populations
% aged 65 and over

2000			2020		
1	Italy	18.2	1	Italy	23.4
2	Greece	17.9	2	Greece	21.8
3	Sweden	17.4		Sweden	21.8
4	Spain	17.0	4	Finland	21.7
5	Belgium	16.7	5	Germany	20.8
6	Euro-11	16.4	6	Euro-11	20.7
	EU15	16.4	7	EU15	20.4
	Germany	16.4	8	Belgium	20.3
9	United Kingdom	16.0	9	Spain	20.2
10	Bulgaria	15.9	10	Denmark	19.9
	France	15.9		Netherlands	19.9
12	Portugal	15.7	12	Switzerland	19.8
13	Norway	15.4	13	France	19.6
14	Denmark	15.2	14	Czech Republic	19.5
15	Finland	14.9	15	Slovenia	19.2
16	Croatia	14.8	16	Norway	19.1
17	Austria	14.7	17	United Kingdom	19.0
	Hungary	14.7	18	Croatia	18.9
	Switzerland	14.7	19	Portugal	18.5
20	Luxembourg	14.4	20	Austria	18.5

Median[a] age

Oldest, 2000	
1 Italy	40.6
2 Germany	40.0
3 Sweden	39.9
4 Greece	39.4
Finland	39.4
6 Belgium	39.3
7 Denmark	39.0
8 Croatia	38.8
Bulgaria	38.8
10 EU15	38.3
Switzerland	38.3
12 United Kingdom	38.2
13 Hungary	38.1
Slovenia	38.1
15 Euro-11	38.0

Oldest, 2020	
1 Italy	48.1
2 Germany	45.6
Spain	45.6
4 Greece	45.4
5 Netherlands	44.2
Switzerland	44.2
7 Austria	43.9
8 Belgium	43.8
9 Slovenia	43.5
10 Euro-11	43.2
11 EU15	43.1
12 Denmark	42.8
Portugal	42.8
14 Czech Republic	42.4
15 Finland	42.3
Sweden	42.3

Youngest, 2000	
1 Turkey	25.6
2 Albania	26.7
3 Azerbaijan	27.0
4 Armenia	30.4
5 Moldova	31.6
6 Macedonia	32.2
7 Ireland	32.3
8 Iceland	32.9
9 Cyprus	33.3
10 Slovakia	34.0
11 Georgia	34.1
12 Romania	34.9
13 Bosnia	35.1
Poland	35.1
15 Serbia & Montenegro	35.6

Youngest, 2020	
1 Turkey	30.6
2 Albania	30.9
3 Azerbaijan	32.2
4 Armenia	34.8
5 Macedonia	35.5
6 Moldova	35.6
7 Cyprus	36.1
8 Georgia	36.3
Iceland	36.3
10 Ireland	36.7
11 Serbia & Montenegro	37.4
12 Malta	38.6
Russia	38.6
14 Slovakia	39.0
15 Poland	39.2

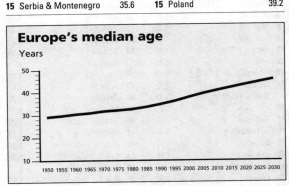

Europe's median age

Years

a Age at which there are an equal number of people above and below.

Matters of breeding

Crude birth rate: countries compared

No. of live births per 1,000 population, 1995–2000

1	Turkey	22.1	24	Croatia	10.6
2	Albania	20.6		Portugal	10.6
3	Azerbaijan	16.8	26	Bosnia	10.5
4	Iceland	15.9	27	EU15	10.4
5	Macedonia	15.8	28	Austria	10.3
6	Cyprus	14.3		Lithuania	10.3
7	Ireland	14.2	30	Sweden	10.2
8	Georgia	14.0	31	Euro-11	10.1
9	Armenia	13.3	32	Hungary	9.9
	Moldova	13.3	33	Belarus	9.8
11	Norway	13.2	34	Ukraine	9.7
12	Malta	12.9	35	Russia	9.6
	Serbia & Montenegro	12.9	36	Greece	9.3
14	Luxembourg	12.3	37	Germany	9.2
15	Denmark	12.2		Romania	9.2
	France	12.2		Slovenia	9.2
17	United Kingdom	11.9		Spain	9.2
18	Netherlands	11.6	41	Italy	9.0
19	Finland	11.4	42	Czech Republic	8.9
20	Switzerland	11.1		Estonia	8.9
21	Poland	11.0	44	Bulgaria	8.8
22	Slovakia	10.8		Latvia	8.8
23	Belgium	10.7			

Fertility rate: countries compared

Average no. of children per woman, 1995–2000

1	Albania	2.50	24	Switzerland	1.47
	Turkey	2.50	25	EU15	1.44
3	Iceland	2.10	26	Lithuania	1.43
4	Macedonia	2.06	27	Austria	1.41
5	Cyprus	2.03	28	Slovakia	1.39
6	Azerbaijan	1.99	29	Euro-11	1.38
7	Georgia	1.92		Ukraine	1.38
8	Ireland	1.90	31	Hungary	1.37
9	Malta	1.89		Portugal	1.37
10	Norway	1.85	33	Belarus	1.36
11	Serbia & Montenegro	1.84	34	Bosnia	1.35
12	Moldova	1.76		Russia	1.35
13	Finland	1.73	36	Germany	1.30
14	Denmark	1.72	37	Estonia	1.29
	United Kingdom	1.72	38	Greece	1.28
16	France	1.71	39	Slovenia	1.26
17	Armenia	1.70	40	Latvia	1.25
18	Luxembourg	1.67	41	Bulgaria	1.23
19	Sweden	1.57	42	Italy	1.20
20	Croatia	1.56	43	Czech Republic	1.19
21	Belgium	1.55	44	Romania	1.17
22	Poland	1.53	45	Spain	1.15
23	Netherlands	1.50			

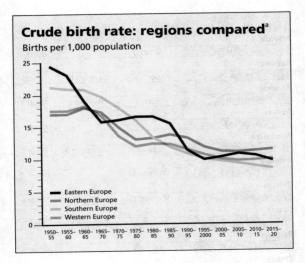

Crude birth rate: regions compared[a]

Births per 1,000 population

- Eastern Europe
- Northern Europe
- Southern Europe
- Western Europe

1950–55, 1955–60, 1960–65, 1965–70, 1970–75, 1975–80, 1980–85, 1985–90, 1990–95, 1995–2000, 2000–05, 2005–10, 2010–15, 2015–20

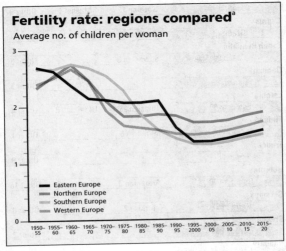

Fertility rate: regions compared[a]

Average no. of children per woman

- Eastern Europe
- Northern Europe
- Southern Europe
- Western Europe

1950–55, 1955–60, 1960–65, 1965–70, 1970–75, 1975–80, 1980–85, 1985–90, 1990–95, 1995–2000, 2000–05, 2005–10, 2010–15, 2015–20

a UN definitions are:
Eastern Europe – Belarus; Bulgaria; Czech Republic; Hungary; Moldova; Poland; Romania; Russia; Slovakia; Ukraine
Northern Europe – Denmark; Estonia; Finland; Iceland; Ireland; Latvia; Lithuania; Norway; Sweden; United Kingdom
Southern Europe – Albania; Bosnia; Croatia; Greece; Italy; Macedonia; Malta; Portugal; Serbia & Montenegro; Slovenia; Spain
Western Europe – Austria; Belgium; France; Germany; Luxembourg; Netherlands; Switzerland

Who lives where

Ethnic breakdown
% of total population

Albania

Albanian 95	Greek 3		Other 2

Andorra

Spanish 61	Andorran 30	French 6	Other 3

Armenia

Armenian 93	Azeri 3	Russian 2	Other 2

Austria

Austrian 99		Other 1

Azerbaijan

Azeri 90	Russian 3	Armenian 2	Other 5

Belgium

Fleming 55	Walloon 33	Other 12

Belarus

Belarussian 78	Russian 13	Polish 4	Other 4

Bosnia

Serbian 40	Muslim 38	Croatian 17	Other 5

Bulgaria

Bulgarian 85	Turkish 9	Other 6

Croatia

Croatian 78	Serbian 12	Muslim 1	Other 9

Cyprus

Greek 78	Turkish 18	Other 4

Czech Republic

Czech 94	Slovakian 3	Other 3

Denmark

Danish 95	Other 5

Estonia

Estonian 65	Russian 28	Ukrainian 3	Other 4

Finland

Finnish 93	Swedish 6	Other 1

France

French 91	Other 9

Georgia

Georgian 70	Armenian 8	Russian 6	Other 16

Germany

German 92	Turkish 2	Other 6

Greece

Greek 98	Other 2

Hungary

Hungarian 90	Gypsy 4	German 3	Other 3

Iceland

Icelandic 98	Other 2

Ireland

Irish 94	Other 6

Italy

Italian 98	Other 2

Latvia

Latvian 57	Russian 30	Belarussian 4	Other 9

Liechtenstein

German 88	Italian 3		Other 9

Lithuania

Lithuanian 81	Russian 8	Polish 7	Other 4

Luxembourg

Luxembourger 73	Portuguese 9	Italian 5	Other 13

Macedonia

Macedonian 66	Albanian 23	Turkish 4	Other 7

Malta

Maltese 95	English 2		Other 3

Moldova

Moldovan 65	Ukrainian 14	Russian 13	Other 8

Monaco

French 47	Monegasque 16	Italian 16	Other 21

Netherlands

Dutch 94			Other 6

Norway

Norwegian 97			Other 3

Poland

Polish 98	German 1		Other 1

Portugal

Portugese 98			Other 2

Romania

Romanian 89	Hungarian 9		Other 2

Russia

Russian 82	Tatar 4	Ukrainian 3	Other 11

San Marino

Sanmarinesi 87	Italian 12		Other 1

Serbia and Montenegro

Serbian 63	Albanians 14	Montenegrian 6	Other 17

Slovakia

Slovakian 86	Hungarian 11	Gypsy 1	Other 2

Slovenia

Slovene 91	Croatian 3	Serbian 2	Other 4

Spain

Spanish 73	Catalan 16	Galician 8	Other 3

Sweden

Swedish 91			Other 9

Switzerland

German 65	French 18	Italian 10	Other 7

Turkey

Turkish 80	Kurdish 20		

Ukraine

Ukrainian 73	Russian 22		Other 5

United Kingdom

English 82	Scottish 10	Welsh 2	Other 6

Migration

The recent picture
Net migration rate, per 1,000 population, 1999 estimated

Albania	-2.93	Liechtenstein	5.90
Armenia	-8.26	Lithuania	-1.58
Austria	1.32	Luxembourg	7.78
Azerbaijan	-5.76	Macedonia	-0.83
Belarus	3.13	Malta	1.24
Belgium	1.01	Moldova	-0.92
Bosnia	33.42	Monaco	4.17
Bulgaria	-0.66	Netherlands	1.99
Croatia	1.81	Norway	1.62
Cyprus	0.44	Poland	-0.40
Czech Republic	0.91	Portugal	-1.51
Denmark	3.22	Romania	-0.87
Estonia	-3.08	Russia	2.05
Finland	0.40	San Marino	4.23
France	0.53	Slovakia	0.29
Georgia	-4.69	Slovenia	0.23
Germany	2.12	Spain	0.66
Greece	4.04	Sweden	1.68
Hungary	0.50	Switzerland	0.49
Iceland	-2.17	Turkey	0.00
Ireland	-1.31	Ukraine	0.63
Italy	0.17	United Kingdom	1.11
Latvia	-1.25		

Average annual migration rate, per 1,000 population, 1995–2000 projection

Albania	-19.1	Latvia	-9.5
Armenia	-8.7	Lithuania	-1.4
Austria	4.9	Luxembourg	8.6
Azerbaijan	-5.6	Macedonia	-2.0
Belarus	0.4	Malta	1.9
Belgium	1.3	Moldova	-2.3
Bosnia	27.1	Netherlands	1.3
Bulgaria	-1.8	Norway	2.3
Croatia	0.0	Poland	-0.4
Cyprus	3.9	Portugal	0.5
Czech Republic	0.6	Romania	-1.3
Denmark	2.1	Russia	2.7
Estonia	-7.8	Serbia & Montenegro	-1.9
Finland	1.0	Slovakia	0.0
France	0.7	Slovenia	0.5
Georgia	-15.7	Spain	0.5
Germany	2.9	Sweden	3.4
Greece	3.3	Switzerland	4.3
Hungary	0.0	Turkey	1.0
Iceland	0.0	Ukraine	0.4
Ireland	0.8	United Kingdom	0.7
Italy	1.2		

Looking back

	1960–69	
	Av. ann. migration rate per 1,000 pop.	Av. ann. net migration, '000s
Austria	0.75	5.45
Belgium	1.65	15.62
Denmark	0.20	0.10
Finland	-3.30	-15.06
France	4.20	204.78
Germany	2.55	193.88
Greece	-4.50	-38.48
Iceland	-1.50	-0.29
Ireland	-6.25	-17.98
Italy	-1.80	-93.80
Liechtenstein	12.30	0.23
Luxembourg	4.55	1.51
Malta	-14.18	-4.51
Netherlands	0.55	6.76
Norway	0.00	0.00
Portugal	-13.90	-126.89
Spain	-2.20	-70.59
Sweden	2.25	17.40
Switzerland	2.85	16.69
United Kingdom	0.55	29.98

	1970–79		1980–89	
	Av. ann. migration rate per 1,000 pop.	Av. ann. net migration, '000s	Av. ann. migration rate per 1,000 pop.	Av. ann. net migration, '000s
Austria	1.05	7.96	1.75	13.23
Belgium	0.80	7.84	0.05	0.49
Denmark	0.85	4.30	0.70	3.58
Finland	-0.60	-2.83	0.65	3.19
France	1.40	73.78	0.95	52.41
Germany	1.20	94.41	2.10	163.10
Greece	1.65	14.93	2.10	20.86
Iceland	-2.70	-0.59	0.20	0.05
Ireland	3.25	10.33	-5.70	-20.25
Italy	-0.35	-19.40	-0.25	-14.15
Liechtenstein	13.00	0.31	2.15	0.06
Luxembourg	7.50	2.72	3.50	1.28
Malta	-3.46	-1.07	0.29	0.10
Netherlands	2.30	31.40	1.45	21.01
Norway	0.90	3.61	1.40	5.81
Portugal	2.25	20.46	-2.00	-19.81
Spain	-0.05	-1.78	-0.30	-11.52
Sweden	1.45	11.88	1.75	14.61
Switzerland	-2.00	-12.68	3.20	20.92
United Kingdom	-0.40	-22.57	0.40	22.75

Who speaks what

First language most spoken in Europe

		No. of people million	% of pop. of Europe			No. of people million	% of pop. of Europe
1	Russian	170.00	21.7	19	Swedish	9.26	1.2
2	German	98.00	12.5	20	Lombard	9.11	1.2
3	French	62.76	8.0	21	Bulgarian	8.97	1.1
4	English	61.91	7.9	22	Tatar	8.00	1.0
5	Turkish	59.00	7.5	23	Azerbaijani	7.06	0.9
6	Polish	44.00	5.6	24	Nap.-Calab.	7.05	0.9
7	Italian	42.30	5.4	25	Slovak	5.11	0.7
8	Ukrainian	41.20	5.3	26	Albanian	5.10	0.7
9	Spanish	28.30	3.6	27	Danish	5.07	0.6
10	Romanian	26.00	3.3	28	Finnish	5.02	0.6
11	Serbo-Croat	21.00	2.7	29	Sicilian	4.67	0.6
12	Dutch	20.00	2.6	30	Catalan	4.31	0.6
13	Hungarian	14.50	1.9	31	Armenian	4.30	0.5
14	Greek	12.00	1.5	32	Norwegian	4.28	0.5
15	Kurdish	11.62	1.5	33	Georgian	4.21	0.5
16	Portuguese	11.55	1.5	34	Galician	3.19	0.4
17	Czech	10.53	1.3	35	Lithuanian	3.04	0.4
18	Belarussian	10.20	1.3	36	Venetian	2.21	0.3

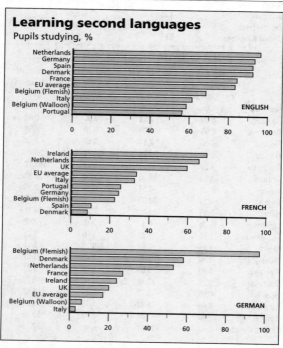

Learning second languages
Pupils studying, %

ENGLISH
Netherlands, Germany, Spain, Denmark, France, EU average, Belgium (Flemish), Italy, Belgium (Walloon), Portugal

FRENCH
Ireland, Netherlands, UK, EU average, Italy, Portugal, Germany, Belgium (Flemish), Spain, Denmark

GERMAN
Belgium (Flemish), Denmark, Netherlands, France, Ireland, UK, EU average, Belgium (Walloon), Italy

Part III

THE ECONOMY

Economic strength

Largest economies
GDP, $bn at market exchange rates
1998

1	Germany	2,180	21	Ukraine		49
2	France[a]	1,465	22	Hungary		46
3	United Kingdom	1,264	23	Romania		31
4	Italy	1,157	24	Serbia & Montenegro[b]		25
5	Spain	555	25	Belarus		22
6	Netherlands	389	26	Croatia		21
7	Russia	332	27	Slovakia		20
8	Switzerland	284	28	Luxembourg		19
9	Belgium	259		Slovenia		19
10	Sweden	227	30	Bulgaria		10
11	Austria	217	31	Cyprus		9
12	Turkey	201		Lithuania		9
13	Denmark	175	33	Iceland		8
14	Norway	152	34	Latvia		6
15	Poland	151	35	Estonia		5
16	Finland	125		Georgia		5
17	Greece	123	37	Azerbaijan		4
18	Portugal	106		Bosnia[b]		4
19	Ireland	69		Malta		4
20	Czech Republic	53				

1990

1	Germany	1,504	13	Denmark	129
2	France	1,195	14	Norway	115
3	Italy	1,094	15	Greece	83
4	United Kingdom	984	16	Portugal	67
5	Spain	492	17	Poland	59
6	Netherlands	284	18	Ireland	45
7	Sweden	230	19	Romania	38
8	Switzerland	228	20	Hungary	33
9	Belgium	194	21	Luxembourg	9
10	Austria	158	22	Iceland	6
11	Turkey	150		Cyprus	6
12	Finland	135	24	Malta	2

1980

1	Western Germany	758.5	11	Turkey	61.6
2	France	601.6	12	Denmark	61.5
3	United Kingdom	476.9	13	Ex-Yugoslavia	56.7
4	Italy	359.2	14	Norway	52.4
5	Spain	195.7	15	Romania	50.9
6	Netherlands	155.7	16	Finland	46.4
7	Sweden	114.2	17	Greece	39.9
8	Belgium	109.6	18	Portugal	22.4
9	Switzerland	101.4	19	Hungary	20.7
10	Austria	70.6	20	Ireland	16.3

a Including French Guiana, Guadeloupe, Martinique and Réunion.   b Estimate.

Largest economies
GDP, $bn at PPP exchange rates
1998

1	Germany	1,819	21	Finland	107
2	France	1,246	22	Hungary	103
3	United Kingdom	1,201	23	Ireland	80
4	Italy	1,185	24	Belarus	65
5	Russia	948	25	Slovakia	52
6	Spain	638	26	Bulgaria	40
7	Turkey	408	27	Croatia	30
8	Netherlands	348	28	Slovenia	28
9	Poland	295	29	Lithuania	24
10	Belgium	237	30	Georgia	18
11	Austria	187	31	Azerbaijan	17
12	Sweden	183	32	Luxembourg	14
13	Switzerland	181		Latvia	14
14	Ukraine	161	34	Cyprus	13
15	Greece	147	35	Estonia	11
	Portugal	147	36	Albania	9
17	Denmark	128		Malta	9
18	Czech Republic	127		Macedonia	9
	Romania	127	39	Moldova	8
20	Norway	117		Armenia	8

1990

1	France	1,006.9	13	Austria	135.4
2	Italy	928.2	14	Portugal	104.1
3	United Kingdom	924.8	15	Greece	100.8
4	Russia	913.8	16	Czech Republic	97.3
5	Spain	477.3	17	Romania	94.5
6	Turkey	257.7	18	Denmark	90.4
7	Netherlands	238.9	19	Finland	83.0
8	Ukraine	221.1	20	Norway	70.2
9	Belgium	179.1	21	Hungary	67.1
10	Poland	176.2	22	Belarus	60.1
11	Switzerland	151.8	23	Bulgaria	42.3
12	Sweden	143.8	24	Ireland	41.4

1980

1	France	523.5	13	Romania	61.8
2	Italy	489.2	14	Greece	56.5
3	Russia	473.2	15	Portugal	51.3
4	United Kingdom	468.8	16	Denmark	48.6
5	Spain	233.4	17	Finland	40.1
6	Netherlands	126.4	18	Hungary	37.8
7	Poland	112.5	19	Norway	36.4
8	Turkey	102.2	20	Bulgaria	20.9
9	Belgium	97.7	21	Ireland	19.1
10	Switzerland	81.1	22	Georgia	18.3
11	Sweden	77.5	23	Armenia	9.0
12	Austria	70.8	24	Latvia	7.2

Strongest growth
Average annual growth in GDP
1990–98

1	Ireland	7.7	**17**	France	1.5
2	Poland	4.6		Germany	1.5
3	Turkey	4.2		Slovakia	1.5
4	Norway	3.9	**20**	Italy	1.2
5	Denmark	2.9		Sweden	1.2
6	Netherlands	2.6	**22**	Czech Republic	0.9
7	Albania	2.3	**23**	Hungary	0.5
	Portugal	2.3	**24**	Switzerland	0.4
9	United Kingdom	2.2	**25**	Croatia	-0.4
10	Finland	2.0	**26**	Romania	-0.7
	Slovenia	2.0	**27**	Estonia	-2.2
12	Austria	1.9	**28**	Bulgaria	-3.1
	Spain	1.9	**29**	Armenia	-4.7
14	Greece	1.7	**30**	Lithuania	-5.0
	Macedonia	1.7	**31**	Latvia	-6.3
16	Belgium	1.6	**32**	Russia	-7.0

1980–90

1	Turkey	5.3		United Kingdom	3.2
2	Bulgaria	4.0	**9**	Portugal	2.9
3	Latvia	3.4	**10**	Norway	2.8
4	Armenia	3.3		Russia	2.8
	Finland	3.3	**12**	Denmark	2.4
6	Ireland	3.2		France	2.4
	Spain	3.2		Italy	2.4

1970–79

1	Malta	10.84	**11**	Austria	3.72
2	Iceland	6.54	**12**	Cyprus	3.34
3	Hungary	5.50	**13**	Finland	3.24
4	Greece	5.04	**14**	Belgium	3.19
5	Portugal	4.87	**15**	Netherlands	3.15
6	Norway	4.81	**16**	Germany	2.88
7	Ireland	4.69	**17**	Denmark	2.56
8	France	4.14	**18**	United Kingdom	2.40
9	Spain	3.78	**19**	Sweden	1.99
10	Italy	3.73	**20**	Switzerland	1.05

EU GDP: who contributes what
%, 1998

1	Germany	26.0	**9**	Austria	2.6
2	France	17.5	**10**	Denmark	2.1
3	United Kingdom	15.1	**11**	Finland	1.5
4	Italy	13.8		Greece	1.5
5	Spain	6.6	**13**	Portugal	1.3
6	Netherlands	4.6	**14**	Ireland	0.8
7	Belgium	3.1	**15**	Luxembourg	0.2
8	Sweden	2.7			

Living standards

Human development index
1997

1	Norway	92.7	22	Czech Republic	83.3
2	Belgium	92.3	23	Slovakia	81.3
	Sweden	92.3	24	Poland	80.2
4	Netherlands	92.1	25	Hungary	79.5
5	Iceland	91.9	26	Croatia	77.3
6	France	91.8		Estonia	77.3
	United Kingdom	91.8	28	Belarus	76.3
8	Switzerland	91.4	29	Lithuania	76.1
9	Finland	91.3	30	Bulgaria	75.8
10	Germany	90.6	31	Romania	75.2
11	Denmark	90.5	32	Russia	74.7
12	Austria	90.4	33	Macedonia	74.6
13	Luxembourg	90.2	34	Latvia	74.4
14	Ireland	90.0	35	Georgia	72.9
	Italy	90.0	36	Armenia	72.8
16	Spain	89.4		Turkey	72.8
17	Cyprus	87.0	38	Ukraine	72.1
18	Greece	86.7	39	Albania	69.9
19	Portugal	85.8	40	Azerbaijan	69.5
20	Malta	85.0	41	Moldova	68.3
21	Slovenia	84.5			

1990

1	Norway	97.8	16	Spain	91.6
2	Switzerland	97.7	17	Cyprus	91.2
3	Sweden	97.6	18	Greece	90.1
4	France	96.9	19	Ex-Czechoslovakia	89.7
5	Netherlands	96.8	20	Hungary	89.3
6	United Kingdom	96.2	21	Poland	87.4
7	Iceland	95.8	22	Ex-Soviet Union	87.3
8	Germany	95.5	23	Bulgaria	86.5
9	Finland	95.3	24	Ex-Yugoslavia	85.7
10	Denmark	95.3	25	Malta	85.4
11	Belgium	95.0	26	Portugal	85.0
12	Austria	95.0	27	Albania	79.1
13	Luxembourg	92.9	28	Romania	73.3
14	Italy	92.2	29	Turkey	67.1
15	Ireland	92.1			

Note: GDP or GDP per head is often taken as a measure of how developed a country is but its usefulness is limited as it refers only to economic welfare. In 1990 the UN Development Programme published its first estimate of a Human Development Index, which combined statistics on two other indicators – adult literacy and life expectancy – with income levels to give a better, though still far from perfect, indicator of human development. In 1991 average years of schooling was combined with adult literacy to give a knowledge variable. The index is shown here scaled from 0 to 100; countries scoring over 80 are considered to have high human development, those scoring from 50–79 have medium human development.

GDP per head
$

1998

1	Luxembourg	45,100	22	Czech Republic	5,150
2	Switzerland	39,980	23	Croatia	4,620
3	Norway	34,310	24	Hungary	4,510
4	Denmark	33,040	25	Poland	3,910
5	Iceland	27,830	26	Slovakia	3,700
6	Austria	26,830	27	Estonia	3,360
7	Germany	26,570	28	Turkey	3,160
8	Sweden	25,580	29	Lithuania	2,540
9	Belgium	25,380	30	Latvia	2,420
10	Netherlands	24,780	31	Serbia & Montenegro[a]	2,400
11	Finland	24,280	32	Russia	2,260
12	France	24,210	33	Romania	1,360
13	United Kingdom	21,410	34	Macedonia	1,290
14	Italy	20,090	35	Bulgaria	1,220
15	Ireland	18,710	36	Bosnia[a]	1,120
16	Spain	14,100	37	Ukraine	980
17	Cyprus	11,920	38	Georgia	970
18	Greece	11,740	39	Albania	810
19	Portugal	10,670	40	Azerbaijan	480
20	Malta	10,100	41	Armenia	460
21	Slovenia	9,780	42	Moldova	380

1980

1	Switzerland	19,620	11	Finland	10,710
2	Luxembourg	17,010	12	United Kingdom	8,580
3	Sweden	15,410	13	Italy	7,900
4	Norway	15,360	14	Spain	5,740
5	Iceland	15,230	15	Ireland	5,650
6	Denmark	14,420	16	Greece	5,510
7	Belgium	13,190	17	Cyprus	3,590
8	Netherlands	12,980	18	Malta	3,370
9	France	12,680	19	Portugal	2,910
10	Austria	10,930	20	Hungary	2,060

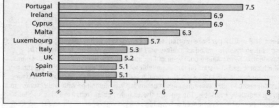

Fastest growth

GDP per head, 1980–98 average annual % increase, $ terms

Portugal	7.5
Ireland	6.9
Cyprus	6.9
Malta	6.3
Luxembourg	5.7
Italy	5.3
UK	5.2
Spain	5.1
Austria	5.1

a Estimate.

GDP per head in PPP
$

	1980	1990	1995	1998
Albania	...	2,653	2,782	2,864
Armenia	...	3,166	1,894	2,074
Austria	9,754	18,153	22,017	23,145
Azerbaijan	...	4,791	1,942	2,168
Belgium	10,293	18,404	22,630	23,622
Bulgaria	2,699	4,920	5,426	4,683
Croatia	...	6,728	5,768	6,698
Cyprus	5,163	12,810	16,884	17,599
Czech Republic	...	12,368	12,401	12,197
Denmark	9,655	17,404	22,678	23,855
Estonia	...	7,775	6,440	7,563
Finland	8,591	16,708	18,119	20,641
France	9,594	17,193	20,410	21,214
Georgia	6,157	8,304	2,626	3,429
Germany	...	...	21,378	22,026
Greece	6,632	11,137	13,266	13,994
Hungary	5,069	8,612	8,941	9,832
Iceland	11,148	19,403	22,120	24,774
Ireland	5,241	10,093	14,991	17,991
Italy	9,099	16,764	20,209	20,365
Latvia	4,063	8,117	4,939	5,777
Lithuania	...	8,328	5,558	6,283
Luxembourg	11,832	28,167	35,801	36,703
Macedonia	...	...	4,147	4,224
Malta	3,608	8,160	11,115	22,901
Moldova	2,537	...	2,273	1,995
Netherlands	9,469	16,818	20,842	22,325
Norway	9,632	17,842	24,378	26,196
Poland	3,331	5,033	6,499	7,543
Portugal	5,200	10,774	13,491	14,569
Romania	4,111	6,114	6,387	5,572
Russia	...	9,855	6,960	6,180
Slovakia	...	8,653	8,480	9,624
Slovenia	...	...	13,122	14,400
Spain	6,378	12,332	15,032	15,960
Sweden	9,753	17,013	19,228	19,848
Switzerland	13,853	24,254	26,574	26,876
Turkey	2,360	4,711	5,873	6,594
Ukraine	...	6,517	3,674	3,130
United Kingdom	8,435	15,946	19,422	20,314

Richest and poorest EU regions
GDP per head in PPP as % of EU average, 1995–97

Richest			Poorest		
1	Inner London	229	1	Ipeiros	43
2	Hamburg	198	2	Azores	50
3	Luxembourg	172	3	Voreio Aigaio	51
4	Brussels	170	4	Extremadura	54

Agriculture's contribution

Agricultural output
As % of GDP
1998 or latest year available

1	Albania	63	20	Estonia	5
2	Armenia	41		Slovakia	5
3	Georgia	32		Slovenia	5
4	Moldova	31	23	Denmark	4
5	Bulgaria	23		Finland	4
6	Greece	21		Poland	4
7	Azerbaijan	19		Portugal	4
8	Romania	15	27	Italy	3
	Turkey	15		Netherlands	3
10	Belarus	14		Spain	3
	Lithuania	14		Switzerland	3
12	Croatia	12	31	France	2
	Macedonia	12		Norway	2
	Ukraine	12		Sweden	2
15	Russia	9		United Kingdom	2
16	Ireland	8	35	Austria	1
17	Latvia	7		Belgium	1
18	Czech Republic	6		Germany	1
	Hungary	6			

1980

1	Albania	34	10	Ex-Czechoslovakia	7
2	Greece	27	11	Denmark	6
3	Turkey	26		Italy	6
4	Georgia	24	13	Austria	4
5	Armenia	18		France	4
6	Bulgaria	14		Norway	4
7	Finland	12		Sweden	4
	Latvia	12	17	Netherlands	3
9	Russia	9	18	United Kingdom	2

1965

1	Turkey	34		Denmark	9
2	Greece	24	9	France	8
3	Ex-Yugoslavia	23		Norway	8
4	Finland	16	11	Sweden	6
5	Spain	15	12	Belgium	5
6	Italy	11	13	Germany	4
7	Austria	9	14	United Kingdom	3

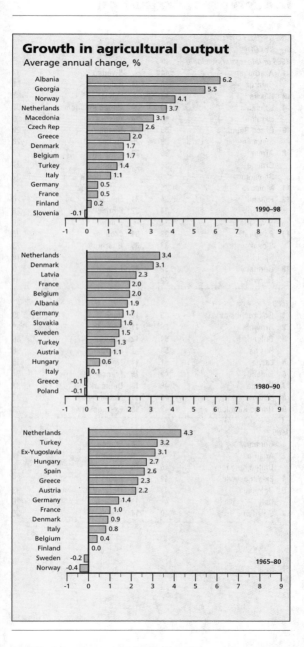

Growth in agricultural output
Average annual change, %

1990–98

Albania	6.2
Georgia	5.5
Norway	4.1
Netherlands	3.7
Macedonia	3.1
Czech Rep	2.6
Greece	2.0
Denmark	1.7
Belgium	1.7
Turkey	1.4
Italy	1.1
Germany	0.5
France	0.5
Finland	0.2
Slovenia	-0.1

1980–90

Netherlands	3.4
Denmark	3.1
Latvia	2.3
France	2.0
Belgium	2.0
Albania	1.9
Germany	1.7
Slovakia	1.6
Sweden	1.5
Turkey	1.3
Austria	1.1
Hungary	0.6
Italy	0.1
Greece	-0.1
Poland	-0.1

1965–80

Netherlands	4.3
Turkey	3.2
Ex-Yugoslavia	3.1
Hungary	2.7
Spain	2.6
Greece	2.3
Austria	2.2
Germany	1.4
France	1.0
Denmark	0.9
Italy	0.8
Belgium	0.4
Finland	0.0
Sweden	-0.2
Norway	-0.4

Industry's contribution

Industrial output
As % of GDP
1998 or latest year available

1	Azerbaijan	44		Sweden	32
	Belarus	44	21	Italy	31
3	Russia	42		Latvia	31
4	Lithuania	40		United Kingdom	31
	Ukraine	40	24	Austria	30
6	Czech Republic	39	25	Denmark	29
	Slovenia	39	26	Turkey	28
8	Armenia	36	27	Belgium	27
	Greece	36		Estonia	27
	Romania	36		Macedonia	27
11	Moldova	35		Netherlands	27
12	Finland	34	31	Bulgaria	26
	Hungary	34	32	France	26
	Switzerland	34		Poland	26
15	Portugal	33	34	Croatia	25
	Slovakia	33	35	Georgia	23
	Spain	33	36	Albania	18
18	Germany	32	37	Ireland	9
	Norway	32			

1980

1	Ex-Czechoslovakia	63	10	Italy	39
2	Armenia	58	11	Sweden	37
3	Bulgaria	54	12	Austria	36
	Russia	54		Georgia	36
5	Latvia	51	14	Norway	35
6	Finland	49	15	France	34
7	Greece	48	16	Denmark	33
8	Albania	45	17	Netherlands	32
9	United Kingdom	43	18	Ex-Yugoslavia	23

1965

1	Germany	53	8	France	39
2	Austria	46	9	Finland	37
	United Kingdom	46	10	Denmark	36
4	Ex-Yugoslavia	42		Spain	36
5	Belgium	41	12	Norway	33
	Italy	41	13	Greece	26
7	Sweden	40	14	Turkey	25

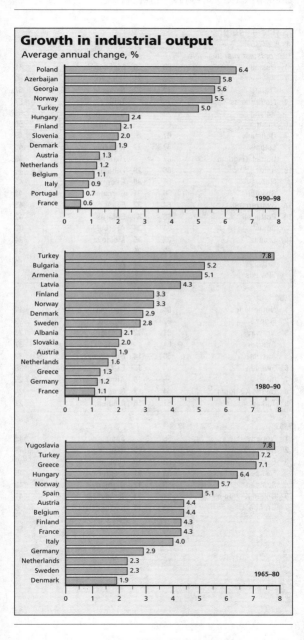

Growth in industrial output

Average annual change, %

1990–98

Poland	6.4
Azerbaijan	5.8
Georgia	5.6
Norway	5.5
Turkey	5.0
Hungary	2.4
Finland	2.1
Slovenia	2.0
Denmark	1.9
Austria	1.3
Netherlands	1.2
Belgium	1.1
Italy	0.9
Portugal	0.7
France	0.6

1980–90

Turkey	7.8
Bulgaria	5.2
Armenia	5.1
Latvia	4.3
Finland	3.3
Norway	3.3
Denmark	2.9
Sweden	2.8
Albania	2.1
Slovakia	2.0
Austria	1.9
Netherlands	1.6
Greece	1.3
Germany	1.2
France	1.1

1965–80

Yugoslavia	7.8
Turkey	7.2
Greece	7.1
Hungary	6.4
Norway	5.7
Spain	5.1
Austria	4.4
Belgium	4.4
Finland	4.3
France	4.3
Italy	4.0
Germany	2.9
Netherlands	2.3
Sweden	2.3
Denmark	1.9

Services' contribution

Services' output
As % of GDP
1998 or latest year available

1	Ireland	83	**20**	Macedonia	61
2	Belgium	72	**21**	Hungary	60
	France	72	**22**	Slovenia	57
4	Netherlands	70		Turkey	57
	Poland	70	**24**	Czech Republic	55
6	Austria	68	**25**	Bulgaria	50
7	Denmark	67	**26**	Russia	49
	Estonia	67	**27**	Romania	48
	United Kingdom	67		Ukraine	48
10	Italy	66	**29**	Lithuania	46
	Norway	66	**30**	Georgia	45
	Sweden	66	**31**	Germany	44
13	Switzerland	64	**32**	Greece	43
14	Portugal	63	**33**	Belarus	42
	Spain	63	**34**	Azerbaijan	36
16	Croatia	62	**35**	Moldova	34
	Finland	62	**36**	Armenia	23
	Latvia	62	**37**	Albania	19
	Slovakia	62			

1980

1	Netherlands	64	**10**	Georgia	40
2	France	62	**11**	Finland	39
3	Norway	61	**12**	Russia	37
	Denmark	61		Latvia	37
5	Austria	60	**14**	Bulgaria	32
6	Sweden	59	**15**	Ex-Czechoslovakia	30
7	Italy	55	**16**	Armenia	25
8	United Kingdom	54	**17**	Greece	24
9	Turkey	51	**18**	Albania	21

1965

1	Norway	59		Spain	49
2	Denmark	55	**9**	Italy	48
3	Belgium	53	**10**	Finland	47
	France	53	**11**	Austria	45
	Sweden	53	**12**	Germany	43
6	United Kingdom	51	**13**	Turkey	41
7	Greece	49	**14**	Ex-Yugoslavia	35

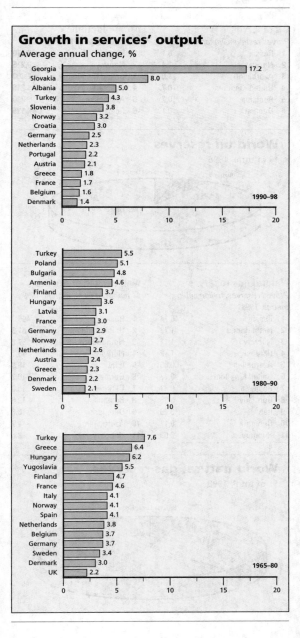

Growth in services' output

Average annual change, %

Georgia — 17.2
Slovakia — 8.0
Albania — 5.0
Turkey — 4.3
Slovenia — 3.8
Norway — 3.2
Croatia — 3.0
Germany — 2.5
Netherlands — 2.3
Portugal — 2.2
Austria — 2.1
Greece — 1.8
France — 1.7
Belgium — 1.6
Denmark — 1.4

1990–98

0   5   10   15   20

Turkey — 5.5
Poland — 5.1
Bulgaria — 4.8
Armenia — 4.6
Finland — 3.7
Hungary — 3.6
Latvia — 3.1
France — 3.0
Germany — 2.9
Norway — 2.7
Netherlands — 2.6
Austria — 2.4
Greece — 2.3
Denmark — 2.2
Sweden — 2.1

1980–90

0   5   10   15   20

Turkey — 7.6
Greece — 6.4
Hungary — 6.2
Yugoslavia — 5.5
Finland — 4.7
France — 4.6
Italy — 4.1
Norway — 4.1
Spain — 4.1
Netherlands — 3.8
Belgium — 3.7
Germany — 3.7
Sweden — 3.4
Denmark — 3.0
UK — 2.2

1965–80

0   5   10   15   20

Energy

Oil reserves
Proved reserves, bn tonnes, 1998

1	Russia	6.7
2	Norway	1.4
3	Azerbaijan	1.0
4	United Kingdom	0.7
5	Romania	0.2
6	Denmark	0.1

Oil production
'000 barrels daily, 1998

1	Russia	6,170
2	Norway	3,215
3	United Kingdom	2,800
4	Denmark	245
5	Azerbaijan	230
6	Romania	135

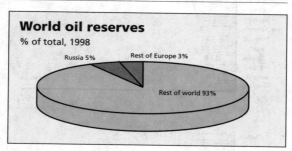

World oil reserves
% of total, 1998

Russia 5%
Rest of Europe 3%
Rest of world 93%

Natural gas reserves
Proved reserves, trillion cubic metres, 1998

1	Russia	48.14
2	Netherlands	1.79
3	Norway	1.17
4	Ukraine	1.12
5	Azerbaijan	0.85
6	United Kingdom	0.77
7	Romania	0.37
8	Germany	0.35
9	Italy	0.23
10	Denmark	0.11
11	Hungary	0.09

Natural gas production
M tonnes of oil equivalent, 1998

1	Russia	496.2
2	United Kingdom	81.3
3	Netherlands	57.2
4	Norway	43.1
5	Italy	16.8
6	Germany	15.2
7	Ukraine	15.0
8	Romania	12.6
9	Denmark	6.8
10	Azerbaijan	4.7
11	Hungary	3.0

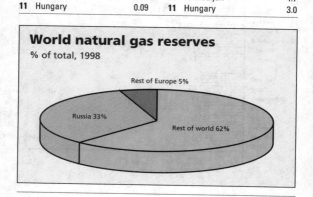

World natural gas reserves
% of total, 1998

Rest of Europe 5%
Russia 33%
Rest of world 62%

Coal reserves
Proved reserves
M tonnes, 1998

1	Russia	157,010
2	Germany	67,000
3	Ukraine	34,356
4	Poland	14,309
5	Czech Republic	6,177
6	Hungary	4,461
7	Romania	3,611
8	Greece	2,874
9	Bulgaria	2,711
10	United Kingdom	1,500
11	Turkey	1,075
12	Spain	660

Coal production
M tonnes of oil equivalent, 1998

1	Russia	104.6
2	Poland	76.3
3	Germany	61.3
4	Ukraine	39.6
5	Czech Republic	25.8
6	United Kingdom	25.1
7	Turkey	16.8
8	Spain	12.0
9	Greece	8.3
10	Bulgaria	4.9
	Romania	4.9
12	Hungary	4.0

World coal reserves
% of total, 1998

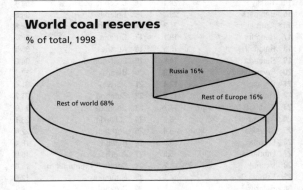

Russia 16%

Rest of Europe 16%

Rest of world 68%

Nuclear power consumption
M tonnes of oil equivalent, 1998

1	France	100.0	9	Switzerland	6.3
2	Germany	41.7	10	Finland	5.7
3	Russia	26.9	11	Bulgaria	5.0
4	United Kingdom	25.8	12	Hungary	3.6
5	Ukraine	19.4	13	Czech Republic	3.4
6	Sweden	18.2	14	Slovakia	2.9
7	Spain	15.2	15	Romania	1.4
8	Belgium[a]	11.7	16	Netherlands	0.6

a Includes Luxembourg.

Who produces most

M tonnes of coal equivalent, 1996

1	Russia	1,430.2
2	United Kingdom	382.5
3	Norway	296.3
4	Germany	197.9
5	France	171.1
6	Poland	135.7
7	Netherlands	114.2
8	Ukraine	111.3
9	Czech Republic	45.1
10	Italy	44.3
11	Romania	42.8
12	Spain	41.4
13	Sweden	34.0
14	Turkey	28.4
15	Denmark	23.3
16	Azerbaijan	21.3
17	Hungary	19.1
18	Belgium	16.5
19	Bulgaria	14.8
20	Switzerland	13.0
21	Greece	12.4
22	Finland	11.9
23	Serbia & Montenegro	11.7
24	Austria	8.2
25	Slovakia	6.8
26	Croatia	5.8
27	Lithuania	5.5
28	Ireland	5.2
29	Estonia	4.1
30	Belarus	3.9
31	Slovenia	3.2

Who uses most

M tonnes of coal equivalent, 1996

1	Russia	896.2
2	Germany	478.0
3	United Kingdom	328.0
4	France	326.6
5	Italy	230.3
6	Ukraine	223.2
7	Poland	144.3
8	Spain	127.0
9	Netherlands	125.1
10	Turkey	78.6
11	Belgium	73.3
12	Romania	60.8
13	Sweden	60.2
14	Czech Republic	58.4
15	Finland	39.5
16	Hungary	36.8
17	Greece	35.7
18	Austria	35.3
19	Switzerland	34.0
20	Belarus	32.7
21	Norway	31.4
22	Bulgaria	31.2
23	Denmark	24.0
24	Slovakia	23.1
25	Portugal	22.6
26	Ireland	16.4
27	Azerbaijan	16.0
28	Serbia & Montenegro	15.4
29	Lithuania	12.4
30	Croatia	9.7
31	Slovenia	8.0

Highest consumption per head

Kg of coal equivalent, 1996

1	Luxembourg	11,292	16	Denmark	4,583
2	Netherlands	8,035	17	Austria	4,360
3	Finland	7,707	18	Slovakia	4,329
4	Iceland	7,438	19	Ukraine	4,325
5	Norway	7,221	20	Slovenia	4,151
6	Belgium	7,215	21	Italy	4,024
7	Sweden	6,826	22	Poland	3,738
8	Russia	6,050	23	Bulgaria	3,686
9	Germany	5,836	24	Hungary	3,661
10	Czech Republic	5,695	25	Greece	3,402
11	United Kingdom	5,620	26	Lithuania	3,339
12	France	5,597	27	Spain	3,202
13	Estonia	4,741	28	Belarus	3,164
14	Switzerland	4,692	29	Cyprus	2,879
15	Ireland	4,629	30	Romania	2,685

Biggest importers
M tonnes of coal equivalent, 1996

1	Germany	327.5
2	Italy	219.5
3	France	209.3
4	Netherlands	143.2
5	Ukraine	118.7
6	Spain	113.6
7	United Kingdom	103.8
8	Belgium	98.6
9	Turkey	57.9
10	Sweden	43.9
11	Poland	39.4
12	Russia	39.2
13	Belarus	34.7
14	Greece	33.3
15	Estonia	31.3
16	Finland	30.9
17	Austria	30.6
18	Czech Republic	29.3
19	Romania	27.2
20	Portugal	26.1
21	Denmark	25.2
22	Switzerland	25.1
23	Hungary	23.0
24	Slovakia	21.6
25	Bulgaria	21.5
26	Ireland	13.4
27	Lithuania	11.3
28	Croatia	8.0
29	Norway	7.1
30	Moldova	6.9

Biggest exporters
M tonnes of coal equivalent, 1996

1	Russia	539.5
2	Norway	263.7
3	United Kingdom	145.7
4	Netherlands	124.6
5	France	32.4
6	Germany	30.7
7	Belgium	29.4
8	Poland	28.2
9	Italy	25.1
10	Denmark	19.0
11	Sweden	14.2
12	Czech Republic	12.2
13	Spain	7.9
14	Finland	6.9
15	Belarus	5.8
16	Greece	5.4
	Romania	5.4
18	Lithuania	4.7
19	Ukraine	3.7
20	Azerbaijan	3.4
21	Portugal	3.3
22	Slovakia	2.9
23	Bulgaria	2.6
24	Croatia	2.5
25	Hungary	2.3
26	Switzerland	2.2
27	Austria	1.8
	Turkey	1.8
29	Ireland	1.3
30	Estonia	0.8

Leading electricity generators
M tonnes of coal equivalent, 1996

1	France	156.51	17	Czech Republic	5.09
2	Germany	63.21	18	Slovakia	4.75
3	Russia	57.16	19	Austria	4.38
4	United Kingdom	35.88	20	Romania	2.45
5	Sweden	33.61	21	Slovenia	2.15
6	Spain	26.44	22	Portugal	1.96
7	Ukraine	20.02	23	Netherlands	1.61
8	Belgium	16.27	24	Serbia & Montenegro	1.38
9	Switzerland	13.00	25	Armenia	1.06
10	Norway	12.78	26	Iceland	1.02
11	Italy	10.41	27	Croatia	0.90
12	Finland	8.70	28	Georgia	0.75
13	Bulgaria	6.99	29	Albania	0.68
14	Turkey	5.49	30	Greece	0.55
15	Hungary	5.30	31	Poland	0.48
16	Lithuania	5.29	32	Latvia	0.23

Current account balances

Recent picture
Current account balance, 1998

		As % of GDP				$m
1	Switzerland	8.64	1	France	40,160
2	Netherlands	6.18	2	Switzerland	24,547
3	Finland	5.94	3	Netherlands	24,056
4	Belgium & Lux	4.67	4	Italy	19,998
5	France	2.74	5	Belgium & Lux	12,094
6	Sweden	2.05	6	Finland	7,432
7	Italy	1.73	7	Sweden	4,639
8	Ireland	1.16	8	Turkey	1,871
9	Turkey	0.93	9	Russia	1,644
10	Russia	0.50	10	Ireland	806
11	Slovenia	-0.02	11	Slovenia	-4
12	United Kingdom	-0.06	12	Bulgaria	-62
13	Germany	-0.16	13	Albania	-65
14	Spain	-0.29	14	Malta	-164
15	Bulgaria	-0.61	15	Macedonia	-288
16	Denmark	-1.17	16	Moldova	-347
17	Norway	-1.42	17	Armenia	-390
18	Austria	-2.13	18	Georgia	-416
19	Albania	-2.41	19	Iceland	-467
20	Czech Republic	-2.63	20	Estonia	-478
21	Ukraine	-2.63	21	Cyprus	-561
22	Belarus	-3.87	22	Latvia	-713
23	Greece	-3.94	23	United Kingdom	-810
24	Malta	-4.31	24	Belarus	-862
25	Poland	-4.56	25	Bosnia	-1,097
26	Hungary	-5.04	26	Ukraine	-1,296
27	Iceland	-6.14	27	Lithuania	-1,298
28	Cyprus	-6.24	28	Azerbaijan	-1,365
29	Portugal	-6.81	29	Czech Republic	-1,392
30	Croatia	-7.46	30	Croatia	-1,552
31	Georgia	-7.86	31	Spain	-1,606
32	Romania	-9.54	32	Denmark	-2,053
33	Estonia	-9.75	33	Slovakia	-2,126
34	Slovakia	-10.68	34	Norway	-2,161
35	Macedonia	-11.07	35	Hungary	-2,304
36	Latvia	-12.08	36	Romania	-2,918
37	Lithuania	-13.81	37	Germany	-3,440
38	Moldova	-20.43	38	Austria	-4,609
39	Armenia	-22.96	39	Greece	-4,860
40	Bosnia	-26.76	40	Poland	-6,901
41	Azerbaijan	-35.91	41	Portugal	-7,250
	Euro area[a]	1.03		Euro area[a]	67,550

a Excludes transactions between member states.

Looking back
Current account balance as % GDP

Top 10, 1990			Bottom 10, 1990		
1	Poland	5.20	1	Romania	-8.51
2	Norway	3.46	2	Russia[b]	-7.10
3	Netherlands	3.25	3	Slovakia	-7.00
4	Switzerland	3.07	4	Bulgaria	-6.30
5	Germany[a]	2.58	5	Finland	-5.15
6	Belgium & Lux	1.89	6	Greece	-4.32
7	Hungary	1.15	7	Spain	-3.66
8	Denmark	1.06	8	Cyprus	-3.42
9	Austria	0.74	9	United Kingdom	-3.40
10	Portugal	-0.27	10	Sweden	-3.00

Top 10, 1980			Bottom 10, 1980		
1	Malta	3.42	1	Ireland	-11.07
2	Norway	1.87	2	Romania	-7.06
3	United Kingdom	1.27	3	Poland	-6.02
4	Cyprus	-0.01	4	Greece	-5.50
5	Switzerland	-0.20	5	Austria	-5.03
6	Netherlands	-0.58	6	Portugal	-4.24
7	France	-0.63	7	Belgium & Lux	-4.18
8	Western Germany	-1.64	8	Denmark	-3.70
9	Italy	-2.34	9	Sweden	-3.47
10	Iceland	-2.35	10	Finland	-2.73

Top 10, 1970			Bottom 10, 1970		
1	Belgium & Lux	2.78	1	Ireland	-5.00
2	Switzerland	1.71	2	Greece	-4.24
3	United Kingdom	1.60	3	Denmark	-3.44
4	Italy	0.80	4	Finland	-2.20
5	Hungary	0.63	5	Norway	-2.17
6	Western Germany	0.46	6	Malta	-2.11
7	Iceland	0.42	7	Netherlands	-1.75
8	Spain	0.21	8	Sweden	-0.80
9	Cyprus	0.00	9	Austria	-0.52
10	France	-0.14	10	Turkey	-0.34

Top 5, 1960			Bottom 5, 1960		
1	Malta	8.69	1	Iceland	-4.10
2	Spain	3.78	2	Norway	-2.47
3	Netherlands	3.13	3	Greece	-1.57
4	Western Germany	1.53	4	Austria	-1.42
5	Switzerland	1.09	5	United Kingdom	-1.00

a Includes Eastern Germany from July 1990.
b Convertible currencies only.

Biggest visible traders

Recent picture
Exports plus imports, 1998

	Average as % of GDP				$bn
1	Ireland	76.97	1	Germany	1,000.94
2	Estonia	66.28	2	United Kingdom	577.58
3	Slovakia	59.78	3	France	577.23
4	Macedonia	58.32	4	Italy	449.51
5	Malta	55.80	5	Netherlands	324.19
6	Belgium & Lux	53.92	6	Belgium & Lux	300.02
7	Czech Republic	52.25	7	Spain	238.34
8	Lithuania	50.22	8	Switzerland	186.73
9	Moldova	49.26	9	Sweden	152.73
10	Slovenia	48.88	10	Russia	132.75
11	Hungary	47.97	11	Austria	129.31
12	Latvia	43.66	12	Ireland	106.68
13	Bulgaria	43.41	13	Denmark	92.20
14	Netherlands	41.66	14	Norway	79.71
15	Bosnia	41.34	15	Poland	77.77
16	Belarus	34.99	16	Turkey	76.77
17	Sweden	33.71	17	Finland	74.30
18	Switzerland	32.86	18	Portugal	64.31
19	Croatia	32.16	19	Czech Republic	55.38
20	Azerbaijan	31.60	20	Hungary	43.85
21	Romania	31.42	21	Ukraine	29.98
22	Ukraine	30.47	22	Greece[a]	26.53
23	Armenia	30.45	23	Slovakia	23.79
24	Portugal	30.22	24	Romania	19.23
25	Austria	29.84	25	Slovenia	18.97
26	Finland	29.69	26	Belarus	15.60
27	Serbia & Montenegro	28.31	27	Croatia	13.38
28	Iceland	27.67	28	Lithuania	9.44
29	Denmark	26.31	29	Bulgaria	8.77
30	Norway	26.22	30	Serbia & Montenegro	7.70
31	Poland	25.70	31	Estonia	6.50
32	Cyprus	25.36	32	Latvia	5.15
33	Germany	22.96	33	Cyprus	4.56
34	United Kingdom	22.84	34	Malta	4.24
35	Spain	21.46	35	Iceland	4.21
36	Russia	20.00	36	Bosnia	3.39
37	France	19.70	37	Macedonia	3.03
38	Italy	19.43	38	Azerbaijan	2.40
39	Turkey	19.15	39	Moldova	1.68
40	Albania	18.88	40	Georgia	1.36
41	Georgia	12.83	41	Armenia	1.04
42	Greece	10.75	42	Albania	1.02
	Euro area[b]	12.21		Euro area[b]	1,597.25

a 1997
b Excludes transactions between member states.

Looking back

Exports plus imports, $m

1990

1	France	451,024	11	Austria	90,411
2	Germany	410,104	12	Denmark	67,361
3	United Kingdom	408,149	13	Norway	61,278
4	Italy	352,454	14	Finland	53,572
5	Germany	346,153	15	Ireland	44,412
6	Netherlands	257,873	16	Portugal	41,680
7	Belgium & Lux	237,405	17	Turkey	35,261
8	Spain	143,357	18	Ex-Yugoslavia	33,179
9	Switzerland	133,465	19	Greece	27,882
10	Sweden	111,804	20	Poland	22,040

1980

1	Western Germany	380,862	11	Denmark	36,089
2	France	250,896	12	Norway	35,488
3	United Kingdom	225,679	13	Poland	30,881
4	Italy	178,845	14	Finland	29,785
5	Netherlands	173,438	15	Romania	25,052
6	Belgium & Lux	136,400	16	Ex-Yugoslavia	24,054
7	Switzerland	65,973	17	Ireland	19,551
8	Sweden	64,344	18	Hungary	17,857
9	Spain	54,798	19	Greece	15,701
10	Austria	41,933	20	Portugal	13,949

1970

1	Western Germany	64,175	11	Spain	7,135
2	United Kingdom	41,294	12	Austria	6,406
3	France	36,998	13	Norway	6,157
4	Netherlands	28,917	14	Finland	4,944
5	Italy	28,179	15	Ex-Yugoslavia	4,553
6	Belgium & Lux	22,854	16	Romania	3,968
7	Sweden	13,802	17	Hungary	3,603
8	Switzerland	11,441	18	Ireland	2,742
9	Denmark	7,763	19	Greece	2,601
10	Poland	7,156	20	Portugal	2,502

1960

1	United Kingdom	23,637	6	Belgium & Lux	7,640
2	Western Germany	21,588	7	Sweden	5,467
3	France	13,149	8	Switzerland	4,066
4	Netherlands	8,559	9	Denmark	3,301
5	Italy	8,391	10	Austria	2,536

Visible trade balances

Recent picture
Visible trade balance, 1998

	As % of GDP				$m
1	Ireland	33.74	1	Germany	79,040
2	Finland	9.99	2	Italy	35,631
3	Sweden	7.78	3	France	26,170
4	Russia	5.08	4	Ireland	23,381
5	Netherlands	4.62	5	Netherlands	17,990
6	Germany	3.63	6	Sweden	17,632
7	Italy	3.08	7	Russia	16,851
8	Belgium & Lux	2.70	8	Finland	12,492
9	Denmark	2.13	9	Belgium & Lux	7,514
10	France	1.79	10	Denmark	3,723
11	Norway	1.03	11	Norway	1,566
12	Switzerland	0.35	12	Switzerland	988
13	Austria	-1.69	13	Iceland	-352
14	United Kingdom	-2.69	14	Bulgaria	-381
15	Spain	-3.37	15	Moldova	-388
16	Bulgaria	-3.76	16	Macedonia	-398
17	Slovenia	-3.99	17	Armenia	-578
18	Iceland	-4.63	18	Malta	-594
19	Czech Republic	-4.89	19	Albania	-604
20	Hungary	-5.15	20	Georgia	-760
21	Ukraine	-5.25	21	Slovenia	-775
22	Belarus	-6.09	22	Azerbaijan	-1,046
23	Turkey	-7.15	23	Estonia	-1,115
24	Serbia & Montenegro	-7.48	24	Latvia	-1,130
25	Poland	-8.48	25	Belarus	-1,359
26	Romania	-8.58	26	Lithuania	-1,518
27	Portugal	-11.54	27	Bosnia	-1,756
28	Slovakia	-11.81	28	Serbia & Montenegro	-1,900
29	Greece[a]	-12.46	29	Slovakia	-2,351
30	Georgia	-14.35	30	Hungary	-2,354
31	Macedonia	-15.29	31	Cyprus	-2,426
32	Malta	-15.63	32	Ukraine	-2,584
33	Lithuania	-16.15	33	Czech Republic	-2,595
34	Latvia	-19.15	34	Romania	-2,625
35	Croatia	-20.04	35	Austria	-3,654
36	Albania	-22.36	36	Croatia	-4,169
37	Estonia	-22.75	37	Portugal	-12,277
38	Moldova	-22.85	38	Poland	-12,836
39	Cyprus	-27.01	39	Turkey	-14,332
40	Azerbaijan	-27.53	40	Greece[a]	-15,375
41	Armenia	-33.97	41	Spain	-18,707
42	Bosnia	-42.83	42	United Kingdom	-34,010
	Euro area[b]	2.04		Euro area[b]	133,300

a 1997
b Excludes transactions between member states.

Looking back
Visible trade balance as % of GDP

Top 10, 1990

1	Ireland	8.80
2	Norway	6.73
3	Poland	6.09
4	Netherlands	4.25
5	Germany	3.83
6	Denmark	3.78
7	Hungary	1.62
8	Sweden	1.61
9	Iceland	1.27
10	Belgium & Lux	0.87

Bottom 10, 1990

1	Cyprus	-27.98
2	Malta	-24.22
3	Greece	-12.35
4	Portugal	-9.94
5	Romania	-8.74
6	Turkey	-6.35
7	Spain	-5.93
8	Austria	-4.40
9	Bulgaria	-4.17
10	United Kingdom	-3.33

Top 10, 1980

1	Norway	3.29
2	Western Germany	0.98
3	United Kingdom	0.62
4	Iceland	0.61
5	Cyprus	-0.03
6	Netherlands	-0.06
7	Hungary	-0.65
8	Finland	-1.33
9	Sweden	-1.76
10	France	-2.12

Bottom 10, 1980

1	Malta	-30.57
2	Portugal	-15.72
3	Greece	-13.80
4	Ireland	-11.53
5	Austria	-8.44
6	Spain	-5.54
7	Switzerland	-5.17
8	Romania	-4.85
9	Italy	-3.51
10	Belgium & Lux	-3.27

Top 10, 1970

1	Western Germany	3.07
2	Belgium & Lux	1.80
3	Sweden	0.91
4	Iceland	0.54
5	France	0.18
6	United Kingdom	0.00
7	Cyprus	-0.02
8	Italy	-0.38
9	Finland	-1.62
10	Hungary	-1.84

Bottom 10, 1970

1	Malta	-41.40
2	Ireland	-10.91
3	Norway	-10.32
4	Greece	-9.00
5	Switzerland	-5.09
6	Spain	-5.07
7	Denmark	-4.80
8	Austria	-4.67
9	Netherlands	-2.70
10	Turkey	-1.89

Top 5, 1960

1	Western Germany	2.91
2	Spain	0.40
3	Belgium & Lux	0.12
4	Finland	-0.04
5	Sweden	-0.81

Bottom 5, 1960

1	Malta	-47.82
2	Cyprus	-17.23
3	Norway	-10.18
4	Ireland	-10.05
5	Greece	-7.13

Biggest invisible traders

Recent picture
Invisible trade, total credits and debits, 1998

	Average % of GDP				$m
1	Ireland	41.41	1	United Kingdom	519,360
2	Malta	41.33	2	Germany	377,400
3	Belgium & Lux	35.36	3	France	272,540
4	Estonia	27.94	4	Italy	245,883
5	Cyprus	27.27	5	Belgium & Lux	196,729
6	Netherlands	23.78	6	Netherlands	185,069
7	United Kingdom	20.54	7	Spain	113,556
8	Bulgaria	20.30	8	Switzerland	113,511
9	Switzerland	19.98	9	Austria	85,303
10	Austria	19.68	10	Sweden	78,586
11	Latvia	18.33	11	Ireland	57,397
12	Sweden	17.35	12	Denmark	53,669
13	Moldova	16.43	13	Russia	49,265
14	Croatia	16.37	14	Norway	43,374
15	Czech Republic	16.12	15	Turkey	41,128
16	Iceland	15.98	16	Finland	25,749
17	Denmark	15.32	17	Portugal	25,333
18	Azerbaijan	14.77	18	Poland	23,254
19	Norway	14.27	19	Greece[a]	17,985
20	Hungary	14.24	20	Czech Republic	17,085
21	Slovakia	14.07	21	Hungary	13,011
22	Armenia	13.51	22	Ukraine	7,582
23	Lithuania	13.20	23	Croatia	6,808
24	Portugal	11.90	24	Slovakia	5,600
25	Slovenia	11.23	25	Cyprus	4,898
26	Italy	10.63	26	Slovenia	4,358
27	Finland	10.29	27	Romania	4,106
28	Turkey	10.26	28	Bulgaria	4,100
29	Spain	10.23	29	Malta	3,141
30	Macedonia	10.15	30	Estonia	2,738
31	France	9.30	31	Lithuania	2,482
32	Georgia	8.78	32	Iceland	2,429
33	Germany	8.66	33	Latvia	2,163
34	Ukraine	7.71	34	Belarus	1,533
35	Poland	7.68	35	Azerbaijan	1,122
36	Russia	7.42	36	Georgia	931
37	Greece[a]	7.29	37	Moldova	559
38	Romania	6.71	38	Macedonia	528
39	Albania	5.75	39	Armenia	459
40	Belarus	3.44	40	Albania	311
	Euro area[b]	7.48		Euro area[b]	978,850

a 1997
b Excludes transactions between member states.

Looking back
Invisible trade, total credits and debits, $m

1990			1980		
1	United Kingdom	387,040	1	United Kingdom	176,733
2	France	367,691	2	France	114,816
3	Germany[a]	248,320	3	Germany[a]	102,430
4	Belgium & Lux	183,770	4	Belgium & Lux	62,545
5	Italy	153,636	5	Netherlands	59,289
6	Netherlands	114,273	6	Italy	49,524
7	Switzerland	78,711	7	Switzerland	29,321
8	Spain	63,158	8	Spain	22,133
9	Austria	56,708	9	Austria	21,159
10	Sweden	54,635	10	Norway	19,508
11	Denmark	40,778	11	Sweden	18,362
12	Norway	35,615	12	Denmark	15,199
13	Finland	23,091	13	Finland	7,131
14	Ireland	18,458	14	Poland	6,676
15	Turkey	15,429	15	Greece	6,152
16	Portugal	11,918	16	Ireland	5,492
17	Greece	11,899	17	Portugal	4,485
18	Poland	10,639	18	Hungary	3,688
19	Hungary	7,271	19	Romania	3,031
20	Cyprus	3,116	20	Turkey	2,500
21	Malta	1,636	21	Cyprus	1,821
22	Romania	1,586	22	Malta	935
23	Iceland	1,492	23	Iceland	683

1970			1960		
1	United Kingdom	20,961	1	United Kingdom	11,034
2	France	14,267	2	Germany[a]	6,000
3	Italy	13,588	3	Italy	3,043
4	Netherlands	8,188	4	Netherlands	2,131
5	Belgium & Lux	6,185	5	Belgium & Lux	1,764
6	Poland	5,417	6	Sweden	1,539
7	Switzerland	5,179	7	Norway	1,486
8	Norway	3,698	8	Switzerland	1,438
9	Sweden	3,427	9	Denmark	805
10	Austria	2,393	10	Spain	614
11	Denmark	2,205	11	Austria	576
12	Germany[a]	1,951	12	Finland	402
13	Spain	1,782	13	Greece	387
14	Ireland	1,277	14	Ireland	286
15	Finland	1,016	15	Turkey	237
16	Greece	847	16	Malta	101
17	Hungary	608	17	Cyprus	86
18	Turkey	508	18	Iceland	58
19	Cyprus	188			
20	Iceland	177			
21	Malta	151			

a Western only up to June 1990.

Invisible trade balances

The recent picture
Invisible trade balance
1998

		As % of GDP				$m
1	Cyprus	19.52		1	United Kingdom	44,000
2	Estonia	9.97		2	Switzerland	27,295
3	Switzerland	9.61		3	France	23,080
4	Malta	9.48		4	Spain	13,676
5	Croatia	9.18		5	Netherlands	13,249
6	Latvia	5.64		6	Turkey	10,476
7	Turkey	5.22		7	Belgium & Lux	8,997
8	United Kingdom	3.48		8	Poland	3,038
9	Netherlands	3.41		9	Greece[a]	3,005
10	Slovenia	3.40		10	Croatia	1,910
11	Belgium & Lux	3.23		11	Cyprus	1,753
12	Georgia	2.56		12	Portugal	995
13	Spain	2.46		13	Austria	959
14	Greece[a]	2.44		14	Czech Republic	795
15	Poland	2.01		15	Slovenia	659
16	Belarus	1.80		16	Ukraine	506
17	France	1.57		17	Estonia	489
18	Czech Republic	1.50		18	Belarus	401
19	Albania	1.29		19	Malta	360
20	Ukraine	1.03		20	Latvia	333
21	Portugal	0.94		21	Georgia	136
22	Bulgaria	0.89		22	Bulgaria	90
23	Armenia	0.58		23	Albania	35
24	Austria	0.44		24	Armenia	10
25	Lithuania	-0.16		25	Lithuania	-15
26	Italy	-0.70		26	Moldova	-42
27	Slovakia	-0.71		27	Iceland	-99
28	Iceland	-1.30		28	Slovakia	-142
29	Norway	-1.41		29	Macedonia	-218
30	Hungary	-2.12		30	Azerbaijan	-382
31	Germany	-2.39		31	Hungary	-969
32	Denmark	-2.42		32	Romania	-1,046
33	Moldova	-2.45		33	Norway	-2,136
34	Finland	-3.19		34	Finland	-3,993
35	Romania	-3.42		35	Denmark	-4,239
36	Sweden	-4.22		36	Italy	-8,147
37	Russia	-4.46		37	Sweden	-9,554
38	Macedonia	-8.38		38	Russia	-14,793
39	Azerbaijan	-10.06		39	Ireland	-24,063
40	Ireland	-34.72		40	Germany	-52,180
	Euro area[b]	7.36			Euro area[b]	481,783

a 1997
b Excludes transactions between member states.

Looking back
Invisible trade balance as % of GDP

Top 10, 1990			Bottom 10, 1990		
1	Cyprus	24.09	1	Ireland	-14.50
2	Malta	18.05	2	Poland	-5.14
3	Switzerland	7.28	3	Finland	-4.97
4	Austria	5.14	4	Russia	-4.87
5	Greece	2.26	5	Sweden	-3.70
6	Belgium & Lux	2.16	6	Iceland	-3.42
7	Spain	1.70	7	Hungary	-2.85
8	Turkey	1.62	8	Bulgaria	-2.60
9	Portugal	1.48	9	Denmark	-2.40
10	France	0.96	10	Norway	-1.99

Top 10, 1980			Bottom 10, 1980		
1	Malta	29.39	1	Ireland	-5.78
2	Switzerland	6.09	2	Poland	-4.16
3	Greece	5.59	3	Iceland	-2.92
4	Austria	3.50	4	Romania	-2.21
5	Spain	2.13	5	Hungary	-2.17
6	France	2.11	6	Finland	-1.18
7	United Kingdom	1.50	7	Western Germany	-1.03
8	Italy	0.93	8	Sweden	-0.73
9	Netherlands	0.24	9	Denmark	-0.70
10	Belgium & Lux	0.13	10	Norway	-0.52

Top 10, 1970			Bottom 10, 1970		
1	Malta	22.23	1	Sweden	-1.25
2	Switzerland	8.38	2	Western Germany	-1.19
3	Norway	8.25	3	Turkey	-1.03
4	Austria	4.09	4	Finland	-0.53
5	Spain	3.50	5	Iceland	-0.04
6	Ireland	3.26	6	Cyprus	0.01
7	United Kingdom	1.96	7	France	0.29
8	Denmark	1.64	8	Hungary	0.76
9	Belgium & Lux	1.58	9	Italy	0.97
10	Greece	1.29	10	Netherlands	1.06

Top 5, 1960			Bottom 5, 1960		
1	Malta	43.44	1	Finland	-0.87
2	Cyprus	8.38	2	Turkey	-0.59
3	Norway	8.02	3	Western Germany	-0.25
4	Ireland	6.60	4	Sweden	0.28
5	Netherlands	4.14	5	Belgium & Lux	0.74

Who exports to whom

Most important export destinations
Exports to main partners and to EU 15 countries as % of total exports

1998	Main ptnrs	EU 15	1998	Main ptnrs	EU 15
Albania		88.6	**Estonia**		55.1
Italy	58.8		Finland	18.9	
Greece	12.9		Sweden	16.7	
Armenia		25.8	**Finland**		53.0
Belgium	20.8		Germany	11.7	
Iran	16.7		Sweden	9.5	
Austria		63.2	**France**		63.2
Germany	36.4		Germany	16.0	
Italy	8.8		United Kingdom	10.0	
Azerbaijan		8.0	**Georgia**		21.1
Georgia	36.4		Turkey	25.1	
Russia	20.3		Russia	16.9	
Belarus		7.4	**Germany**		50.7
Russia	65.2		France	11.1	
Ukraine	5.5		United States	9.4	
Belgium		76.5	**Greece**		53.3
Germany	18.7		Germany	18.4	
France	17.7		Italy	11.9	
Bulgaria		51.6	**Hungary**		72.7
Italy	13.1		Germany	36.1	
Germany	10.9		Austria	10.6	
Croatia		45.8	**Iceland**		61.9
Italy	18.5		United Kingdom	18.9	
Germany	17.4		Germany	14.8	
Cyprus		39.3	**Ireland**		61.7
Russia	10.1		United Kingdom	22.0	
Greece	9.7		Germany	15.6	
Czech Republic		64.2	**Italy**		53.7
Germany	38.5		Germany	16.5	
Slovakia	10.7		France	12.8	
Denmark		66.2	**Latvia**		56.6
Germany	21.1		Germany	15.6	
Sweden	11.0		United Kingdom	30.2	

1970	Main ptnrs	EU 15	1970	Main ptnrs	EU 15
Austria		56.3	**Germany, Western**[a]		59.4
Western Germany	23.7		France	12.4	
Switzerland	10.4		Netherlands	10.6	
Belgium & Lux		78.1	**Greece**		56.6
Western Germany	24.1		Western Germany	20.2	
France	19.9		Italy	10.0	
Denmark		63.3	**Iceland**		40.3
United Kingdom	18.6		United States	30.0	
Sweden	16.6		United Kingdom	13.2	
Finland		63.7	**Ireland**		73.1
United Kingdom	17.4		United Kingdom	60.8	
Sweden	15.1		United States	9.2	
France		59.6	**Italy**		55.3
Western Germany	20.4		Western Germany	21.6	
Italy	11.0		France	12.8	

1998	Main ptnrs	EU 15
Lithuania		38.0
Russia	16.5	
Germany	13.1	
Luxembourg		83.2
Germany	24.9	
France	20.0	
Macedonia		51.8
Germany	22.3	
United States	12.5	
Malta		41.5
France	11.3	
Germany	11.0	
Moldova		13.6
Russia	49.6	
United States	12.2	
Netherlands		73.3
Germany	26.4	
United Kingdom	11.1	
Norway		77.1
United Kingdom	17.1	
Germany	12.4	
Poland		68.3
Germany	19.8	
Italy	5.9	
Portugal		81.5
Germany	19.8	
Spain	15.5	
Romania		64.6
Italy	22.3	
Germany	19.5	

1998	Main ptnrs	EU 15
Russia		32.7
Germany	8.2	
Ukraine	7.8	
Serbia & Montenegro		81.0
Italy	28.9	
Germany	26.4	
Slovakia		55.7
Germany	28.8	
Czech Republic	20.3	
Slovenia		65.5
Germany	28.4	
Italy	13.8	
Spain		70.8
France	19.5	
Germany	13.6	
Sweden		55.2
Germany	10.9	
United Kingdom	8.9	
Switzerland		60.1
Germany	23.1	
United States	11.0	
Turkey		50.1
Germany	20.2	
United States	8.3	
Ukraine		16.9
Russia	23.0	
China	5.8	
United Kingdom		48.2
United States	13.4	
Germany	11.4	

1970	Main ptnrs	EU 15
Netherlands		76.9
Western Germany	32.6	
Belgium & Lux	13.9	
Norway		78.6
United Kingdom	17.9	
Western Germany	17.9	
Portugal		52.6
United Kingdom	20.3	
Angola	12.5	
Spain		52.3
United States	14.2	
Western Germany	11.8	

1970	Main ptnrs	EU 15
Sweden		71.6
United Kingdom	12.5	
Western Germany	11.7	
Switzerland		60.4
Western Germany	14.8	
Italy	9.4	
Turkey		52.6
Western Germany	19.9	
United States	9.5	
United Kingdom		44.7
United States	11.7	
Western Germany	6.2	

a Trade between Western and Eastern Germany is excluded.

Who imports from where

Most important sources of imports

Imports from main partners and from EU 15 countries as % of total imports

1998	Main ptnrs	EU 15	1998	Main ptnrs	EU 15
Albania		78.6	**Estonia**		60.1
Italy	38.6		Finland	22.6	
Greece	24.4		Russia	11.1	
Armenia		24.8	**Finland**		55.2
Russia	17.7		Germany	15.2	
Belgium	6.7		Sweden	11.6	
Austria		68.6	**France**		62.4
Germany	42.5		Germany	17.3	
Italy	8.3		Italy	9.9	
Azerbaijan		25.1	**Georgia**		25.2
Turkey	22.5		Turkey	13.6	
Russia	9.8		Azerbaijan	11.4	
Belarus		18.2	**Germany**		48.5
Russia	54.7		France	11.1	
Germany	8.9		United States	8.3	
Belgium		71.3	**Greece**		66.9
Germany	17.9		Italy	16.3	
Netherlands	16.8		Germany	15.3	
Bulgaria		46.5	**Hungary**		64.1
Russia	21.0		Germany	28.2	
Germany	13.9		Austria	9.6	
Croatia		58.1	**Iceland**		58.8
Germany	20.5		Germany	11.6	
Italy	19.0		United States	10.5	
Cyprus		54.8	**Ireland**		52.5
United States	12.5		United Kingdom	33.4	
United Kingdom	11.3		United States	16.2	
Czech Republic		64.2	**Italy**		56.8
Germany	34.5		Germany	18.8	
Slovakia	7.2		France	13.2	
Denmark		71.2	**Latvia**		55.2
Germany	22.1		Germany	16.8	
Sweden	12.7		Russia	11.8	

1970	Main ptnrs	EU 15	1970	Main ptnrs	EU 15
Austria		68.5	**Germany, Western**[a]		57.4
Western Germany	41.3		France	12.7	
Switzerland	7.4		Netherlands	12.2	
Belgium & Lux		69.2	**Greece**		56.9
Western Germany	23.4		Western Germany	18.6	
France	17.1		Japan	12.7	
Denmark		53.4	**Iceland**		63.6
Western Germany	18.8		Western Germany	15.1	
Sweden	15.9		United Kingdom	14.2	
Finland		61.9	**Ireland**		72.9
Western Germany	16.5		United Kingdom	51.7	
Sweden	16.1		Western Germany	6.8	
France		58.9	**Italy**		51.0
Western Germany	22.1		Western Germany	19.8	
Belgium & Lux	11.2		France	13.2	

1998	Main ptnrs	EU 15	1998	Main ptnrs	EU 15
Lithuania		47.2	**Russia**		36.3
Russia	21.1		Germany	12.6	
Germany	18.2		Belarus	10.5	
Luxembourg		96.1	**Serbia & Montenegro**		73.3
Belgium	37.5		Germany	23.4	
Germany	27.4		Italy	21.1	
Macedonia		52.7	**Slovakia**		50.1
France	14.4		Germany	25.7	
Germany	13.8		Czech Republic	18.4	
Malta		82.7	**Slovenia**		69.4
Italy	28.5		Germany	20.6	
France	17.8		Italy	16.8	
Moldova		25.4	**Spain**		67.4
Russia	24.9		France	18.3	
Ukraine	13.9		Germany	15.6	
Netherlands		53.9	**Sweden**		64.2
Germany	19.3		Germany	17.8	
United States	10.6		United Kingdom	9.6	
Norway		70.2	**Switzerland**		73.3
Sweden	15.5		Germany	30.4	
Germany	14.2		France	10.9	
Poland		65.9	**Turkey**		52.4
Germany	26.4		Germany	15.9	
Italy	9.4		Italy	9.2	
Portugal		77.2	**Ukraine**		21.6
Spain	24.0		Russia	48.1	
Germany	14.9		Germany	8.6	
Romania		57.9	**United Kingdom**		43.8
Italy	17.5		United States	13.8	
Germany	17.4		Germany	12.1	

1970	Main ptnrs	EU 15	1970	Main ptnrs	EU 15
Netherlands		66.8	**Sweden**		64.3
Western Germany	27.1		Western Germany	18.9	
Belgium & Lux	16.8		United Kingdom	13.8	
Norway		68.4	**Switzerland**		78.7
Sweden	20.1		Western Germany	30.5	
Western Germany	14.3		France	12.3	
Portugal		57.1	**Turkey**		45.3
Western Germany	15.1		United States	18.2	
United Kingdom	13.9		Western Germany	17.3	
Spain		44.7	**United Kingdom**		36.7
United States	18.9		United States	13.0	
Western Germany	12.6		Canada	7.6	

a Trade between Western and Eastern Germany is excluded.

Top traders by sector

Food

		As % of world exports/imports		
	Value, $bn			
	1998	1980	1990	1998
Exporters				
1 United States	54.33	17.6	13.5	12.3
2 France	37.33	8.0	10.5	8.5
3 Netherlands	28.86	6.6	8.3	6.5
4 Germany	24.69	4.5	6.3	5.6
5 Belgium & Lux	18.32	2.7	3.5	4.1
6 United Kingdom	17.52	3.5	4.1	4.0
7 Spain	16.14	1.7	2.6	3.6
8 Canada	15.66	3.5	3.5	3.5
EU15	187.66	34.8[a]	45.7	42.3
Intra-exports	134.97	23.5[a]	33.7	30.5
Extra-exports	52.69	11.3[a]	12.0	11.9
Importers				
1 United States	46.07	8.5	8.8	9.7
2 Japan	44.46	7.0	9.9	9.4
3 Germany	39.41	9.4	10.4	8.3
4 United Kingdom	29.69	6.4	6.7	6.3
5 France	27.61	5.7	6.6	5.8
6 Italy	22.80	5.3	6.3	4.8
7 Netherlands	17.86	4.8	4.6	3.8
8 Belgium & Lux	17.48	3.3	3.4	3.7

Textiles

		As % of world exports/imports		
	Value, $bn			
	1998	1980	1990	1998
Exporters				
1 Germany	13.26	11.3	13.4	8.8
2 Italy	13.03	7.4	9.1	8.6
3 China[b]	12.82	4.5	6.9	8.5
4 South Korea	11.28	4.0	5.8	7.5
5 Taiwan	11.02	3.2	5.9	7.3
6 United States	9.22	6.7	4.8	6.1
7 France	7.57	6.1	5.8	5.0
EU15	60.6	46.3[a]	48.6	40.1
Intra-exports	37.68	29.1[a]	34.1	25.3
Extra-exports	22.92	17.1[a]	14.5	15.2
Importers				
1 United States	13.46	4.3	6.1	8.6
2 China[b]	11.08	1.9	4.8	7.0
3 Germany	10.99	11.7	10.8	7.0
4 United Kingdom	8.31	6.1	6.4	5.3
5 France	7.5	7.0	6.9	4.8
6 Italy	6.61	4.5	5.6	4.2
7 Belgium & Lux	4.42	4.0	3.3	2.8

Clothing

	Value, $bn	As % of world exports/imports		
	1998	1980	1990	1998
Exporters				
1 China	30.05	4.0	8.9	16.7
2 Italy	14.74	11.2	11.0	8.2
3 Hong Kong[c]	9.67	11.4	8.6	5.4
4 United States	8.79	3.1	2.4	4.9
5 Germany	7.68	7.7	7.3	4.3
6 Turkey	7.06	0.3	3.1	3.9
7 Mexico[b]	6.60	0.0	0.5	3.7
8 France	5.75	5.6	4.3	3.2
EU15	51.17	38.0[a]	37.7	28.5
Intra-exports	35.37	25.9[a]	27.2	19.7
Extra-exports	15.80	12.1[a]	10.5	8.8
Importers				
1 United States	55.72	15.9	23.6	29.9
2 Germany	22.35	19.1	17.9	12.0
3 Japan	14.72	3.5	7.7	7.9
4 United Kingdom	11.98	6.6	6.1	6.4
5 France	11.64	6.0	7.3	6.3
6 Italy	5.86	1.8	2.3	3.1
7 Belgium & Lux	5.30	4.2	3.1	2.8
8 Netherlands	5.27	6.6	4.2	2.8

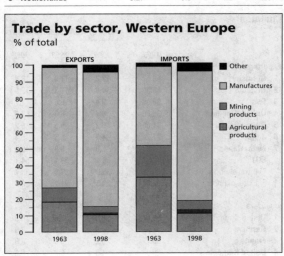

Trade by sector, Western Europe
% of total

EXPORTS IMPORTS

Other
Manufactures
Mining products
Agricultural products

1963 1998 1963 1998

a EU12.
b Includes significant shipments through processing zones.
c Domestic exports, ie, excluding re-exports.
d Imports are valued fob.

Automotive products

	Value, $bn	As % of world exports/imports		
	1998	1980	1990	1998
Exporters				
1 **Germany**	99.56	21.0	21.9	19.0
2 Japan	77.61	19.8	20.8	14.8
3 United States	61.06	11.9	10.2	11.6
4 Canada	49.92	6.9	8.9	9.5
5 **France**	38.65	9.9	8.2	7.4
6 Spain	27.11	1.8	3.7	5.2
7 **United Kingdom**	26.17	5.8	4.4	5.0
8 **Belgium & Lux**	25.36	4.9	5.7	4.8
EU15	267.67	49.4[a]	53.8	51.0
Intra-exports	189.31	28.5[a]	39.5	36.1
Extra-exports	78.36	20.9[a]	14.3	14.9
Importers				
1 United States	129.83	19.7	24.3	24.3
2 Germany	48.25	6.0	9.4	9.0
3 Canada[d]	39.98	8.4	7.5	7.5
4 **United Kingdom**	38.27	5.5	7.0	7.2
5 France	28.54	5.3	6.6	5.3
6 Italy	25.02	5.4	5.5	4.7
7 **Belgium & Lux**	23.26	5.2	5.7	4.4
8 Spain	22.47	0.8	3.1	4.2

Chemicals

	Value, $bn	As % of world exports/imports		
	1998	1980	1990	1998
Exporters				
1 **Germany**	69.57	17.2	17.9	13.8
2 United States	69.30	14.8	13.3	13.8
3 France	38.99	9.4	9.6	7.7
4 **United Kingdom**	36.86	8.7	8.0	7.3
5 **Belgium & Lux**	31.00	5.3	5.6	6.2
6 Japan	27.24	4.7	5.3	5.4
7 **Netherlands**	26.97	8.0	6.8	5.4
EU15	272.32	58.4[a]	59.1	54.1
Intra-exports	169.38	35.0[a]	37.9	33.7
Extra-exports	102.94	23.3[a]	21.2	20.5
Importers				
1 United States	56.44	6.0	7.6	10.9
2 Germany	41.26	8.9	10.2	7.9
3 France	35.77	8.2	8.0	6.9
4 **United Kingdom**	29.96	4.9	6.2	5.8
5 Italy	27.87	5.4	6.4	5.4
6 **Belgium & Lux**	27.33	4.0	4.4	5.3
7 Japan	20.57	4.0	4.9	4.0

Machinery and transport equipment

		Value, $bn	As % of world exports/imports		
		1998	1980	1990	1998
Exporters					
1	United States	358.20	16.4	15.1	16.5
2	**Germany**	275.80	16.3	17.2	12.7
3	Japan	268.50	14.5	16.7	12.4
4	**France**	131.90	7.0	6.5	6.1
5	**United Kingdom**	130.60	7.6	6.2	6.0
6	**Italy**	94.50	4.8	5.2	4.4
7	Canada	88.20	3.2	3.9	4.1
	EU15	910.36	43.0[a]	47.8	42.0
	Intra-exports	539.34	20.9[a]	29.8	24.9
	Extra-exports	371.02	22.1[a]	18.0	17.1
Importers					
1	United States	431.60	11.7	17.2	19.6
2	**Germany**	168.40	6.4	9.3	7.6
3	**United Kingdom**	141.30	5.6	6.8	6.4
4	**France**	111.90	5.3	6.4	5.1
5	Canada[d]	105.20	4.9	4.7	4.8
6	Japan	74.90	1.5	2.9	3.4
7	**Italy**	72.80	3.7	4.4	3.3

Office machines and telecoms equipment

		Value, $bn	As % of world exports/imports		
		1998	1980	1990	1998
Exporters					
1	United States	113.89	20.2	17.3	16.7
2	Japan	85.03	21.1	22.4	12.5
3	**United Kingdom**	43.25	6.4	6.4	6.3
4	Taiwan	38.44	3.2	4.7	5.6
5	Singapore[c]	36.81	2.5	4.9	5.4
6	Malaysia	34.61	1.4	2.7	5.1
7	**Germany**	34.21	9.9	7.5	5.0
	EU15	202.35	32.6[a]	31.1	29.7
	Intra-exports	133.41	19.3[a]	22.0	19.6
	Extra-exports	68.93	13.3[a]	9.1	10.1
Importers					
1	United States	155.91	15.4	20.7	22.5
2	**United Kingdom**	47.44	6.8	7.8	6.8
3	**Germany**	45.82	9.4	9.6	6.6
4	Japan	36.55	2.5	3.7	5.3
5	**Netherlands**	31.73	3.7	4.0	4.6
6	**France**	30.93	6.2	5.9	4.5
7	Taiwan	23.79	1.4	2.4	3.4

See page 75 for footnotes.

Inflation

Snapshots
Consumer price inflation, %

1999

1	Belarus	293.7	19	Latvia	2.4
2	Russia	85.7	20	Norway	2.3
3	Turkey	64.9		Portugal	2.3
4	Moldova	45.9		Spain	2.3
5	Romania	45.8	23	Netherlands	2.2
6	Ukraine[a]	15.9	24	Czech Republic	2.1
7	Slovakia	10.6		Malta	2.1
8	Hungary	10.3	26	Cyprus	1.7
9	Armenia[b]	8.7		Italy	1.7
10	Poland	7.3	28	Ireland	1.6
11	Slovenia	6.6		United Kingdom	1.6
12	Sri Lanka	4.7	30	Finland	1.2
13	Croatia	3.7	31	Belgium	1.1
14	Georgia[b]	3.6	32	Luxembourg	1.0
15	Estonia	3.3	33	Lithuania	0.8
16	Iceland	3.2		Switzerland	0.8
17	Greece	2.6	35	Austria	0.6
18	Denmark	2.5		Germany	0.6

1990

1	Ex-Yugoslavia	583.1	14	Switzerland	5.4
2	Poland	555.4	15	Cyprus	4.5
3	Turkey	60.3	16	Romania	4.2
4	Hungary	29.0	17	Norway	4.1
5	Greece	20.4	18	Luxembourg	3.7
6	Iceland	15.5	19	Belgium	3.5
7	Portugal	13.4	20	France	3.4
8	Sweden	10.5	21	Austria	3.3
9	Ex-Czechoslovakia	10.0		Ireland	3.3
10	United Kingdom	9.5	23	Malta	3.0
11	Spain	6.7	24	Germany	2.7
12	Italy	6.5	25	Denmark	2.6
13	Finland	6.1	26	Netherlands	2.5

1980 / 1970

1980			**1970**		
1	Turkey	110.2	1	Iceland	13.1
2	Iceland	58.5	2	Norway	10.6
3	Ex-Yugoslavia	30.9	3	Ex-Yugoslavia	9.5
4	Greece	24.9	4	Ireland	8.2
5	Italy	21.3	5	Sweden	7.0
6	Ireland	18.2	6	Turkey	6.9
7	United Kingdom	18.0	7	Denmark	6.5
8	Portugal	16.6	8	United Kingdom	6.4
9	Malta	15.7	9	France	5.8
10	Spain	15.6	10	Spain	5.7
11	Sweden	13.7	11	Italy	4.8
12	Cyprus	13.5	12	Luxembourg	4.6
	France	13.5	13	Portugal	4.5

Highest averages
Average annual consumer price inflation, %

1990–99

1	Ukrainec	431.3	14	Turkey	78.7
2	Armeniad	405.4	15	Latvia	73.0
3	Georgiad	395.6	16	Albania	39.3
4	Belarus	353.4	17	Slovenia	36.2
5	Azerbaijanc	333.6	18	Poland	29.0
6	Russia	190.8	19	Hungary	21.3
7	Moldova	151.8	20	Slovakia	15.3
8	Bulgaria	123.5	21	Czech Republic	14.4
9	Macedoniad	116.3	22	Greece	10.0
10	Romania	113.9	23	Portugal	5.1
11	Croatia	105.9	24	Italy	3.9
12	Lithuania	105.1		Spain	3.9
13	Estonia	80.3	26	Cyprus	3.8

1980–90

1	Poland	69.9	10	Norway	7.6
2	Turkey	45.8		Sweden	7.6
3	Iceland	33.4	12	Finland	6.7
4	Greece	19.0	13	United Kingdom	6.6
5	Portugal	17.1	14	France	6.3
6	Hungary	10.7	15	Denmark	5.9
7	Italy	9.6	16	Cyprus	4.9
8	Spain	9.3	17	Belgium	4.5
9	Ireland	7.7	18	Luxembourg	4.4

1970–80

1	Iceland	34.0	10	Denmark	9.9
2	Turkey	27.7	11	France	9.7
3	Portugal	18.1	12	Sweden	9.1
4	Spain	15.3	13	Norway	8.4
5	Greece	14.4	14	Cyprus	7.9
6	Italy	13.9	15	Belgium	7.4
7	Ireland	13.7	16	Netherlands	7.3
	United Kingdom	13.7	17	Malta	6.7
9	Finland	11.2	18	Luxembourg	6.6

1960–70

1	Iceland	11.6	10	France	4.0
2	Spain	6.2		Sweden	4.0
3	Denmark	5.9		Turkey	4.0
4	Finland	5.0	13	Italy	3.6
5	Ireland	4.7		Austria	3.6
6	Norway	4.5	15	Switzerland	3.3
7	Netherlands	4.3	16	Belgium	3.0
8	Portugal	4.2	17	Germany	2.6
9	United Kingdom	4.1		Luxembourg	2.6

a 1997 b 1998 c 1990–97 d 1990–98

Exchange rates

Currency units per dollar

	1960	1965	1970	1975	1980
Austria	26.04	25.89	25.88	18.51	13.81
Belgium & Lux	49.70	49.64	49.68	39.53	31.52
Cyprus	0.36	0.36	0.42	0.39	0.36
Denmark	6.91	6.89	7.49	6.18	6.02
Finland	3.21	3.22	4.18	3.85	3.84
France	4.90	4.90	5.55	4.49	4.52
Germany	4.17	4.01	3.65	2.62	1.96
Greece	30.00	30.00	30.00	35.65	46.54
Hungary			60.00	43.51	32.21
Iceland	0.38	0.43	0.88	1.71	6.24
Ireland	0.36	0.36	0.42	0.49	0.53
Italy	620.60	624.70	623.00	683.60	930.50
Malta	0.36	0.36	0.42	0.40	0.35
Netherlands	3.77	3.61	3.60	2.69	2.13
Norway	7.15	7.15	7.14	5.59	5.18
Poland			-	-	-
Portugal	28.83	28.83	28.75	27.47	53.04
Romania			6.00	20.00	18.00
Spain	60.15	59.99	69.72	59.77	79.25
Sweden	5.18	5.18	5.17	4.39	4.37
Switzerland	4.31	4.32	4.32	2.62	1.76
Turkey	9.02	9.04	9.00	15.20	90.10
United Kingdom	0.36	0.36	0.42	0.49	0.42

Changing values
Currencies change against the dollar, %
1990–2000

1	Latvia	38.99	17	Norway	-33.52
2	Lithuania	-5.23	18	Sweden	-36.30
3	United Kingdom	-22.14	19	Portugal	-37.67
4	Switzerland	-22.70	20	Slovakia	-38.74
5	Estonia	-22.80	21	Finland	-42.89
6	Iceland	-26.66	22	Italy	-45.40
7	France	-26.85	23	Spain	-45.69
8	Czech Republic	-27.31	24	Greece	-56.24
9	Austria	-27.40	25	Slovenia	-74.26
10	Denmark	-27.54	26	Hungary	-77.83
11	Belgium & Lux	-28.17	27	Poland	-78.19
12	Netherlands	-28.27	28	Albania	-93.22
13	Germany	-28.74	29	Russia	-98.52
14	Cyprus	-29.92	30	Turkey	-99.52
15	Malta	-31.24	31	Bulgaria	-99.63
16	Ireland	-33.49	32	Romania	-99.83

Note: Andorra uses the Spanish peseta; Liechtenstein uses the Swiss franc; the Luxembourg franc is at parity with the Belgian franc, which, in turn, is also legal tender in Luxembourg; Monaco uses the French franc; San Marino and the Vatican use the Italian lira.

1985	1990	1995	June 2000 per $	June 2000 per euro
17.28	10.68	10.09	14.71	13.76
50.36	30.98	29.42	43.13	40.35
0.54	0.43	0.46	0.61	0.57
8.97	5.78	5.55	7.98	7.46
5.42	3.63	4.36	6.36	5.95
7.56	5.13	4.90	7.01	6.56
2.46	1.49	1.43	2.09	1.96
147.76	157.63	237.04	360.20	336.97
47.35	61.45	139.47	277.16	259.28
42.06	55.39	65.23	75.53	70.66
0.80	0.56	0.62	0.84	0.79
1,678.50	1,130.20	1,584.70	2,070.11	1,936.58
0.42	0.30	0.35	0.44	0.41
2.77	1.69	1.60	2.36	2.20
7.58	5.91	6.32	8.89	8.32
0.01	0.95	2.47	4.36	4.08
157.49	133.60	149.41	214.34	200.52
15.73	34.71	2,578.00	20,750.00	19,411.63
154.15	96.61	121.41	177.89	166.41
7.62	5.70	6.66	8.95	8.37
2.08	1.30	1.15	1.68	1.57
576.90	2,930.10	59,650.00	614,615.00	574,972.33
0.69	0.52	0.65	0.67	0.62

Currency units per dollar

	1992 per $	1995 per $	June 2000 per $	June 2000 per euro
Albania	102.90	94.24	147.60	138.08
Armenia	2.07	402.00	531.10	496.84
Azerbaijan	48.60	4,440.00	4,378.00	4,095.62
Belarus	15.00	11,500.00	969.00	906.50
Bosnia			2.11	1.98
Bulgaria	24.49	70.70	1,904.35	1,781.52
Croatia	0.80	5.32	8.29	7.76
Czech Republic	28.90	26.60	38.52	36.03
Estonia	12.91	11.46	16.72	15.64
Georgia		1.25	1.99	1.86
Latvia	0.84	0.54	0.60	0.57
Lithuania	3.79	4.00	4.00	3.74
Macedonia		37.98	59.85	55.99
Moldova	0.41	4.50	12.61	11.80
Russia	0.42	4.64	28.43	26.60
Serbia & Montenegro			12.18	11.39
Slovakia	28.90	29.57	45.70	42.76
Slovenia	98.70	125.99	220.28	206.07
Ukraine	0.01	1.79	5.44	5.09

Burgernomics

Over/under valuation of national currencies (as measured by *The Economist*'s Big Mac index, see Glossary, page 12, for explanation) in April 2000, compared to that of the US$, %

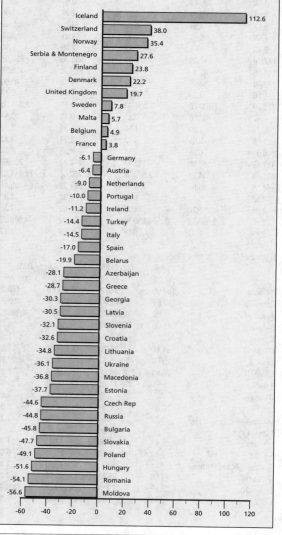

Iceland	112.6
Switzerland	38.0
Norway	35.4
Serbia & Montenegro	27.6
Finland	23.8
Denmark	22.2
United Kingdom	19.7
Sweden	7.8
Malta	5.7
Belgium	4.9
France	3.8
Germany	-6.1
Austria	-6.4
Netherlands	-9.0
Portugal	-10.0
Ireland	-11.2
Turkey	-14.4
Italy	-14.5
Spain	-17.0
Belarus	-19.9
Azerbaijan	-28.1
Greece	-28.7
Georgia	-30.3
Latvia	-30.5
Slovenia	-32.1
Croatia	-32.6
Lithuania	-34.8
Ukraine	-36.1
Macedonia	-36.8
Estonia	-37.7
Czech Rep	-44.6
Russia	-44.8
Bulgaria	-45.8
Slovakia	-47.7
Poland	-49.1
Hungary	-51.6
Romania	-54.1
Moldova	-56.6

Part IV

GOVERNMENT FINANCE

General government revenue

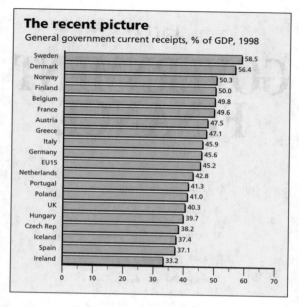

The recent picture

General government current receipts, % of GDP, 1998

Sweden	58.5
Denmark	56.4
Norway	50.3
Finland	50.0
Belgium	49.8
France	49.6
Austria	47.5
Greece	47.1
Italy	45.9
Germany	45.6
EU15	45.2
Netherlands	42.8
Portugal	41.3
Poland	41.0
UK	40.3
Hungary	39.7
Czech Rep	38.2
Iceland	37.4
Spain	37.1
Ireland	33.2

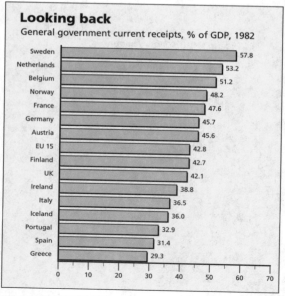

Looking back

General government current receipts, % of GDP, 1982

Sweden	57.8
Netherlands	53.2
Belgium	51.2
Norway	48.2
France	47.6
Germany	45.7
Austria	45.6
EU 15	42.8
Finland	42.7
UK	42.1
Ireland	38.8
Italy	36.5
Iceland	36.0
Portugal	32.9
Spain	31.4
Greece	29.3

General government spending

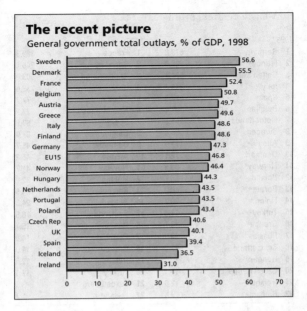

The recent picture
General government total outlays, % of GDP, 1998

Sweden	56.6
Denmark	55.5
France	52.4
Belgium	50.8
Austria	49.7
Greece	49.6
Italy	48.6
Finland	48.6
Germany	47.3
EU15	46.8
Norway	46.4
Hungary	44.3
Netherlands	43.5
Portugal	43.5
Poland	43.4
Czech Rep	40.6
UK	40.1
Spain	39.4
Iceland	36.5
Ireland	31.0

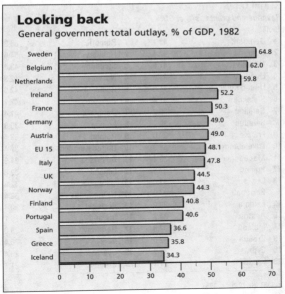

Looking back
General government total outlays, % of GDP, 1982

Sweden	64.8
Belgium	62.0
Netherlands	59.8
Ireland	52.2
France	50.3
Germany	49.0
Austria	49.0
EU 15	48.1
Italy	47.8
UK	44.5
Norway	44.3
Finland	40.8
Portugal	40.6
Spain	36.6
Greece	35.8
Iceland	34.3

Central government revenue

How much central governments raise
$bn

1998			1988		
1	Germany	678.8	1	France	399.3
2	France[a]	598.0	2	Germany	346.1
3	United Kingdom	524.2	3	United Kingdom	303.0
4	Italy	343.4	4	Italy	239.6
5	Spain	117.3	5	Sweden	77.7
6	Belgium[a]	107.4	6	Netherlands	77.2
7	Netherlands	105.8	7	Spain	67.9
8	Sweden	88.8	8	Belgium	67.0
9	Austria[a]	77.9	9	Denmark	45.7
10	Denmark[b]	72.1	10	Austria	45.2
11	Norway[a]	66.5	11	Norway	41.7
12	Poland	56.7	12	Finland	32.8
13	Portugal[a]	40.2	13	Romania	25.5
14	Finland[a]	39.7	14	Bulgaria	24.3
15	Turkey[c]	33.5	15	Switzerland	18.5
16	Greece[c]	33.1	16	Hungary	15.7
17	Russia	30.9	17	Portugal	14.8
18	Switzerland	27.1	18	Greece	14.0
19	Hungary	19.0	19	Ireland	12.5
20	Czech Republic	16.4	20	Turkey	12.4
21	Ireland	12.0	21	Luxembourg	3.3
22	Romania[c]	9.8	22	Iceland	1.7

...and relative revenue
Revenue and grants as % of GDP

1998			1988		
1	Denmark[b]	43.1	1	Bulgaria	86.3
2	Bulgaria	42.4	2	Hungary	54.6
3	Norway[a]	41.8	3	Sweden	43.4
4	Hungary	41.6	4	Norway	42.9
5	United Kingdom	41.5	5	Romania	42.5
6	Slovenia	41.4	6	Belgium	42.1
7	Belgium[a]	39.2	7	Denmark	41.4
	Sweden	39.2	8	France	39.9
9	France	39.0	9	Ireland	38.4
10	Luxembourg[b]	38.9	10	United Kingdom	37.4
11	Macedonia[b]	38.4	11	Austria	34.9
12	Poland	37.5	12	Finland	32.8
13	Latvia	37.0	13	Luxembourg	32.6
	Portugal[a]	37.0	14	Netherlands	32.4
15	Estonia	35.0	15	Portugal	30.4
16	Austria[a]	34.2	16	Iceland	30.1
17	Iceland	32.5	17	Germany	29.0
18	Croatia	32.0	18	Italy	28.4
19	Cyprus	31.7	19	Cyprus	25.4
20	Finland[a]	31.2	20	Greece	21.7

a 1997 b 1995 c 1996

Central government spending

How much central governments spend

$bn

1998			*1988*		
1	Germany	691.0	1	France	416.4
2	France[a]	650.6	2	Germany	365.2
3	United Kingdom	516.1	3	Italy	333.1
4	Italy	371.6	4	United Kingdom	290.0
5	Spain	124.3	5	Netherlands	87.5
6	Belgium[a]	112.3	6	Belgium	76.9
7	Netherlands	108.3	7	Sweden	72.8
8	Sweden	88.0	8	Spain	66.2
9	Austria[a]	83.4	9	Austria	51.5
10	Denmark[b]	75.6	10	Denmark	43.3
11	Norway[a]	65.4	11	Norway	41.9
12	Poland	58.3	12	Finland	32.4
13	Turkey[c]	48.7	13	Bulgaria	26.3
14	Greece[c]	45.1	14	Romania	22.0
15	Russia	43.9	15	Greece	21.4
16	Finland[a]	42.6	16	Portugal	18.5
17	Portugal[a]	42.3	17	Switzerland	17.1
18	Switzerland	26.9	18	Hungary	15.7
19	Hungary	21.9	19	Turkey	15.1
20	Czech Republic	17.3	20	Ireland	13.4
21	Ireland	11.2	21	Luxembourg	3.2
	Romania[c]	11.2	22	Iceland	1.9

...and relative spending

Spending and lending minus repayments as % of GDP

1998			*1988*		
1	Hungary	48.0	1	Bulgaria	93.1
2	Denmark[b]	45.2	2	Hungary	54.8
3	France[a]	42.4	3	Belgium	48.3
4	Slovenia	42.0	4	Norway	43.1
5	Norway[a]	41.1	5	France	41.6
6	Belgium[a]	41.0	6	Ireland	41.4
7	United Kingdom	40.8	7	Sweden	40.6
8	Bulgaria	39.0	8	Austria	39.8
	Portugal[a]	39.0	9	Italy	39.5
10	Sweden	38.8	10	Denmark	39.2
11	Poland	38.5	11	Portugal	37.9
12	Macedonia[c]	38.2	12	Netherlands	36.7
13	Greece[c]	37.8		Romania	36.7
14	Cyprus	37.2	14	United Kingdom	35.8
15	Latvia	36.9	15	Iceland	34.1
16	Austria[a]	36.6	16	Greece	33.1
17	Luxembourg[c]	36.3	17	Finland	32.4
18	Estonia	35.0	18	Luxembourg	31.2
19	Romania[c]	34.1	19	Germany	30.6
20	Albania	33.7	20	Cyprus	29.8

a 1997 b 1995 c 1996

Spending on what?

General public services

Central government spending, % of total

	1986			1998	
1	Turkey	31.6	1	Croatia	19.6
2	Greece	19.8	2	Azerbaijan[d]	11.3
3	Luxembourg	13.6	3	Georgia	10.6
4	Malta	9.8	4	Luxembourg[e]	10.2
	Netherlands[a]	9.8	5	Russia[e]	9.2
6	Switzerland[b]	9.5	6	Malta	7.9
7	Cyprus	7.8	7	Denmark[e]	7.4
8	Finland	7.7	8	Bulgaria	7.2
9	Ireland	7.4		Latvia	7.2
	Denmark	7.4	10	Finland	7.0
11	Italy	6.9		Slovakia	7.0
12	Estonia[a]	6.2	12	Netherlands	6.4
	Portugal	6.2	13	Cyprus	6.3
14	France	5.6	14	Sweden	6.2
15	Norway	5.0	15	Albania	5.8
16	Austria	5.0		Iceland[f]	5.8
17	Bulgaria[c]	4.5	17	Norway[f]	5.4
	Iceland	4.5	18	Hungary	5.1
19	Sweden	3.9	19	Estonia	4.9
	Germany	3.9	20	Lithuania	4.6
21	United Kingdom	3.6	21	United Kingdom	4.3
22	Belgium	3.1	22	Poland	3.9
23	Spain	3.0		Switzerland[f]	3.9
24	Croatia[a]	2.0	24	Greece[f]	3.7
25	Romania	0.5		Turkey[g]	3.7

Public order

Central government spending, % of total

	1986			1998	
1	Croatia[a]	8.1	1	Austria	11.5
2	Greece	8.0	2	Georgia	10.6
3	Cyprus	7.5	3	Lithuania	7.9
4	Iceland	4.8	4	Estonia	7.3
5	Switzerland[b]	4.5	5	Bulgaria	6.3
6	Luxembourg	4.2	6	Latvia	6.1
7	Estonia[a]	3.6	7	Azerbaijan[d]	6.0
	Netherlands[a]	3.6	8	Albania	5.8
9	Spain	3.4	9	Cyprus	5.6
10	United Kingdom	3.1	10	Slovakia	5.4
11	Malta	2.8	11	Belarus	5.3
12	Sweden	2.7	12	Turkey[g]	5.0
13	Austria	2.5	13	Russia[e]	4.9
14	Denmark	2.3	14	Czech Republic	4.5
15	Bulgaria[c]	1.9		Iceland[f]	4.5
	Norway	1.9		Poland	4.5
			17	Malta	4.0

Note: These figures are for central government spending. In countries such as Germany a lot of government spending is done at the regional level.

Education
Central government spending, % of total

1986			1998		
1	Bulgaria[c]	25.3	1	Ireland	13.1
2	Switzerland[b]	22.1	2	Malta	12.2
3	Greece	16.6	3	Cyprus	11.9
	Luxembourg	16.6	4	Turkey[g]	11.2
5	Iceland	14.0	5	Slovakia	10.3
6	Finland	13.9	6	Iceland[f]	10.2
7	Turkey	12.6	7	Finland	10.1
8	Belgium	12.2	8	Netherlands	10.0
9	Ireland	11.8	9	Czech Republic	9.7
10	Cyprus	10.4	10	Denmark[e]	9.4
11	Austria	9.7		Romania[f]	9.4

Health
Central government spending, % of total

1986			1998		
1	Iceland	24.5	1	Iceland[f]	24.1
2	Bulgaria[c]	23.3	2	Switzerland[f]	19.7
3	Germany	18.3	3	Czech Republic	17.9
4	Croatia[a]	16.3	4	Estonia	16.4
5	Switzerland[b]	16.0	5	Ireland	15.7
6	France	15.5	6	Lithuania	15.5
7	United Kingdom	13.4	7	Slovakia	15.2
8	Spain	12.5	8	United Kingdom	15.0
9	Ireland	12.4	9	Netherlands	14.8
10	Austria	12.2	10	Austria	14.4
11	Finland	10.6	11	Croatia	14.1

Social security
Central government spending, % of total

1986			1998		
1	Germany	49.0	1	Switzerland[f]	50.5
2	Sweden	46.4	2	Poland	49.9
3	Austria	46.3	3	Sweden	43.9
4	France	44.6	4	Denmark[e]	43.2
5	Estonia[a]	41.9	5	Austria	42.0
6	Belgium	41.6	6	Latvia	40.8
7	Croatia[a]	39.0	7	Finland	39.2
8	Spain	36.4	8	Spain[g]	38.5
9	Denmark	36.4	9	Norway[f]	38.4
10	Italy	35.1	10	Netherlands	37.4
	Malta	35.1	11	Czech Republic	36.4
12	Finland	34.4		United Kingdom	36.4
13	Norway	33.0	13	Belarus	36.3
14	United Kingdom	31.9	14	Croatia	36.0
15	Netherlands[a]	25.4	15	Malta	34.4
			16	Azerbaijan[d]	33.1

a 1991 b 1990 c 1988 d 1999 forecast. e 1995 f 1997 g 1996

Debt: rich countries

Total debt

General government gross financial liabilities as % of GDP

		1998	1990	1980
1	Italy	118.2	103.7	58.1
2	Belgium	116.2	125.2	78.2
3	Greece	105.4	89.0	22.9
4	Sweden	73.7	42.9	44.3
5	Spain	70.3	48.5	18.3
6	Netherlands	65.0	75.6	46.9
7	France	64.9	39.5	30.9
8	Austria	63.3	57.9	37.3
	Germany	63.3	42.0	31.1
10	Denmark	59.6	65.8	44.7
11	Portugal	57.7	65.3	32.8
12	United Kingdom	56.4	39.1	54.0
13	Ireland	52.6	92.6	72.7
14	Finland	49.7	14.5	14.1

Net debt

General government net financial liabilities as % of GDP

		1998	1990	1980
1	Belgium	112.9	115.5	68.7
2	Italy	105.9	83.7	53.0
3	Netherlands	54.0	35.4	24.6
4	Spain	51.3	31.5	6.1
5	Germany	46.6	17.8	9.3
6	Austria	44.0	38.4	20.0
7	France	42.3	16.1	-3.3
8	United Kingdom	41.9	18.6	36.2
9	Denmark	35.8	33.0	14.2
10	Iceland	32.1	19.5	3.3
11	Sweden	15.7	-7.8	-13.9
12	Finland	-5.5	-35.7	-30.7

Interest payments

General government net interest payments as % of GDP

		1998	1990	1980
1	Greece	8.9	10.0	2.3
2	Italy	7.6	8.9	4.2
3	Belgium	7.2	9.6	5.3
4	Netherlands	4.2	4.1	2.4
5	Spain	4.0	3.0	0.3
6	Austria	3.6	3.2	1.7
7	Portugal	3.4	8.1	2.8
8	France	3.1	2.3	0.8
9	Germany	3.0	1.9	1.3
	Sweden	3.0	0.1	-0.4
11	United Kingdom	2.8	2.3	3.1
12	Ireland	2.4	6.2	3.6
13	Denmark	2.4	3.7	0.5
14	Finland	1.8	-1.7	-1.0

Debt: poor countries

External debt
$bn, 1998

1	Russia	183.6			Slovakia	9.9
2	Turkey	102.0		10	Romania	9.5
3	Poland	47.7		11	Croatia	8.3
4	Hungary	28.6		12	Macedonia	2.4
5	Czech Republic	25.3		13	Lithuania	1.9
6	Serbia & Montenegro	13.7		14	Georgia	1.7
7	Ukraine	12.7		15	Belarus	1.1
8	Bulgaria	9.9		16	Moldova	1.0

As % of GDP, 1998

1	Macedonia	92.6		8	Czech Republic	45.5
2	Bulgaria	83.0		9	Croatia	39.4
3	Russia	69.4		10	Georgia	31.9
4	Hungary	62.2		11	Poland	30.6
5	Moldova	62.1		12	Ukraine	29.8
6	Turkey	50.2		13	Albania	26.4
7	Slovakia	49.0		14	Azerbaijan	16.9

As % of exports, 1998

1	Russia	207		9	Poland	100
2	Georgia	183		10	Romania	97
3	Bulgaria	169		11	Croatia	83
4	Armenia	165		12	Slovakia	74
5	Turkey	151		13	Czech Republic	71
6	Macedonia	150		14	Azerbaijan	66
7	Moldova	115		15	Albania	64
8	Hungary	107		16	Lithuania	37

Interest payments
$bn, 1998

1	Russia	5,787.4		9	Croatia	328.8
2	Turkey	4,870.0		10	Macedonia	101.9
3	Poland	1,624.0		11	Lithuania	67.9
4	Czech Republic	1,519.9		12	Belarus	64.6
5	Hungary	1,494.3		13	Serbia & Montenegro	56.7
6	Slovakia	580.9		14	Georgia	45.7
7	Romania	548.4		15	Moldova	43.7
8	Bulgaria	524.8		16	Estonia	39.0

As % of GDP, 1998

1	Bulgaria	4.4		10	Romania	1.5
2	Macedonia	3.9		11	Poland	1.0
3	Hungary	3.3		12	Georgia	0.9
4	Slovakia	2.9		13	Albania	0.8
5	Czech Republic	2.7		14	Estonia	0.7
6	Moldova	2.6			Lithuania	0.7
7	Turkey	2.4		16	Azerbaijan	0.5
8	Russia	2.2			Latvia	0.5
9	Croatia	1.6				

Aid

Givers

Official Development Assistance (ODA) from
Development Assistance Committee (DAC) countries to developing countries
$bn

1987–88			1998		
1	France	5.36	1	France	5.74
2	Germany	4.56	2	Germany	5.58
3	Italy	2.90	3	United Kingdom	3.86
4	United Kingdom	2.26	4	Netherlands	3.04
5	Netherlands	2.16	5	Italy	2.28
6	Sweden	1.45	6	Denmark	1.70
7	Norway	0.94	7	Sweden	1.57
8	Denmark	0.89	8	Spain	1.38
9	Belgium	0.64	9	Norway	1.32
10	Switzerland	0.58	10	Switzerland	0.90
11	Finland	0.52	11	Belgium	0.88
12	Austria	0.25	12	Austria	0.46
13	Spain	0.24	13	Finland	0.40
14	Portugal	0.06	14	Portugal	0.26
15	Ireland	0.05	15	Ireland	0.20
16	Luxembourg	0.02	16	Luxembourg	0.11
	Total EU	21.37		Total EU	27.46

% of GDP

1987–88			1998		
1	Norway	1.11	1	Denmark	0.99
2	Netherlands	0.98	2	Norway	0.91
3	Denmark	0.88	3	Netherlands	0.80
4	Sweden	0.87	4	Sweden	0.72
5	France	0.59	5	Luxembourg	0.65
6	Finland	0.55	6	France	0.40
7	Belgium	0.44	7	Belgium	0.35
8	Germany	0.39	8	Finland	0.32
9	Italy	0.37		Switzerland	0.32
10	Switzerland	0.31	10	Ireland	0.30
11	United Kingdom	0.30	11	United Kingdom	0.27
12	Austria	0.21	12	Germany	0.26
13	Ireland	0.20	13	Portugal	0.24
14	Luxembourg	0.19		Spain	0.24
15	Portugal	0.16	15	Austria	0.22
16	Spain	0.08	16	Italy	0.20
	Total EU	0.44		Total EU	0.33

Per head, $, 1998

1	Denmark	322	9	Finland	77
2	Norway	299	10	Germany	68
3	Luxembourg	260	11	United Kingdom	65
4	Netherlands	194	12	Austria	56
5	Sweden	178	13	Ireland	54
6	Switzerland	126	14	Italy	40
7	France	98	15	Spain	35
8	Belgium	87	16	Portugal	26

Receivers

Aid (ODA) received, $m, 1998

1	Russia	1,017	9	Hungary	209
2	Poland	902	10	Slovakia	155
3	Bosnia	876	11	Armenia	138
4	Czech Rep	447	12	Lithuania	128
5	Ukraine	380	13	Serbia & Montenegro	106
6	Romania	356	14	Latvia	97
7	Albania	242	15	Macedonia	92
8	Bulgaria	232	16	Estonia	90

Aid (ODA) as % of GDP, 1998

1	Bosnia[a]	21.37	9	Latvia	1.64
2	Albania	8.96	10	Lithuania	1.36
3	Armenia	8.12	11	Romania	1.16
4	Macedonia	3.54	12	Czech Rep	0.84
5	Azerbaijan	2.34	13	Slovakia	0.78
6	Bulgaria	2.30	14	Ukraine	0.77
7	Moldova	1.94	15	Poland	0.60
8	Estonia	1.84	16	Malta	0.58

Aid (ODA) per head, $, 1998

1	Bosnia	238	9	Lithuania	35
2	Albania	78	10	Slovakia	29
3	Estonia	63	11	Bulgaria	28
4	Malta	58	12	Poland	23
5	Macedonia	46	13	Hungary	21
6	Czech Rep	43	14	Slovenia	20
7	Latvia	40	15	Romania	16
8	Armenia	39	16	Azerbaijan	12

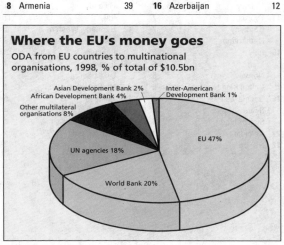

Where the EU's money goes

ODA from EU countries to multinational organisations, 1998, % of total of $10.5bn

Asian Development Bank 2%
African Development Bank 4%
Other multilateral organisations 8%
Inter-American Development Bank 1%
EU 47%
UN agencies 18%
World Bank 20%

a Based on estimated GDP.

Money supply

Narrow money
Average annual % growth

1995–99

1	Belarus[a]	145.8
2	Bulgaria	129.6
3	Turkey[b]	75.6
4	Romania	43.1
5	Moldova[c]	38.9
6	Russia	36.6
7	Ukraine	31.7
8	Hungary	23.6
9	Poland[b]	22.3
10	Slovenia	22.1
11	Estonia	19.7
12	Latvia	15.9
13	Georgia	15.4
	Iceland[b]	15.4
15	Armenia	14.8
16	Cyprus	14.1
17	Greece[d]	13.9
18	Croatia	13.7
19	Macedonia	12.8
20	Azerbaijan	12.1
21	Lithuania	10.9
22	Norway	10.0
23	Switzerland[a]	8.4
24	Euro-11	8.3
25	United Kingdom	7.5
26	Denmark	6.9
27	Czech Republic[e]	4.3
28	Malta[f]	3.4
29	Slovakia	0.6

1990–95

1	Romania	95
2	Turkey	66
3	Poland	32
4	Hungary	15
5	Greece	13
6	Portugal	12
7	Ireland	10
	Iceland	10
9	Austria	9
10	Finland[g]	8
11	Cyprus	7
	Germany	7
	Netherlands	7
13	Italy	5
	Malta	5
	Norway	5
	United Kingdom	5
16	Denmark	4
	Spain	4
	Switzerland	4
21	Belgium	3
22	France	1

1980–90

1	Poland	60
2	Turkey	45
3	Iceland	38
4	Greece	20
	Norway	20
6	Portugal	17
7	Spain	14
8	Denmark	12
9	Cyprus	11
	Finland	11
	Italy	11
12	Germany, Western	9
13	France	8
	Romania	8
15	Ireland	7
	Luxembourg	7
	Netherlands	7
18	Austria	5
19	Belgium	4
	Malta	4
21	Switzerland	2

Broad money
Average annual % growth

1995–99

1	Belarus[a]	164.4	16	Macedonia	16.2
2	Turkey[b]	104.9	17	Azerbaijan	13.5
3	Bulgaria	86.5	18	Lithuania	12.4
4	Romania	65.0	19	Iceland	11.6
5	Moldova[c]	42.9	20	Slovakia	11.3
6	Russia	37.5	21	Greece[d]	10.8
7	Ukraine	33.0	22	Cyprus	9.3
8	Armenia	28.9	23	Malta[f]	8.8
9	Hungary	26.1	24	Switzerland[a]	8.3
10	Estonia	25.7	25	United Kingdom	6.8
11	Poland[b]	25.6	26	Norway	6.2
12	Georgia	24.9	27	Euro-11	4.9
13	Croatia	23.0	28	Czech Republic[e]	4.6
14	Slovenia	20.3	29	Denmark	4.3
15	Latvia	17.3	30	Sweden	3.7

1990–95

1	Romania	102
2	Turkey	93
3	Poland	40
4	Hungary	21
5	Portugal	15
6	Cyprus	14
7	Ireland	13
8	Malta	11
9	Greece	9
	Spain	9
11	Germany	7
	United Kingdom	7
13	Austria	6
	Iceland	6
15	France	4
	Italy	4
	Netherlands	4
	Norway	4
	Switzerland	4
20	Denmark	3
	Sweden	3
22	Belgium	2
	Finland[g]	2

1980–90

1	Poland	62
2	Turkey	58
3	Iceland	42
4	Greece	22
5	United Kingdom	21
6	Portugal	19
7	Cyprus	15
8	Finland	13
9	Spain	12
10	Denmark	11
	Luxembourg	11
	Norway	11
13	Italy	10
	Romania	10
15	Ireland	9
16	Austria	8
	Malta	8
	Sweden	8
19	Belgium	7
	France	7
	Germany, Western	7
	Switzerland	7
23	Netherlands	6

a 1996–99
b 1995–November 1999.
c 1998–99
d 1995–June 1999.
e 1997–November 1999.
f 1995–August 1999.
g 1991–95

Reserves

Recent picture
Total reserves minus gold, $m, December 1999

1	Germany	51,039	19	Portugal	8,321
2	France	39,701	20	Finland	8,102
3	Switzerland	36,321	21	Ireland	5,324
4	Spain	32,567	22	Slovakia	3,371
5	United Kingdom[a]	29,300	23	Slovenia	3,168
6	Poland	24,535	24	Bulgaria	3,083
7	Turkey	23,340	25	Croatia	3,025
8	Italy	22,427	26	Romania	2,690
9	Denmark	22,287	27	Malta[b]	1,875
10	Norway	20,400	28	Cyprus[c]	1,396
11	Greece	18,122	29	Lithuania	1,195
12	Sweden	15,019	30	Ukraine	1,046
13	Austria	14,868	31	Estonia	853
14	Czech Republic	12,882	32	Latvia	840
15	Hungary	10,954	33	Azerbaijan	673
16	Belgium	10,932	34	Iceland	478
17	Netherlands	10,206	35	Macedonia	430
18	Russia	8,457		Euro-11	255,681

Gold
Fine troy ounces, m, December 1999 or latest

1	Germany	111.52	19	Slovakia	1.29
2	France	97.24	20	Norway	1.18
3	Switzerland	83.28	21	Bulgaria	1.03
4	Italy	78.83	22	Cyprus[c]	0.46
5	Netherlands	31.57	23	Czech Republic	0.45
6	United Kingdom[a]	22.99	24	Latvia	0.25
7	Portugal	19.51	25	Ireland	0.19
8	Spain	16.83	26	Lithuania	0.19
9	Russia	13.33	27	Ukraine	0.16
10	Austria	13.10	28	Albania	0.12
11	Belgium	8.30	29	Macedonia	0.10
12	Sweden	5.96	30	Hungary	0.10
13	Greece	4.24	31	Luxembourg	0.08
14	Turkey	3.74	32	Iceland	0.06
15	Romania	3.32	33	Armenia	0.04
16	Poland	3.31	34	Estonia	0.01
17	Denmark	2.00	35	Malta[b]	0.01
18	Finland	1.58		Euro-11	402.77

The world picture
Gold, % of total weight, December 1999

Euro-11	42.7	Other Asia	5.9
Other European Union	3.8	Middle East	3.7
Other industrial countries	37.2	Latin America	2.2
Other Europe	3.1	Africa	1.3

a March.
b October.
c November.

Looking back
Total reserves minus gold, $m

1990

#	Country	Value	#	Country	Value
1	Germany	67,902	13	Finland	9,644
2	Italy	62,927	14	Austria	9,376
3	Spain	51,228	15	Turkey	6,050
4	France	36,778	16	Ireland	5,223
5	United Kingdom	35,850	17	Poland	4,492
6	Switzerland	29,223	18	Greece	3,412
7	Sweden	17,988	19	Cyprus	1,507
8	Netherlands	17,484	20	Malta	1,432
9	Norway	15,332	21	Hungary	1,070
10	Portugal	14,485	22	Romania	524
11	Belgium	12,151	23	Iceland	436
12	Denmark	10,591	24	Luxembourg	81

1980

#	Country	Value	#	Country	Value
1	Germany	48,592	12	Denmark	3,387
2	France	27,340	13	Ireland	2,860
3	Italy	23,126	14	Finland	1,870
4	United Kingdom	20,650	15	Greece	1,346
5	Switzerland	15,656	16	Turkey	1,077
6	Spain	11,863	17	Malta	990
7	Netherlands	11,645	18	Portugal	795
8	Belgium	7,823	19	Cyprus	368
9	Norway	6,048	20	Romania	323
10	Austria	5,280	21	Iceland	174
11	Sweden	3,418	22	Poland	128

1970

#	Country	Value	#	Country	Value
1	Germany	9,630	11	Ireland	681
2	Italy	2,465	12	Portugal	602
3	Switzerland	2,401	13	Sweden	561
4	United Kingdom	1,480	14	Finland	425
5	Netherlands	1,454	15	Denmark	419
6	France	1,428	16	Turkey	304
7	Belgium	1,377	17	Cyprus	194
8	Spain	1,319		Greece	194
9	Austria	1,044	19	Malta	148
10	Norway	787.9	20	Iceland	53

Total reserves minus gold, % of total value, December 1999			
Euro-11	14.1	Other Asia	36.2
Other European Union	4.7	Middle East	5.8
Other industrial countries	22.5	Latin America	8.5
Other Europe	5.9	Africa	2.4

Interest rates

Central bank discount rates
%

End 1999

1	Armenia[a]	65.10	13	Croatia	7.90
2	Romania	35.00	14	Norway	7.50
3	Belarus[c]	23.40	15	Cyprus	7.00
4	Bulgaria[a]	22.12	16	Iceland[b]	6.80
5	Poland	21.50	17	United Kingdom[c]	5.50
6	Hungary[b]	19.00	18	Czech Republic	5.00
7	Albania	18.20		Malta	5.00
8	Greece[b]	14.50	20	Latvia	4.00
9	Azerbaijan[c]	10.00		Euro-11	4.00
10	Macedonia	8.90	22	Denmark	3.00
11	Slovakia	8.80	23	Sweden	1.50
12	Slovenia	8.35	24	Switzerland	0.50

1990

1	Poland	48.00	13	Belgium	10.50
2	Turkey	45.00		Norway	10.50
3	Ex-Yugoslavia	30.00	15	France	9.55
4	Hungary	22.00	16	Denmark	8.50
5	Iceland	21.00		Finland	8.50
6	Greece	19.00	18	Netherlands	7.25
7	Spain	14.71	19	Austria	6.50
8	Portugal	14.50		Cyprus	6.50
9	United Kingdom	14.09	21	Germany	6.00
10	Italy	12.50		Switzerland	6.00
11	Sweden	11.50	23	Malta	5.50
12	Ireland	11.25			

1980

1	Iceland	28.00	11	Spain	10.90
2	Turkey	26.00	12	Sweden	10.00
3	Greece	20.50	13	Finland	9.25
4	Portugal	18.00	14	Norway	9.00
5	Italy	16.50	15	Netherlands	8.00
6	United Kingdom	15.11	16	Germany	7.50
7	Ireland	14.00	17	Austria	6.75
8	Belgium	12.00	18	Cyprus	6.00
9	France	11.90	19	Malta	5.50
10	Denmark	11.00	20	Switzerland	3.00

a End-1997.
b End-1998.
c Refinancing rate.

Money market rates
%

End 1999

1	Turkey	69.77	13	Czech Republic[b]	7.50
2	Romania[a]	65.30	14	Slovenia	6.77
3	Ukraine	63.20	15	Malta[a]	5.15
4	Armenia	30.74	16	United Kingdom	5.00
5	Georgia	30.13	17	Latvia	4.71
6	Moldova	27.20	18	Estonia	3.85
7	Russia	13.70	19	Denmark	3.64
8	Poland	13.40	20	Euro-11	3.44
9	Croatia	12.35	21	Sweden	3.17
10	Iceland	10.13	22	Bulgaria	3.14
11	Greece[a]	9.20	23	Switzerland	1.09
12	Lithuania	7.79			

1990

1	Turkey	47.60	13	Finland	7.50
2	Poland	41.70	14	Germany	7.07
3	Hungary	24.70	15	Italy	6.80
4	Greece	19.52	16	Ireland	6.29
5	Portugal	13.99	17	Belgium	6.13
6	United Kingdom	12.54	18	Luxembourg	6.00
7	Iceland	12.30	19	Cyprus	5.75
8	Spain	10.65	20	France	4.50
9	Sweden	9.93		Malta	4.50
10	Norway	9.68	22	Austria	3.41
11	Switzerland	8.28	23	Netherlands	3.31
12	Denmark	7.90			

1980

1	Iceland	38.80	12	Turkey	8.00
2	Portugal	19.00	13	Germany	7.95
3	Greece	14.50	14	Belgium	7.69
4	United Kingdom	14.13	15	France	7.25
5	Spain	13.05	16	Luxembourg	6.50
6	Italy	12.70	17	Netherlands	5.96
7	Ireland	12.00	18	Cyprus	5.75
8	Sweden	11.25	19	Austria	5.00
9	Denmark	10.80		Malta	5.00
10	Finland	9.00		Norway	5.00
11	Switzerland	8.80	22	Hungary	3.00

a Treasury bill rate.
b Refinancing rate.

Taxation

Total tax revenue
As % of GDP
1998

1	Sweden	53.0		11	Poland	40.0
2	Denmark	49.3		12	Hungary	39.0
3	Finland	46.9		13	Czech Republic	38.3
4	Belgium	46.3		14	United Kingdom	37.6
5	France	45.2		15	Germany	37.1
6	Luxembourg	45.1		16	Portugal	34.9
7	Austria	44.3		17	Switzerland	34.8
8	Norway	43.6		18	Spain	34.2
9	Italy	43.5		19	Greece[a]	33.7
10	Netherlands	41.1			EU15[ab]	41.5

1990

1	Sweden	55.6		11	Germany	36.7
2	Denmark	47.1		12	United Kingdom	36.3
3	Finland	44.9		13	Spain	34.4
4	Netherlands	44.6		14	Ireland	33.6
5	Luxembourg	43.9		15	Iceland	31.4
6	Belgium	43.9		16	Switzerland	30.9
7	France	43.0		17	Portugal	30.2
8	Norway	41.8		18	Greece	29.7
9	Austria	41.0		19	Turkey	20.0
10	Italy	38.9			EU15[b]	40.3

1980

1	Sweden	48.8		11	United Kingdom	35.1
2	Denmark	45.4		12	Ireland	32.6
3	Netherlands	45.2		13	Italy	30.4
4	Belgium	43.7		14	Iceland	29.2
5	Luxembourg	43.0		15	Switzerland	28.9
6	Norway	42.7		16	Portugal	24.7
7	France	41.7		17	Greece	24.3
8	Austria	40.3		18	Spain	23.9
9	Germany	38.2		19	Turkey	17.9
10	Finland	36.9			EU15[b]	36.9

EU15[b] tax revenue by type
% of total, 1997

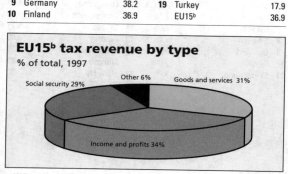

Social security 29% Other 6% Goods and services 31%

Income and profits 34%

a 1997   b Unweighted average.

Part V
LABOUR

The changing workforce

Force in numbers
Total no. in workforce, 1998, m

#	Country		#	Country	
1	Russia	77.9	22	Azerbaijan	3.5
2	Germany	41.0	23	Denmark	3.0
3	Turkey	29.8	24	Slovakia	2.9
4	United Kingdom	29.5	25	Georgia	2.7
5	France	26.5	26	Finland	2.6
6	Italy	25.3	27	Norway	2.3
7	Ukraine	25.1	28	Croatia	2.1
8	Poland	19.7		Moldova	2.1
9	Spain	17.3	30	Armenia	1.9
10	Romania	10.6		Lithuania	1.9
11	Netherlands	7.4	32	Bosnia	1.7
12	Czech Republic	5.8	33	Albania	1.6
13	Belarus	5.3	34	Ireland	1.5
14	Portugal	5.0	35	Latvia	1.3
15	Hungary	4.9	36	Slovenia	1.0
16	Sweden	4.8	37	Macedonia	0.9
17	Greece	4.5	38	Estonia	0.8
18	Belgium	4.2	39	Cyprus	0.4
	Bulgaria	4.2	40	Iceland	0.2
20	Switzerland	3.8		Luxembourg	0.2
21	Austria	3.8	42	Malta	0.1

Most male workforce
Male % of workforce, 1998

#	Country		#	Country	
1	Malta	73		Switzerland	60
2	Ireland	66	13	Albania	59
3	Greece	63		Belgium	59
	Luxembourg	63		Macedonia	59
	Spain	63	16	Germany	58
	Turkey	63	17	Azerbaijan	56
7	Bosnia	62		Croatia	56
	Italy	62		Portugal	56
9	Cyprus	61		Romania	56
10	Austria	60		United Kingdom	56
	Netherlands	60			

Most female workforce
Female % of workforce, 1998

#	Country		#	Country	
1	Latvia	50		Sweden	48
2	Belarus	49	13	Czech Republic	47
	Estonia	49		Georgia	47
	Moldova	49	15	Denmark	46
	Russia	49		Norway	46
	Ukraine	49		Poland	46
7	Armenia	48		Slovenia	46
	Bulgaria	48	19	France	45
	Finland	48		Hungary	45
	Lithuania	48		Iceland	45
	Slovakia	48			

Total no. in workforce, 1985, m

1	Russia	76.2	22	Azerbaijan	2.9
2	Germany	38.1	23	Denmark	2.8
3	United Kingdom	27.8	24	Georgia	2.6
4	Ukraine	26.0		Slovakia	2.6
5	France	24.3	26	Finland	2.5
6	Italy	23.2	27	Croatia	2.2
7	Turkey	21.6	28	Moldova	2.1
8	Poland	19.0	29	Norway	2.0
9	Spain	15.0	30	Bosnia	1.8
10	Romania	10.9		Lithuania	1.8
11	Netherlands	6.2	32	Armenia	1.6
12	Czech Republic	5.4	33	Albania	1.4
13	Belarus	5.2		Latvia	1.4
14	Hungary	5.0	35	Ireland	1.3
15	Portugal	4.8	36	Slovenia	1.0
16	Bulgaria	4.6	37	Estonia	0.8
17	Sweden	4.3		Macedonia	0.8
18	Greece	4.0	39	Cyprus	0.3
19	Belgium	3.9	40	Luxembourg	0.2
20	Austria	3.5	41	Iceland	0.1
21	Switzerland	3.3		Malta	0.1

Male % of workforce, 1985

1	Malta	77	12	Macedonia	62
2	Ireland	70		Switzerland	62
3	Spain	69	14	Albania	61
4	Greece	68	15	Austria	59
5	Turkey	66		Croatia	59
6	Bosnia	65		Germany	59
	Italy	65		Portugal	59
	Luxembourg	65		United Kingdom	59
	Netherlands	65	20	France	58
10	Cyprus	64		Iceland	58
11	Belgium	63			

Female % of workforce, 1985

1	Estonia	50		Czech Republic	47
	Latvia	50		Finland	47
	Ukraine	50	13	Slovakia	46
4	Belarus	49		Slovenia	46
	Lithuania	49		Sweden	46
	Moldova	49	16	Azerbaijan	45
	Russia	49		Denmark	45
8	Armenia	48		Poland	45
	Georgia	48		Romania	45
10	Bulgaria	47	20	Hungary	44

What people do – and did

Agriculture
% of workforce employed in agriculture, latest

Male			Female		
1	Romania	35	1	Turkey	65
2	Turkey	30	2	Romania	43
3	Latvia	23	3	Albania	27
	Lithuania	23	4	Greece	23
5	Albania	22	5	Poland	20
6	Poland	21	6	Latvia	18
7	Greece	18		Lithuania	18
8	Estonia	16	8	Portugal	16
9	Ireland	15	9	Slovenia	13
10	Portugal	12	10	Austria	8
	Slovenia	12		Estonia	8

Industry
% of workforce employed in industry, latest

Male			Female		
1	Macedonia	53	1	Albania	45
2	Croatia	50	2	Macedonia	41
	Czech Republic	50	3	Croatia	34
4	Slovakia	49	4	Slovenia	31
	Slovenia	49	5	Czech Republic	29
6	Germany	46	6	Slovakia	28
7	Albania	45	7	Estonia	27
8	Austria	42	8	Hungary	25
9	Belgium	41	9	Romania	24
	Poland	41	10	Italy	22
11	Hungary	40	11	Lithuania	21
	Portugal	40		Poland	21
				Portugal	21

Services
% of workforce employed in services, latest

Male			Female		
1	Norway	59	1	Norway	87
	Switzerland	59		Sweden	87
	United Kingdom	59	3	United Kingdom	86
4	Denmark	58	4	Denmark	83
5	France	57	5	Switzerland	82
	Sweden	57	6	Belgium	81
7	Belgium	56		Finland	81
8	Italy	55		France	81
9	Greece	54	9	Spain	80
10	Austria	52	10	Germany	79
	Finland	52		Ireland	79
	Spain	52	12	Austria	78
13	Germany	51	13	Italy	72
14	Hungary	50	14	Hungary	71
15	Ireland	49	15	Slovakia	67

% of workforce employed in agriculture, 1980

Male			Female		
1	Albania	54	1	Turkey	88
2	Moldova	46	2	Albania	62
3	Turkey	45	3	Macedonia	47
4	Serbia	34		Serbia	47
5	Georgia	31	5	Romania	45
6	Macedonia	30	6	Azerbaijan	42
7	Belarus	29	7	Moldova	41
8	Poland	28	8	Greece	39
	Azerbaijan	28	9	Bosnia	37
10	Ukraine	26	10	Georgia	34

% of workforce employed in industry, 1980

Male			Female		
1	Czech Republic	67	1	Czech Republic	44
2	Germany	54	2	Hungary	38
3	Austria	51		Armenia	38
4	Estonia	50	4	Slovenia	37
	Romania	50		Russia	37
	Russia	50	6	Estonia	36
7	Latvia	49	7	Latvia	35
	Slovenia	49	8	Slovakia	34
9	Armenia	48	9	Ukraine	33
10	Hungary	47		Germany	33
	Lithuania	47		Belarus	33
12	Poland	46	12	Lithuania	30
	Ukraine	46	13	Romania	29
14	Bosnia	45	14	Poland	28
	Sweden	45	15	Croatia	27

% of workforce employed in services, 1980

Male			Female		
1	Belgium	50	1	Norway	80
	Netherlands	50	2	Sweden	79
	Norway	50	3	Denmark	76
4	France	48	4	Netherlands	74
	Slovakia	48	5	United Kingdom	72
6	Sweden	46	6	France	71
7	Denmark	44	7	Belgium	68
	United Kingdom	44	8	Finland	64
9	Austria	41	9	Austria	62
10	Germany	40	10	Germany	59
	Greece	40	11	Spain	56
	Italy	40	12	Slovakia	54
13	Croatia	39	13	Estonia	52
14	Finland	38	14	Latvia	50
15	Georgia	37		Russia	50

Unemployment

The size of the problem
Total no. unemployed, '000, 1998

1	Russia	8,876	16	Slovakia	297
2	Germany	3,849	17	Finland	285
3	Spain	3,060	18	Sweden	276
4	France	3,050	19	Portugal	248
5	Italy	2,805	20	Lithuania	247
6	Poland	1,808	21	Croatia	199
7	United Kingdom	1,766	22	Austria	165
8	Turkey	1,547	23	Latvia	161
9	Romania	732	24	Denmark	155
10	Bulgaria	497	25	Switzerland	142
11	Greece	440	26	Armenia	139
12	Czech Republic	387	27	Ireland	127
13	Belgium	384	28	Belarus	106
14	Netherlands	337	29	Slovenia	75
15	Hungary	313	30	Norway	75

The burden on the economy
Public expenditure on unemployment benefit as % of GDP, 1998

1	Netherlands	3.14	11	Austria	1.16
2	Finland	2.35	12	Switzerland	1.07
3	Ireland[a]	2.29	13	United Kingdom	0.82
4	Germany	2.29	14	Portugal[b]	0.72
5	Belgium[b]	2.06	15	Italy[a]	0.68
6	Sweden	1.91	16	Greece[b]	0.50
7	Denmark	1.86	17	Norway	0.49
8	Poland[a]	1.77	18	Hungary[b]	0.46
9	Spain	1.64	19	Luxembourg[b]	0.42
10	France[b]	1.50	20	Czech Republic	0.24

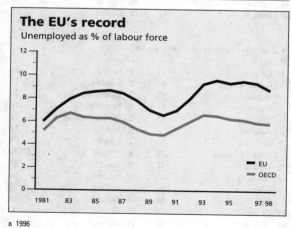

The EU's record
Unemployed as % of labour force

— EU
— OECD

1981 83 85 87 89 91 93 95 97 98

a 1996
b 1997

The problem in proportion
% of workforce unemployed, 1998

1	Spain	18.8		Ireland	7.8
2	Bulgaria[a]	14.4	18	Slovenia	7.7
3	Latvia	13.8	19	Sweden	6.5
4	Lithuania	13.5	20	Romania	6.3
5	Russia	13.3	21	Turkey	6.2
6	Italy[a]	12.3	22	United Kingdom	6.1
7	Slovakia	11.9	23	Denmark	5.5
8	France	11.8	24	Malta[a]	5.0
9	Croatia	11.4		Portugal	5.0
10	Finland	11.3	26	Czech Republic[a]	4.7
11	Poland	10.5	27	Netherlands	4.4
12	Greece[a]	10.3	28	Austria	4.2
13	Germany	9.7	29	Norway[a]	4.1
14	Armenia	9.3		San Marino	4.1
15	Belgium	9.1	31	Switzerland	3.6
16	Hungary	7.8	32	Cyprus	3.3

Looking back

	% of workforce unemployed, 1990			*% of workforce unemployed, 1983*	
1	Macedonia	23.6	1	Macedonia	21.6
2	Spain	15.9	2	Spain	17.0
3	Ireland	13.3	3	Ireland	14.0
4	Italy	10.3	4	United Kingdom	12.4
5	Denmark	9.7	5	Belgium	12.1
6	Albania	9.5	6	Netherlands	12.0
7	France	8.9	7	Turkey	11.2
8	Croatia	8.0	8	Denmark	9.1
9	Netherlands	7.5	9	Italy	8.8
10	Turkey	7.4	10	France	8.3
11	Belgium	7.2	11	Malta	8.1
12	United Kingdom	6.9	12	Greece	7.8
13	Greece	6.4		Portugal	7.8
14	San Marino	5.5	14	Germany	7.7
15	Austria	5.4	15	Croatia	7.0
16	Norway	5.2	16	San Marino	6.9
17	Germany	4.8	17	Albania	6.7
18	Slovenia	4.7	18	Finland	5.4
19	Portugal	4.6	19	Austria	4.8
20	Malta	3.9	20	Sweden	3.9
21	Poland	3.5	21	Norway	3.4
22	Finland	3.4	22	Cyprus	3.3
23	Cyprus	1.8	23	Luxembourg	1.7
	Iceland	1.8	24	Switzerland	1.0
	Sweden	1.8	25	Iceland	0.9
26	Bulgaria	1.7			
	Hungary	1.7			
28	Slovakia	1.5			
29	Luxembourg	1.3			

a 1997

What people earn

Skilled industrial worker
1997, $ '000

	Gross income	Net income
Switzerland	49.8	39.7
Denmark	39.6	23.5
Germany	34.4	20.1
Norway	33.8	24.5
Belgium	32.6	19.7
Austria	30.9	21.9
United Kingdom	28.5	21.6
Netherlands	28.3	19.9
Sweden	27.9	18.2
Finland	27.5	17.6
France	22.0	16.3
Italy	21.9	14.5
Ireland	21.1	16.6
Spain	17.1	13.7
Greece	16.5	12.9
Cyprus	15.1	12.3
Portugal	12.5	10.4
Turkey	11.6	7.8
Czech Republic	4.8	3.8
Russia	4.5	3.6
Poland	3.7	3.0
Hungary	3.3	2.2

School teacher
1997, $ '000

	Gross income	Net income
Switzerland	68.8	51.7
Germany	41.8	32.2
Denmark	38.7	23.1
United Kingdom	32.1	23.8
Ireland	31.8	24.7
Netherlands	29.2	22.3
Norway	28.8	21.1
Sweden	27.1	17.7
Austria	27.0	19.7
Belgium	26.6	16.0
Finland	25.2	16.5
Cyprus	24.9	21.0
Spain	23.5	18.4
France	22.0	17.1
Italy	21.8	14.8
Portugal	18.0	13.6
Greece	14.6	11.7
Turkey	5.4	3.7
Czech Republic	4.2	3.4
Poland	3.1	2.5
Hungary	2.6	1.8
Russia	0.9	0.8

Department manager
1997, $ '000

	Gross income	Net income
Switzerland	104.6	73.5
Belgium	72.2	35.7
France	68.4	45.1
Germany	66.0	36.6
Austria	65.5	43.1
Netherlands	65.2	37.6
Norway	60.9	49.4
Denmark	54.6	29.8
Sweden	54.1	31.1
Finland	53.6	29.5
Ireland	45.3	31.1
United Kingdom	41.7	30.8
Portugal	38.8	25.9
Turkey	36.1	22.1
Italy	32.6	20.4
Cyprus	32.0	24.2
Spain	30.7	21.7
Greece	27.8	20.2
Czech Republic	18.3	12.3
Hungary	7.8	4.2
Poland	7.8	6.1
Russia	7.0	5.2

Secretary
1997, $ '000

	Gross income	Net income
Switzerland	43.0	32.5
Denmark	33.6	19.7
Germany	30.9	18.6
Belgium	27.7	15.9
Norway	27.0	18.7
Austria	26.5	19.0
United Kingdom	24.7	18.5
Sweden	24.3	16.0
France	23.6	15.2
Netherlands	22.3	15.2
Ireland	21.3	15.4
Finland	20.3	13.8
Italy	19.4	13.2
Spain	18.1	14.0
Cyprus	13.8	10.9
Greece	13.0	10.3
Portugal	10.3	7.5
Turkey	8.7	6.0
Czech Republic	5.2	4.0
Russia	4.7	3.4
Poland	3.8	3.1
Hungary	2.7	1.9

Taxing matters

The taxman's take
Marginal rates of personal income taxes, 1999

	Top/bottom rates, %		Top/bottom rates, %
Finland[a]	70[b]/7	Albania	40/1[c]
Sweden[a]	61/25	Azerbaijan	40/1[c]
Netherlands	60/5.1	Belarus	40/12
Belgium	55/25	Cyprus	40/20
France	54/10.5	Czech Republic	40/10
Germany	53/25.9	Poland	40/19
Norway[a]	52.2/44.5	Portugal	40/14
Switzerland[a]	51.5/4	Ukraine	40/1[c]
Austria	50/21	United Kingdom	40/20
Moldova	50/1[c]	Spain	39.6/15
Slovenia	50/17	Croatia	35/20
Denmark[a]	49.2/34.1	Lithuania	35/33
Ireland	46/24	Macedonia	35/15
Italy	46/19	Russia	35/12
Luxembourg	46/6	Armenia	30/15
Greece	45/5	Estonia	26/26
Romania	45/21	Latvia	25/25
Hungary	42/20	Georgia	20/12
Slovakia	42/15	Serbia & Montenegro	20/1[c]

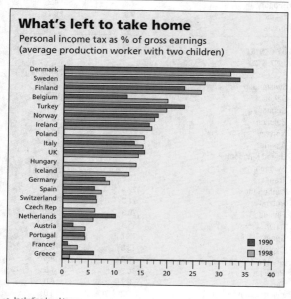

What's left to take home
Personal income tax as % of gross earnings
(average production worker with two children)

Denmark, Sweden, Finland, Belgium, Turkey, Norway, Ireland, Poland, Italy, UK, Hungary, Iceland, Germany, Spain, Switzerland, Czech Rep, Netherlands, Austria, Portugal, France[d], Greece

■ 1990
□ 1998

a Including local taxes.
b Level of ceiling limit on combined local and national income tax.
c Theoretical low level.
d 1991

Strikes

Time out
Working days not worked per 1,000 employees, all industries

1998			1988		
1	Denmark	31.7	1	Spain	1,399
2	Sweden	26.9	2	Iceland	929
3	Finland	26.2	3	Greece	442
4	Belgium	19.8	4	Turkey	264
5	Turkey	19.6	5	Italy	226
6	Norway	17.3	6	Sweden	199
7	Ireland	16.8	7	Ireland	177
8	Poland	15.4	8	United Kingdom	166
9	Italy	15.2	9	France	107
10	United Kingdom	14.3	10	Finland	88
11	Hungary	13.9	11	Portugal	67
12	Iceland	12.5	12	Belgium	66
13	Germany	8.9	13	Norway	45
14	Spain	7.3	14	Denmark	41
15	Switzerland	6.4	15	Austria	3
16	Czech Rep	6.1	16	Germany	2
17	Netherlands	5.8		Netherlands	2
18	Portugal	4.3	18	Luxembourg	0
19	Austria	4.3		Switzerland	0
20	France	2.9			
21	Greece	1.4		EU average	206

Average working days lost
All industries

1993–98			1988–92		
1	Iceland[c]	609	1	Spain	644
2	Spain	262	2	Greece	627
3	Finland	156	3	Turkey	366
4	Italy[c]	151	4	Iceland	341
5	Turkey[c]	147	5	Italy	248
6	Ireland[c]	82	6	Finland	184
7	Norway[c]	77	7	Ireland	165
8	Sweden[c]	54	8	Sweden	102
9	Denmark[c]	48	9	United Kingdom	98
10	Greece[c]	47	10	France	85
11	Russia	46	11	Norway	68
12	Romania[c]	32	12	Portugal	66
13	Netherlands	24	13	Belgium	46
	United Kingdom	24	14	Denmark	33
15	Portugal[c]	23	15	Germany	16
	Poland	23	16	Netherlands	15
17	Hungary	18	17	Austria	7
18	Slovakia[c]	3	18	Luxembourg	0
19	Austria[c]	2		Switzerland	0
20	Switzerland[c]	1			
				EU average	138

a 1997   b 1996   c 1993–97

Work and play

Working hours
Average working hours, 1998

		Per week	Per year
1	Turkey	46.5	2,418
2	Croatia	42.2	2,194
3	Luxembourg[a]	41.1	2,137
4	Greece	41.0	2,132
5	Latvia	40.8	2,122
	Poland	40.8	2,122
7	Slovenia	40.5	2,106
8	Iceland	40.3	2,096
9	United Kingdom	40.2	2,090
10	Cyprus	40.0	2,080
11	Germany	39.8	2,070
12	Czech Republic	39.4	2,049
13	Netherlands[b]	39.2	2,038
14	France[a]	38.9	2,023
15	Belgium	38.3	1,992
16	Portugal	38.0	1,976
17	Lithuania	37.3	1,940
18	Spain	36.7	1,908
	Finland	36.7	1,908
20	Sweden	36.4	1,893
21	Austria	35.5	1,846
22	Norway	35.3	1,836
23	Ireland	34.8	1,810
24	Estonia	34.3	1,784
25	Georgia	33.8	1,758

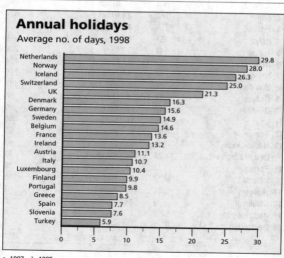

Annual holidays
Average no. of days, 1998

Netherlands	29.8
Norway	28.0
Iceland	26.3
Switzerland	25.0
UK	21.3
Denmark	16.3
Germany	15.6
Sweden	14.9
Belgium	14.6
France	13.6
Ireland	13.2
Austria	11.1
Italy	10.7
Luxembourg	10.4
Finland	9.9
Portugal	9.8
Greece	8.5
Spain	7.7
Slovenia	7.6
Turkey	5.9

a 1997 b 1995

Part VI

BUSINESS AND FINANCE

Agriculture: leading producers

Wheat
'000 tonnes
1998

1	France	39,793
2	Russia	27,012
3	Turkey	21,000
4	Germany	20,187
5	United Kingdom	15,470
6	Ukraine	14,937
7	Poland	9,537
8	Italy	8,338
9	Spain	5,437
10	Romania	5,182
11	Hungary	4,977
12	Denmark	4,928
13	Czech Republic	3,845
14	Bulgaria	3,203
15	Serbia & Montenegro	2,967
16	Sweden	2,249
17	Greece	2,058
18	Belgium & Lux	1,803
19	Slovakia	1,789
20	Austria	1,342

Coarse grains[a]
'000 tonnes
1998

1	France	28,519
2	Germany	24,387
3	Russia	19,544
4	Poland	17,622
5	Spain	16,235
6	Turkey	11,865
7	Italy	10,999
8	Ukraine	10,701
9	Romania	10,264
10	Hungary	8,118
11	United Kingdom	7,313
12	Serbia & Montenegro	5,700
13	Denmark	4,416
14	Belarus	3,705
15	Austria	3,429
16	Sweden	3,369
17	Czech Republic	2,831
18	Finland	2,376
19	Greece	2,302
20	Croatia	2,182

Oilseeds[b]
'000 tonnes
1998

1	France	2,196
2	Germany	1,394
3	Russia	1,363
4	Spain	1,349
5	Italy	1,017
6	Turkey	968
7	Ukraine	966
8	United Kingdom	647
9	Greece	570
10	Romania	492
11	Poland	426
12	Hungary	345
13	Czech Republic	295
14	Bulgaria	221
15	Serbia & Montenegro	146
16	Denmark	137
17	Slovakia	91
18	Austria	90
19	Portugal	89
20	Moldova	82

Sugar beets
'000 tonnes
1998

1	France	31,156
2	Germany	26,787
3	Turkey	20,000
4	Ukraine	15,523
5	Poland	15,171
6	Italy	13,343
7	Russia	10,798
8	United Kingdom	10,002
9	Spain	9,021
10	Netherlands	5,505
11	Belgium & Lux	5,366
12	Czech Republic	3,479
13	Denmark	3,414
14	Hungary	3,361
15	Austria	3,314
16	Sweden	2,639
17	Romania	2,361
18	Greece	1,996
19	Serbia & Montenegro	1,980
20	Moldovia	1,452

a Barley, maize, oats, rye, millet and sorghum.
b Sunflower seed, rapeseed, olives and soyabeans.

Fruit
'000 tonnes
1998

1	Italy	17,760
2	Spain	13,667
3	Turkey	10,389
4	France	10,344
5	Germany	5,012
6	Greece	3,526
7	Russia	2,573
8	Poland	2,519
9	Romania	1,879
10	Ukraine	1,594
11	Hungary	1,562
12	Serbia & Montenegro	1,481
13	Portugal	1,329
14	Austria	1,042
15	Moldovia	956
16	Switzerland	849
17	Bulgaria	726
18	Netherlands	715
19	Belgium & Lux	652
20	Croatia	646

Vegetables
'000 tonnes
1998

1	Turkey	21,777
2	Italy	14,722
3	Spain	11,691
4	Russia	10,884
5	France	8,025
6	Poland	6,387
7	Ukraine	5,515
8	Greece	4,194
9	Netherlands	3,560
10	Romania	3,509
11	Germany	3,140
12	United Kingdom	2,932
13	Portugal	2,459
14	Hungary	1,818
15	Belgium & Lux	1,767
16	Bulgaria	1,714
17	Serbia & Montenegro	1,399
18	Belarus	1,201
19	Albania	626
20	Bosnia	609

Meat
'000 tonnes
1998

1	France	6,522
2	Germany	6,166
3	Russia	4,703
4	Spain	4,689
5	Italy	4,044
6	United Kingdom	3,733
7	Poland	3,004
8	Netherlands	2,995
9	Denmark	1,987
10	Belgium & Lux	1,801
11	Ukraine	1,706
12	Turkey	1,244
13	Romania	1,135
14	Hungary	1,085
15	Serbia & Montenegro	1,031
16	Ireland	1,026
17	Austria	909
18	Czech Republic	846
19	Portugal	690
20	Belarus	675

Milk
'000 tonnes
1998

1	Russia	33,255
2	Germany	28,400
3	France	25,476
4	United Kingdom	14,635
5	Ukraine	13,752
6	Poland	12,597
7	Italy	12,236
8	Netherlands	11,200
9	Turkey	10,060
10	Spain	6,729
11	Belarus	5,232
12	Ireland	5,148
13	Romania	4,784
14	Denmark	4,668
15	Switzerland	3,904
16	Belgium & Lux	3,682
17	Austria	3,278
18	Sweden	3,277
19	Czech Republic	2,734
20	Finland	2,447

Industry: who makes what

Cars
Production, '000s, 1998

1	Germany	5,348	10	Belgium	317
2	France	2,600	11	Netherlands	255
3	Spain	1,940	12	Turkey	240
4	United Kingdom	1,752	13	Romania	109
5	Italy	1,378	14	Hungary	88
6	Russia	834	15	Slovakia[a]	42
7	Poland	506	16	Ukraine	25
8	Czech Republic	337	17	Serbia & Montenegro	11
9	Sweden	325			

Commercial vehicles
Production, '000s, 1998

1	Spain	519	7	Belgium	78
2	Germany	391	8	Turkey	60
3	France	345	9	Poland	46
4	Italy	262	10	Czech Republic	37
5	United Kingdom	232	11	Russia	36
6	Sweden	228	12	Netherlands	25

Steel
Production, m tonnes, 1999

1	Russia	49.8	10	Poland	8.8
2	Germany	42.1	11	Netherlands	6.1
3	Ukraine	27.0	12	Czech Republic	5.6
4	Italy	25.0	13	Austria	5.2
5	France	20.2	14	Sweden	5.1
6	United Kingdom	16.3	15	Romania	4.3
7	Spain	14.6	16	Finland	4.0
8	Turkey	14.4	17	Slovakia	3.6
9	Belgium	11.0	18	Luxembourg	2.6

Shipbuilding
Completions, gross tonnage '000, 1999

1	Italy	777	11	Norway	160
2	Germany	764	12	France	129
3	Poland	606	13	Russia	62
4	Spain	490	14	Ukraine	46
5	Denmark	434	15	Sweden	31
6	Netherlands	330	16	United Kingdom	23
7	Croatia	225	17	Czech Republic	7
8	Finland	224		Serbia & Montenegro	7
9	Romania	223	19	Lithuania	6
10	Turkey	170		Slovakia	6

a 1997

Inventiveness and investment

Patents granted
Average annual number, 1996–97

1	Germany	19,646	11	Belgium	983
2	France	12,597	12	Spain	940
3	Italy	4,551	13	Ireland	485
4	United Kingdom	4,436	14	Norway	393
5	Netherlands	2,238	15	Denmark	384
6	Switzerland	2,004	16	Czech Republic	354
7	Sweden	1,886	17	Hungary	349
8	Austria	1,311	18	Slovenia	244
9	Poland	1,292	19	Greece	102
10	Finland	1,024	20	Luxembourg	84

Spending on research and development
As % of GDP, 1998

1	Sweden	3.85	11	Austria	1.55
2	Finland	2.91	12	Iceland	1.54
3	Switzerland	2.74	13	Ireland	1.52
4	Germany	2.31	14	Slovenia	1.44
5	France	2.24	15	Czech Republic	1.27
6	Netherlands	2.09	16	Italy	1.09
7	Denmark	1.96	17	Russia	0.95
8	United Kingdom	1.82	18	Spain	0.84
9	Norway	1.67	19	Hungary	0.72
10	Belgium	1.59	20	Portugal	0.65

Nobel prizes[a]
*No. awarded in physics, chemistry, physiology or medicine and economics
1901–1999[b]*

1	United Kingdom	67	6	Netherlands	10
2	Germany	46	7	Austria	9
3	France	21	8	Denmark	8
4	Sweden	17		Russia	8
5	Switzerland	15	10	Italy	7

Investment in telecommunications
As % of GDP, 1995–97

1	Czech Republic	1.87	12	Norway	0.50
2	Hungary	1.31	13	Luxembourg	0.49
3	Slovenia	0.65	14	Finland	0.48
4	Greece	0.63	15	Iceland	0.45
	Poland	0.63	16	United Kingdom	0.44
6	Switzerland	0.62	17	Germany	0.43
7	Ireland	0.60	18	Denmark	0.41
8	Portugal	0.53	19	Netherlands	0.39
9	Austria	0.52	20	Italy	0.38
	Sweden	0.52	21	France	0.37
11	Spain	0.51	22	Belgium	0.36

a Prizes by country of residence at time awarded. When prizes have been shared in
  the same field, one credit has been given to each country.
b Economics since 1969.

Service sectors

Working at it
% of labour force in service sector, 1998

1	Netherlands	72.8	19	Greece	57.7
2	Norway	72.1	20	Estonia[d]	57.2
3	Sweden	71.6	21	Latvia	55.0
4	United Kingdom	71.4	22	Russia	53.9
5	Denmark	69.7	23	Croatia	53.4
6	Switzerland[a]	69.1	24	Czech Republic	53.0
7	France[b]	68.7		Slovakia	53.0
8	Luxembourg	66.4	26	Lithuania	52.4
9	Finland	65.9	27	Portugal	50.8
10	Belgium	65.8	28	Poland	48.7
11	Iceland[c]	65.6	29	Slovenia	48.2
12	Austria[a]	63.2	30	Ukraine	46.5
	Germany	63.2	31	Bulgaria	43.5
14	Cyprus	63.0	32	Belarus	40.1
15	Ireland	61.5	33	Moldova	39.7
	Spain	61.5	34	Turkey	34.2
17	Italy[a]	59.2	35	Romania	30.6
18	Hungary	58.2			

% of labour force in trade, restaurants and hotels, 1998

1	Cyprus[b]	26.2
2	Switzerland	23.4
3	Greece[a]	22.6
4	Spain	22.5
5	Austria	21.4
6	Italy[a]	21.2
	Luxembourg[d]	21.2
8	Ireland	20.1
	Netherlands	20.1
10	United Kingdom	19.9
11	Portugal	18.9
12	Croatia	18.7

% of labour force in finance and business services, 1998

1	Switzerland	14.9
2	Netherlands	14.8
3	United Kingdom	14.7
4	Sweden	12.4
5	Denmark	11.4
6	Finland	11.1
	Ireland	11.1
8	Germany	10.7
9	France[c]	10.6
10	Norway	10.2

% of labour force in transport and communication, 1998

1	Estonia	9.3
2	Hungary	8.2
3	Latvia	8.1
4	Russia	7.9
5	Slovakia	7.8
6	Czech Republic[a]	7.7
7	Norway	7.6
8	Finland	7.5
9	Iceland	7.3
10	Bulgaria	7.2

% of labour force in social and personal services, 1998

1	Sweden	37.0
2	Norway	36.0
3	Denmark	35.3
4	France[c]	35.0
5	Belgium	32.6
6	Finland	32.3
7	Netherlands	31.9
8	Iceland	31.8
9	Ukraine	30.4
10	United Kingdom	30.3

a 1997   b 1995   c 1994   d 1990

Tourism receipts

$bn, 1998			*$ per head of population, 1998*	
1	France	29.9	1	Cyprus	2,089
2	Italy	29.8	2	Malta	1,660
3	Spain	29.7	3	Austria	1,383
4	United Kingdom	21.0	4	Switzerland	1,068
5	Germany	16.4	5	Ireland	892
6	Austria	11.2	6	Spain	750
7	Poland	7.9	7	Iceland	673
8	Switzerland	7.8	8	Slovenia	645
	Turkey	7.8	9	Denmark	604
10	Netherlands	6.8	10	Croatia	600
11	Russia	6.5	11	Norway	555
12	Belgium	5.4	12	Belgium	535
	Ukraine	5.4	13	Italy	519
14	Greece	5.2	14	France	509
15	Portugal	4.9	15	Portugal	495
16	Sweden	4.1	16	Greece	491
17	Czech Republic	3.7	17	Sweden	461
18	Ireland	3.3	18	Netherlands	433
19	Denmark	3.2	19	Estonia	381
20	Croatia	2.7	20	Czech Republic	361

Advertising expenditure

$ per head of population, 1998					
1	Switzerland	337	11	Belgium[a]	138
2	Finland	300	12	Ireland	133
3	United Kingdom	297	13	Cyprus[a]	126
4	Denmark	295	14	Spain[a]	114
5	Norway	252	15	Italy	105
6	Germany	244	16	Slovenia	98
7	Netherlands	201	17	Greece	94
8	Sweden	192	18	Portugal	92
9	Austria	175	19	Hungary	51
10	France	151	20	Czech Republic	37

Number of lawyers

Per 100,000 population, 1999					
1	Gibraltar	362	13	Belgium	119
2	Spain	237	14	Italy	99
3	Greece	217	15	Bulgaria	90
4	United Kingdom	202	16	Switzerland	85
5	Liechtenstein[b]	177	17	Norway	79
6	Portugal	172		Hungary	79
7	Iceland	168	19	Monaco	77
8	Luxembourg	167		Denmark	77
9	Cyprus	156	21	Netherlands	66
10	Malta	145	22	France	60
11	Ireland	141	23	Czech Republic	58
12	Germany	125	24	Turkey	54

a 1997 b 1996

Big business

Europe's biggest companies
By sales, 1998, $bn

	Company	Country	Sales	Profits/losses
1	DaimlerChrysler	Germany	154.62	5.66
2	Royal Dutch/Shell Group	UK/Netherlands	93.69	0.35
3	AXA	France	78.73	1.70
4	Volkswagen	Germany	76.31	1.26
5	BP Amoco	UK	68.30	3.26
6	Siemens	Germany	66.04	0.37
7	Allianz	Germany	64.87	2.02
8	ING Group	Netherlands	56.47	2.91
9	Metro	Germany	52.13	0.33
10	Fiat	Italy	51.00	0.69
11	Nestlé	Switzerland	49.50	2.96
12	Credit Suisse	Switzerland	49.14	2.12
13	Assicurazioni Generali	Italy	48.48	1.00
14	Deutsche Bank	Germany	45.17	1.88
15	Unilever	UK/Netherlands	44.91	3.27
16	Veba Group	Germany	43.41	1.33
17	HSBC Holdings	UK	43.34	4.32
18	Renault	France	41.35	1.50
19	Deutsche Telekom	Germany	39.71	2.49
20	Zurich Financial Services	Switzerland	39.12	0.80
21	Royal Philips Electronics	Netherlands	38.46	6.60
22	CGU	UK	37.59	0.83
23	Peugeot	France	37.54	0.54
24	Électricité De France	France	36.67	0.26
25	Rwe Group	Germany	36.60	0.80
26	BMW	Germany	35.89	0.51
27	Elf Aquitaine	France	35.86	0.60
28	Munich Re Group	Germany	35.46	0.49
29	Vivendi	France	35.29	1.25
30	Suez Lyonnaise des Eaux	France	34.87	1.12
31	ABN Amro Holding	Netherlands	34.24	1.99
32	Prudential	UK	33.68	1.46
33	Crédit Agricole	France	33.02	2.09
34	ENI	Italy	32.39	2.59
35	HypoVereinsbank	Germany	31.82	2.13
36	Fortis	Belgium	31.33	1.52
37	Bayer	Germany	31.20	1.79
38	ABB Asea Brown Boveri	Switzerland	30.87	1.31
39	BASF	Germany	30.73	1.89
40	Carrefour	France	30.48	0.72

Note: The e-business readiness rankings opposite, compiled by the Economist Intelligence Unit, cover 60 countries. They consider two factors: the general business environment (based on 70 indicators, including the strength of the economy, the outlook for political stability, the regulatory climate, taxation policies and openness to trade and investment); and connectivity (taking into account criteria such as the state of the telephone network, factors affecting Internet access, dial-up costs and literacy rates).

Europe's biggest employers
1998, '000

	Company	Country	No. of employees
1	DaimlerChrysler	Germany	441.5
2	Siemens	Germany	416.0
3	Volkswagen	Germany	297.9
4	La Poste	France	288.0
5	RAO Gazprom	Russia	278.4
6	Unilever	UK	267.0
7	Deutsche Bahn	Germany	252.5
8	Vivendi	France	235.6
9	Nestlé	Switzerland	231.9
10	Royal Philips Electronics	Netherlands	224.6
11	Deutsche Post	Germany	223.9
12	Fiat	Italy	220.5
13	SNCF	France	210.4
14	Suez Lyonnaise des Eaux	France	201.0
15	ABB Asea Brown Boveri	Switzerland	199.2
16	Deutsche Telekom	Germany	195.9
17	British Post Office	UK	194.0
18	Robert Bosch	Germany	189.5
19	Metro	Germany	181.3
20	France Télécom	France	169.1

E-business readiness
Scores (out of 10), June 2000 (see note opposite)

		General business environment	Connectivity	E-business readiness
1	Sweden	8.26	9	8.6
2	Finland	8.21	9	8.6
3	Norway	8.00	9	8.5
4	Netherlands	8.84	8	8.4
5	United Kingdom	8.80	8	8.4
6	Switzerland	8.42	8	8.2
7	Ireland	8.42	8	8.2
8	Denmark	8.41	8	8.2
9	Germany	8.32	8	8.2
10	France	8.17	8	8.1
11	Belgium	8.17	8	8.1
12	Austria	7.96	8	8.0
13	Italy	7.68	8	7.8
14	Spain	8.01	7	7.5
15	Portugal	7.59	6	6.8
16	Poland	7.15	5	6.1
17	Hungary	7.09	5	6.0
18	Czech Republic	7.07	5	6.0
19	Greece	6.90	5	6.0
20	Slovakia	6.19	5	5.6
21	Turkey	6.06	5	5.5
22	Bulgaria	5.61	5	5.3
23	Romania	5.45	5	5.2

Banking

Europe's biggest banks
By capital, $m, 1998

	Bank	Country	Capital
1	HSBC Holdings	United Kingdom	29,352
2	Credit Agricole	France	25,930
3	UBS	Switzerland	20,525
4	Deutsche Bank	Germany	18,680
5	Credit Suisse Group	Switzerland	17,579
6	ABN Amro Bank	Netherlands	17,471
7	Hypo Vereinsbank	Germany	15,195
8	Radobank Nederland	Netherlands	14,688
9	Banque National de Paris	France	13,552
10	Barclays Bank	United Kingdom	13,495
11	National Westminster Bank	United Kingdom	13,389
12	Dresdner Bank	Germany	13,042
13	ING Bank Group	Netherlands	12,961
14	Societe Generale	France	12,521
15	Lloyds TSB Group	United Kingdom	12,111
16	Commerzbank	Germany	11,760
17	Halifax	United Kingdom	11,564
18	Credit Mutuel	France	10,737
19	Banco Santander	Spain	10,654
20	Groupe Caisse d'Epargne	France	10,124
21	Paribas	France	9,919
22	Fortis Banking Group	Belgium	9,867
23	Sanpaolo IMI	Italy	9,423
24	Westdeutsche Landesbank Girozentrale	Italy	9,204
25	Abbey National	United Kingdom	8,659
26	Unicredito Italiano	Italy	8,420
27	Credit Lyonnais	France	7,749
28	Banco Bilbao Vizcaya	Spain	7,686
29	Groupe Banques Populaires	France	7,272
30	Bayerische Landesbank	Germany	7,124
31	KBC Bank	Belgium	6,921
32	Dexia	European Union	6,547
33	Banco di Roma	Italy	6,196
34	Banca Commerciale Italiana	Italy	5,903
35	Argentenaria	Spain	5,638
36	MeritaNordbanken	Finland	5,566
37	Royal Bank of Scotland	United Kingdom	5,427
38	DG Bank	Germany	5,426
39	Bank Austria	Austria	5,397
40	Bank of Scotland	United Kingdom	5,285
41	LB Baden-Wurttemberg	Germany	5,198
42	Banca Intesa	Italy	4,955
43	Bankgesellschaft Berlin	Germany	4,906
44	Den Danske Bank	Denmark	4,709
45	Banca Monte dei Paschi di Siena	Italy	4,658

Note: capital is essentially equity and reserves.

By assets, $m, 1998

	Bank	Country	Assets
1	Deutsche Bank	Germany	732,534
2	UBS	Switzerland	685,882
3	Hypo Vereinsbank	Germany	538,625
4	ABN Amro Bank	Netherlands	504,122
5	HSBC Holdings	United Kingdom	484,655
6	Credit Suisse Group	Switzerland	473,983
7	Credit Agricole	France	455,792
8	Societe Generale	France	447,545
9	Dresdner Bank	Germany	427,261
10	Westdeutsche Landesbank Girozentrale	Italy	408,372
11	Commerzbank	Germany	381,359
12	Banque National de Paris	France	378,997
13	Barclays Bank	United Kingdom	353,367
14	ING Bank Group	Netherlands	326,813
15	Fortis Banking Group	Belgium	323,567
16	National Westminster Bank	United Kingdom	309,421
17	Paribas	France	309,364
18	Abbey National	United Kingdom	295,756
19	Radobank Nederland	Netherlands	291,353
20	Credit Mutuel	France	286,461

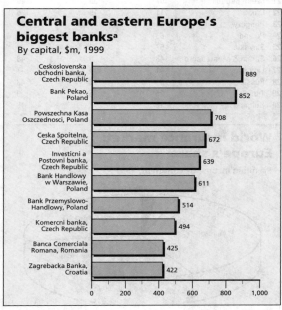

Central and eastern Europe's biggest banks[a]

By capital, $m, 1999

Ceskoslovenska obchodni banka, Czech Republic	889
Bank Pekao, Poland	852
Powszechna Kasa Oszczednosci, Poland	708
Ceska Spoitelna, Czech Republic	672
Investicni a Postovni banka, Czech Republic	639
Bank Handlowy w Warszawie, Poland	611
Bank Przemyslowo-Handlowy, Poland	514
Komercni banka, Czech Republic	494
Banca Comerciala Romana, Romania	425
Zagrebacka Banka, Croatia	422

a Excluding Russia.

Insurance

Who buys most insurance?
Premiums per person, 1997, $

		Non-life	Life	Total
1	Switzerland	1,297	2,993	4,290
2	United Kingdom	731	1,721	2,452
3	France	693	1,511	2,204
4	Netherlands	959	1,233	2,192
5	Denmark	782	1,221	2,003
6	Finland	442	1,368	1,810
7	Ireland	622	1,092	1,714
8	Germany	973	694	1,666
9	Luxembourg	1,059	605	1,664
10	Belgium	909	711	1,620
11	Norway	805	783	1,588
12	Austria	853	517	1,369
13	Sweden	591	625	1,215
14	Italy	454	376	830
15	Spain	385	341	726
16	Iceland	687	29	716
17	Portugal	295	262	557
18	Cyprus	228	257	485
19	Slovenia	269	72	341
20	Greece	101	100	201
21	Czech Republic	107	39	146
22	Croatia	111	15	126
23	Hungary	69	34	103
24	Poland	69	27	96
25	Slovakia	67	26	94
26	Serbia & Montenegro	48	0	48
27	Latvia	41	6	47
28	Russia	34	10	43
29	Turkey	25	5	29
30	Bulgaria	18	2	19

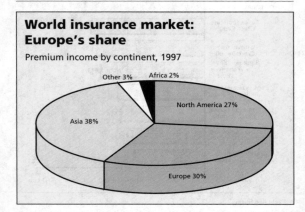

World insurance market: Europe's share

Premium income by continent, 1997

Other 3% | Africa 2% | North America 27% | Asia 38% | Europe 30%

More premium comparisons
Insurance premiums as % of GDP, 1997

		Non-life	Life	Total
1	Switzerland	3.61	8.33	11.94
2	United Kingdom	3.34	7.87	11.22
3	Netherlands	4.12	5.29	9.41
4	France	2.91	6.34	9.25
5	Ireland	3.04	5.33	8.37
6	Finland	1.90	5.87	7.76
7	Belgium	3.82	2.98	6.80
8	Germany	3.81	2.72	6.53
9	Denmark	2.43	3.79	6.22
10	Portugal	2.87	2.55	5.42
11	Spain	2.85	2.53	5.38
12	Austria	3.34	2.02	5.36
13	Sweden	2.29	2.42	4.72
14	Norway	2.31	2.25	4.56
15	Luxembourg	2.88	1.64	4.53
16	Cyprus	2.01	2.28	4.29
17	Italy	2.28	1.89	4.17
18	Slovenia	2.94	0.79	3.73
19	Croatia	2.60	0.34	2.94
20	Czech Republic	2.12	0.77	2.89
21	Serbia & Montenegro	2.73	0.02	2.75
22	Poland	1.97	0.77	2.74
23	Iceland	2.50	0.11	2.61
24	Slovakia	1.87	0.72	2.59
25	Hungary	1.56	0.77	2.33
26	Latvia	1.84	0.25	2.09
27	Greece	0.87	0.87	1.74
28	Bulgaria	1.47	0.12	1.59
29	Russia	1.10	0.31	1.41
30	Turkey	0.83	0.16	0.98

Europe's largest insurance companies
Revenues, $bn, 1998

1	Axa	France	78.73
2	Allianz	Germany	64.86
3	ING Group	Netherlands	56.47
4	Assicurazioni Generali	Italy	48.48
5	Zurich Financial Services	Switzerland	39.12
6	CGU	United Kingdom	37.59
7	Munich Re	Germany	35.47
8	Prudential	United Kingdom	33.68
9	Royal & Sun Alliance	United Kingdom	25.44
10	CNP Assurances	France	24.11
11	Aegon	Netherlands	18.73
12	Norwich Union	United Kingdom	16.90
13	Swiss Reinsurance	Switzerland	16.42
14	Swiss Life	Switzerland	15.52
15	Standard Life Assurance	United Kingdom	14.83

Mergers and acquisitions

Activity in the EU
Mergers and acquisitions, 1996–98

Target	Own country	EU15	Outside EU
		Targeter/Bidder, %	
Austria	27.1	39.3	33.6
Belgium	35.2	37.7	27.1
Denmark	43.9	21.6	34.5
Finland	57.9	20.4	21.7
France	53.6	19.6	26.8
Germany	48.8	19.0	32.2
Greece	70.7	12.1	17.2
Ireland	29.1	22.1	48.8
Italy	46.6	25.6	27.8
Luxembourg	5.0	41.7	53.3
Netherlands	44.4	20.4	35.2
Portugal	18.8	55.2	26.0
Spain	42.6	33.2	24.2
Sweden	42.6	19.1	38.3
United Kingdom	64.3	6.6	29.1
EU15	42.0	26.0	32.0

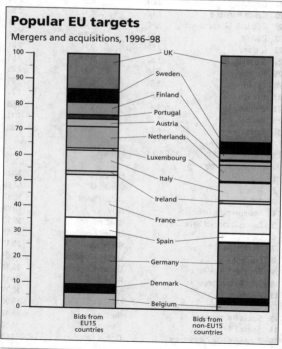

Popular EU targets
Mergers and acquisitions, 1996–98

UK
Sweden
Finland
Portugal
Austria
Netherlands
Luxembourg
Italy
Ireland
France
Spain
Germany
Denmark
Belgium

Bids from EU15 countries

Bids from non-EU15 countries

The big ones
Main EU mergers, demergers and acquisitions, 1992–May 2000

	Date	Target	Bidder	Amount, $m
1	Nov-99	Mannesmann	Vodafone AirTouch	202,785
2	Jan-00	SmithKline Beecham	Glaxo Wellcome	78,385
3	Jul-99	Elf Aquitaine	Total Fina	55,340
4	May-00	Orange (Mannesmann)	France Telecom	45,967
5	Nov-99	National Westminster Bank	Royal Bank of Scotland Grp	38,525
6	Oct-99	Orange	Mannesmann	35,320
7	Feb-99	Telecom Italia	Ing C Olivetti & Co	34,758
8	Dec-98	Astra	Zeneca Group	31,787
9	May-99	Hoechst	Rhône-Poulenc	28,526
10	Mar-96	Ciba-Geigy	Sandoz	28,001
11	Dec-97	Schweizerischer Bankverein	Union Bank of Switzerland	23,009
12	Apr-00	Allied Zurich	Zurich Allied	19,399
13	Oct-99	Ente Nazionale per l'Energia	Investors	18,734
14	Mar-00	Seat Pagine Gialle	Tin.it	18,694
15	Oct-97	BAT Industries-Financial	Zurich Versicherungs	18,355
16	May-97	Guinness	Grand Metropolitan	18,290
17	Aug-99	Promodès	Carrefour	17,531
18	Sep-99	VIAG	VEBA	16,275
19	Oct-95	Lloyds Bank	TSB Group	15,316
20	Jul-99	One 2 One	Deutsche Telekom	13,629
21	Jul-92	Deutsche Telekom	Investors	13,534
22	Jan-95	Wellcome	Glaxo Holdings	13,408
23	Mar-99	Paribas	BNP	13,201
24	Jan-99	Marconi Electronic Systems	British Aerospace	12,863
25	May-99	Banca Commerciale Italiana	Banca Intesa	12,791

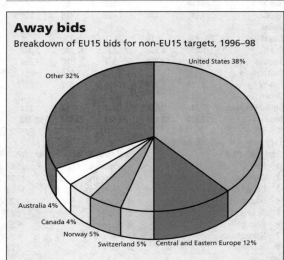

Away bids
Breakdown of EU15 bids for non-EU15 targets, 1996–98

United States 38%
Other 32%
Australia 4%
Canada 4%
Norway 5%
Switzerland 5%
Central and Eastern Europe 12%

Privatisation

How much has been sold
Privatisation proceeds (public offers and private sales), $m

	1988–95	1996	1997	1998	1999
Armenia	...	...	80	30	...
Austria	3,188	948	1,710	2,940	301
Belgium	4,120	680	985	2,271	9
Bulgaria	102	26	386	128	252
Croatia	13	140	...	222	850
Czech Republic	2,231	...	72	216	1,175
Denmark	4,263	185	3,200	...	...
Estonia	0	22	80	25	252
Finland	1,825	1,105	743	2,060	3,685
France	27,739	4,989	7,454	16,768	9,805
Germany	39,662	14,796	6,418	2,611	16,204
Greece	1,216	530	1,359	2,401	3,638
Hungary	4,995	1,004	2,116	315	638
Iceland	...	...	...	102	137
Ireland	1,264	290	...	...	4,183
Italy	20,277	8,189	32,396	16,490	31,410
Latvia	160	16	235	...	...
Lithuania	29	...	9	519	79
Macedonia	...	...	...	...	58
Malta	...	...	...	91	250
Monaco	...	...	...	...	118
Netherlands	11,264	1,040	6	...	6,105
Norway	719	651	...	...	906
Poland	2,253	1,061	2,319	2,334	3,280
Portugal	6,898	2,945	4,944	4,351	2,814
Romania	60	...	396	969	43
Russia	1,215	734	4,102	1,409	200
Serbia	0	...	15	...	...
Slovakia	113	16	11	...	...
Spain	10,099	2,523	12,997	12,440	3,387
Sweden	8,840	1,338	907	180	1,970
Switzerland	...	...	...	5,500	...
Turkey	1,584	255	293	1,967	...
Ukraine	25	...	...	...	...
United Kingdom	63,347	9,534	234	64	719
Total	**217,501**	**53,017**	**83,467**	**76,403**	**92,468**

The biggest privatisers

Total 1988–99, $m			*Total 1988–99, as % of 1998 GDP*	
1	Italy	108,762	1 Portugal	20.63
2	Germany	79,691	2 Hungary	19.84
3	United Kingdom	73,898	3 Monaco[a]	14.75
4	France	66,755	4 Italy	9.40
5	Spain	41,446	5 Malta	8.97
6	Portugal	21,952	6 Bulgaria	8.85
7	Netherlands	18,415	7 Ireland	8.28
8	Sweden	13,235	8 Estonia	7.73

a Estimate.

Big ones

Biggest European privatisations, $bn, 1988–99

1	Italy	Enel	17.46
2	Italy	Telecom Italia	14.90
3	Germany	Deutsche Telekom 1	13.30
4	Germany	Deutsche Telekom 2	11.80
5	France	France Telecom	10.20
6	United Kingdom	BritishTelecom (BT2)	9.99
7	United Kingdom	BritishTelecom (BT3)	8.06
8	Italy	ENI 3	7.80
9	Spain	Endesa	7.60
10	Italy	ENI 4	7.30
11	France	France Telecom	7.10
12	France	Elf Aquitaine	6.82
13	Germany	Vereinigte Energiewerke	5.70
14	Switzerland	Swisscom	5.50
15	Italy	ENI 2	5.06
16	Italy	Cariplo bank	5.00
17	France	Banque Nationale de Paris	4.81
18	Spain	Endesa	4.56
19	United Kingdom	British Steel	4.50
20	Italy	Autostrade	4.42
21	Spain	Telefonica	4.36
22	Portugal	Gescartao	4.32
23	Ireland	Telecom Eireann	4.18
24	Italy	ENI 1	3.97
25	Sweden	Procordia	3.82
26	Netherlands	Koninklijke PTT Nederland (KPN1)	3.75
27	France	Credit Lyonnais	3.70
28	United Kingdom	Scottish Power	3.67
29	Netherlands	Koninklijke PTT Nederland (KPN2)	3.44
30	Denmark	Tele Danmark	3.33

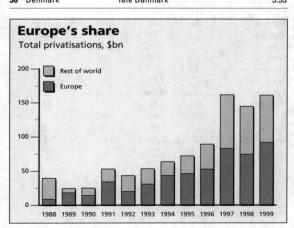

Europe's share
Total privatisations, $bn

Rest of world
Europe

1988 1989 1990 1991 1992 1993 1994 1995 1996 1997 1998 1999

Foreign direct investment

Inward

	Inflows, $m			Stock, $bn[a]
	1987–92 av.	1995	1998	1998
Albania	...	70	45	0.4
Armenia	...	24	232	0.4
Austria	648	1,904	5,915	25.4
Azerbaijan	...	155	1,085	2.9
Belarus	...	15	144	0.5
Belgium & Lux	7,214	10,811	20,889	164.1
Bulgaria	...	90	401	1.4
Croatia	...	101	873	2.4
Cyprus	83	119	200	2.2
Czech Republic	...	2,561	2,540	13.5
Denmark	897	4,139	6,623	31.8
Estonia	...	201	581	1.8
Finland	377	1,044	11,115	15.5
France	12,092	23,681	28,039	179.2
Georgia	...	5	251	0.4
Germany	2,560	12,026	19,877	228.8
Greece	938	1,053	700	22.0
Hungary	675	4,453	1,935	18.3
Iceland	-2	13	112	0.4
Ireland	615	1,447	6,820	23.9
Italy	4,317	4,878	2,611	105.4
Latvia	...	180	274	1.5
Lithuania	...	73	926	1.6
Macedonia	...	10	119	0.2
Malta	46	183	130	1.6
Moldova	...	67	85	0.3
Netherlands	7,147	12,151	31,859	169.5
Norway	320	2,393	3,597	24.3
Poland	183	3,659	5,129	21.7
Portugal	1,676	685	1,771	21.1
Romania	...	420	2,063	4.3
Russia	...	2,016	2,183	13.4
Slovakia	...	195	466	2.1
Slovenia	37	176	165	2.4
Spain	9,943	6,839	11,307	118.9
Sweden	2,070	14,454	19,358	53.8
Switzerland	2,490	3,599	3,707	60.1
Turkey	578	885	807	7.4
Ukraine	...	267	743	2.8
United Kingdom	22,156	20,404	63,124	326.8

Outward

	Outflows, $m			Stock, $bn[a]
	1987–92 av.	1995	1998	1998
Albania	...	12	1	0.1
Austria	1,030	1,131	3,013	16.8
Belarus	...	...	2	...
Belgium & Lux	6,174	11,712	23,111	128.8
Bulgaria	...	8	...	...
Croatia	...	6	92	0.7
Cyprus	6	7	2	0.5
Czech Republic	...	37	55	0.7
Denmark	1,496	2,969	4,008	35.8
Estonia	...	2	6	0.2
Finland	1,440	1,494	19,812	32.8
France	22,492	15,760	40,587	242.3
Georgia	...	...	8	...
Germany	17,112	39,052	86,591	390.1
Greece	26	66	-47	0.9
Hungary		43	481	1.3
Iceland	11	25	99	0.4
Ireland	379	820	705	6.5
Italy	4,964	6,925	12,076	170.7
Latvia	...	-65	54	0.3
Lithuania	...	1	4	...
Macedonia	...	...	1	...
Malta	...	56	40	0.2
Moldova	...	...	-1	...
Netherlands	12,317	20,022	38,310	263.0
Norway	1,057	2,865	2,544	33.0
Poland	9	42	163	0.8
Portugal	245	688	2,946	7.5
Romania	...	3	23	0.1
Russia	...	358	1,027	7.4
Slovakia	...	8	92	0.3
Slovenia	10	6	11	0.4
Spain	2,249	4,131	18,387	68.4
Sweden	7,442	11,215	22,465	93.5
Switzerland	6,131	12,210	17,416	176.7
Turkey	14	113	307	0.9
Ukraine	...	10	-4	0.1
United Kingdom	26,393	44,424	114,195	498.6

a Stock figures in some countries based on accumulated flows for available years.

Stockmarkets

Largest by market capitalisation
End 1999, $bn

1	United Kingdom	2,933.28	16	Norway	63.70
2	France	1,475.46	17	Ireland	42.46
3	Germany	1,432.19	18	Luxembourg	35.94
4	Italy	728.27	19	Austria	33.03
5	Netherlands	695.21	20	Poland	29.58
6	Switzerland	693.13	21	Hungary	16.32
7	Spain	431.67	22	Czech Republic	11.80
8	Sweden	373.28	23	Serbia & Montenegro	10.82
9	Finland	349.41	24	Cyprus	8.08
10	Greece	204.21	25	Iceland	4.81
11	Belgium	184.94	26	Croatia	2.58
12	Turkey	112.72	27	Slovenia	2.18
13	Denmark	105.29	28	Estonia	1.79
14	Russia	72.21		United States	16,635.11
15	Portugal	66.49		Japan	4,546.94

Largest by annual value traded
1999, $m

1	Germany	1,357,841	16	Hungary	14,395
2	Netherlands	941,804	17	Austria	12,705
3	France	769,951	18	Poland	11,149
4	Spain	744,315	19	Czech Republic	9,038
5	Switzerland	538,955	20	Russia	2,839
6	Italy	536,475	21	Cyprus	2,095
7	Sweden	238,237	22	United Kingdom	1,377
8	Greece	188,722	23	Luxembourg	1,041
9	Finland	111,585	24	Slovenia	733
10	Turkey	81,277	25	Slovakia	474
11	Denmark	61,297	26	Romania	317
12	Belgium	59,129	27	Lithuania	290
13	Norway	54,135	28	Estonia	285
14	Ireland	50,531		United States	18,574,100
15	Portugal	40,796		Japan	1,849,228

Largest by number of companies listed
End 1999

1	United Kingdom	1,945	14	Denmark	233
2	France	968	15	Poland	221
3	Germany	933	16	Russia	207
4	Bulgaria	860	17	Norway	195
5	Slovakia	845	18	Belgium	172
6	Spain	718	19	Czech Republic	164
7	Romania	582	20	Finland	147
8	Netherlands	344	21	Portugal	125
9	Turkey	285		Ukraine	125
10	Greece	281	23	Austria	97
11	Sweden	277	24	Armenia	95
12	Italy	241		United States	7,651
13	Switzerland	239		Japan	2,470

1990, $bn

1	United Kingdom	848.87
2	Germany[b]	355.07
3	France	314.38
4	Switzerland	160.04
5	Italy	148.77
6	Netherlands	119.83
7	Spain	111.40
8	Sweden	92.10
9	Belgium	65.45
10	Denmark	39.06
11	Norway	26.13
12	Finland	22.72
13	Turkey	19.07
14	Greece	15.23
15	Austria	11.48

1980, $bn

1	United Kingdom	205.20
2	Germany[b]	71.70
3	France	54.60
4	Switzerland	37.60
5	Netherlands	29.30
6	Italy	25.30
7	Spain	16.60
8	Sweden	12.90
9	Belgium	10.00
10	Denmark	5.40
11	Greece	3.02
12	Austria	2.00
13	Turkey	0.48

1990, $m

1	Germany[b]	501,805
2	United Kingdom	278,740
3	France	116,893
4	Italy	42,566
5	Spain	40,967
6	Netherlands	40,199
7	Austria	18,609
8	Sweden	15,718
9	Norway	13,996
10	Denmark	11,105
11	Belgium	6,425
12	Turkey	5,841
13	Finland	3,933
14	Portugal	1,687

1980, $m

1	Switzerland	96,262
2	United Kingdom	35,791
3	Germany[b]	15,248
4	France	10,118
5	Italy	8,574
6	Netherlands	5,099
7	Sweden	1,796
8	Spain	981
9	Belgium	838
10	Austria	105
11	Greece	86
12	Denmark	58

1990

1	United Kingdom	1,701
2	France	578
3	Spain	427
4	Germany[b]	413
5	Netherlands	260
6	Denmark	258
7	Italy	220
8	Switzerland	182
	Belgium	182
10	Portugal	181

1980

1	United Kingdom	2,655
2	France	586
3	Spain	496
4	Germany[b]	459
5	Belgium	225
6	Denmark	218
7	Netherlands	214
8	Italy	134
9	Greece	116
10	Sweden	103

a 1996
b Western Germany.

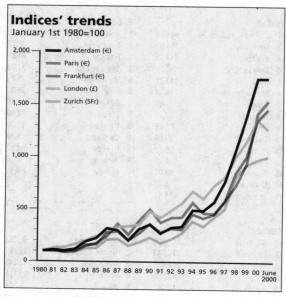

Indices' trends
January 1st 1980=100

- Amsterdam (€)
- Paris (€)
- Frankfurt (€)
- London (£)
- Zurich (SFr)

1980 81 82 83 84 85 86 87 88 89 90 91 92 93 94 95 96 97 98 99 00 June 2000

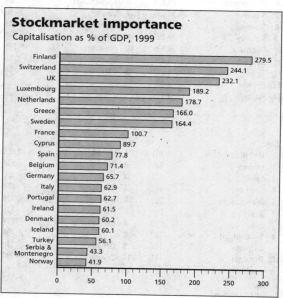

Stockmarket importance
Capitalisation as % of GDP, 1999

Country	%
Finland	279.5
Switzerland	244.1
UK	232.1
Luxembourg	189.2
Netherlands	178.7
Greece	166.0
Sweden	164.4
France	100.7
Cyprus	89.7
Spain	77.8
Belgium	71.4
Germany	65.7
Italy	62.9
Portugal	62.7
Ireland	61.5
Denmark	60.2
Iceland	60.1
Turkey	56.1
Serbia & Montenegro	43.3
Norway	41.9

Part VII
TOURISM AND TRANSPORT

Tourism

Most popular destinations

Tourist arrivals, '000s

	1998			% increase on year earlier	
1	France	70,000	1	Albania	42.1
2	Spain	47,749	2	Lithuania	39.9
3	Italy	34,829	3	Belarus	39.8
4	United Kingdom	25,745	4	Armenia	39.1
5	Poland	18,780	5	Netherlands	19.0
6	Austria	17,352	6	Iceland	14.9
7	Germany	16,511	7	Estonia	13.0
8	Czech Republic	16,325	8	Portugal	11.0
9	Russia	15,805	9	Spain	10.4
10	Hungary	15,000	10	Slovakia	10.1
11	Portugal	11,295	11	Ireland	8.5
12	Greece	10,916	12	Greece	8.4
13	Switzerland	10,900	13	Sweden	7.5
14	Netherlands	9,320	14	Croatia	7.3
15	Turkey	8,960		Monaco	7.3
16	Ukraine	6,208	16	Cyprus	6.5
17	Belgium	6,179	17	Malta	6.4
18	Ireland	6,064	18	Norway	4.7
19	Croatia	4,112	19	Germany	4.3
20	Bulgaria	3,000	20	Austria	4.2
21	Romania	2,966	21	France	4.0
22	Norway	2,829	22	Liechtenstein	3.5
23	Sweden	2,568	23	Russia	3.0
24	Cyprus	2,223	24	Switzerland	2.8
25	Denmark	2,073	25	Azerbaijan	2.4
26	Finland	1,858		Belgium	2.4
27	Lithuania	1,416	27	Luxembourg	2.3
28	Malta	1,182	28	Italy	2.2
29	Slovenia	977	29	Finland	1.4
30	Slovakia	896	30	Georgia	1.3

Biggest spenders

Spending on tourism, $m, 1998

1	Germany	46,939	16	Ireland	2,374
2	United Kingdom	32,267	17	Finland	2,063
3	France	17,791	18	Czech Republic	1,869
4	Italy	17,579	19	Greece	1,756
5	Netherlands	11,174	20	Turkey	1,754
6	Austria	9,511	21	Hungary	1,205
7	Belgium	8,842	22	Croatia	600
8	Russia	8,279	23	Slovenia	575
9	Sweden	7,723	24	Slovakia	475
10	Switzerland	7,126	25	Romania	451
11	Spain	5,005	26	Iceland	396
12	Ukraine	4,482	27	Latvia	305
13	Denmark	4,462	28	Lithuania	292
14	Poland	4,430	29	Cyprus	282
15	Portugal	2,535	30	Georgia	262

Biggest earners
Earnings from tourism, $m

1998		
1	France	29,931
2	Italy	29,809
3	Spain	29,737
4	United Kingdom	20,978
5	Germany	16,429
6	Austria	11,184
7	Poland	7,946
8	Switzerland	7,815
9	Turkey	7,809
10	Netherlands	6,803
11	Russia	6,508
12	Belgium	5,437
13	Ukraine	5,407
14	Greece	5,182
15	Portugal	4,853
16	Sweden	4,189
17	Czech Republic	3,719
18	Ireland	3,252
19	Denmark	3,211
20	Croatia	2,733
21	Hungary	2,504
22	Norway	2,212
23	Cyprus	1,671
24	Finland	1,631
25	Slovenia	1,117
26	Malta	656
27	Estonia	534
28	Slovakia	489
29	Lithuania	460
30	Bulgaria	437

% change on year earlier		
1	Albania	100.0
2	Armenia	42.9
3	Greece	37.4
4	Lithuania	27.8
5	Iceland	19.7
6	Bulgaria	18.4
7	Estonia	14.8
8	Portugal	14.3
9	Sweden	12.3
10	Spain	11.6
11	Croatia	8.0
12	Netherlands	7.6
13	France	6.9
14	United Kingdom	4.7
15	Luxembourg	4.0
16	Belgium	3.2
17	Ireland	2.0
18	Czech Republic	2.0
19	Cyprus	2.0
20	Austria	1.8
21	Georgia	1.7
22	Ukraine	1.3
23	Malta	1.2
24	Denmark	0.8
25	Italy	0.3
26	Bosnia	0.0
27	Moldova	0.0
28	Norway	-0.2
29	Germany	-0.4
30	Finland	-0.8

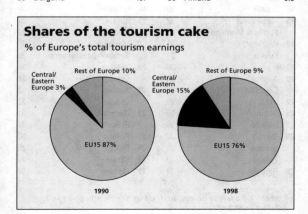

Shares of the tourism cake

% of Europe's total tourism earnings

Central/Eastern Europe 3%
Rest of Europe 10%
EU15 87%

1990

Central/Eastern Europe 15%
Rest of Europe 9%
EU15 76%

1998

Road transport

Longest road networks
Km

1	France	893,300	16	Netherlands	125,575
2	Germany	656,140	17	Greece	117,000
3	Italy	654,676	18	Ireland	92,500
4	Russia[a]	570,719	19	Norway	90,741
5	Turkey	382,059	20	Finland	77,895
6	Poland	381,046	21	Denmark	71,437
7	United Kingdom	371,603	22	Lithuania	71,375
8	Spain	346,858	23	Switzerland	71,059
9	Sweden	210,907	24	Portugal	68,732
10	Hungary	188,203	25	Belarus	63,355
11	Ukraine	176,310	26	Belarus	63,355
12	Romania	153,359	27	Latvia	59,178
13	Belgium	145,850	28	Serbia & Montenegro	49,525
14	Austria	133,361	29	Estonia	49,480
15	Czech Republic	127,693	30	Bulgaria	36,759

Car congestion
Private cars per km of road

1	Monaco	422
2	Malta	88
3	Slovakia	68
4	Germany	64
5	United Kingdom	60
6	Bulgaria	49
	Netherlands	49
8	Switzerland	48
9	Italy	47
	Luxembourg	47
11	Portugal	45
12	Spain	44
13	Slovenia	41
14	Croatia	36
15	Macedonia	32
	Serbia & Montenegro	32
17	Belgium	31
	Russia	31
19	France	30
20	Austria	29
	Czech Republic	29
22	Ukraine	28
23	Denmark	26
	Finland	26
25	Cyprus	23
	Greece	23
	Poland	23
28	Georgia	21

Vehicle congestion
All vehicles per km of road

1	Monaco	480
2	Malta	109
3	Slovakia	77
4	United Kingdom	67
5	Germany	66
6	Netherlands	58
7	Bulgaria	56
8	Spain	53
9	Italy	52
	Switzerland	52
11	Luxembourg	51
12	Portugal	50
13	Slovenia	44
14	Croatia	40
15	Russia	39
16	France	35
	Macedonia	35
	Serbia & Montenegro	35
19	Belgium	34
	Cyprus	34
21	Austria	32
	Czech Republic	32
23	Denmark	31
	Greece	31
25	Finland	30
26	Poland	28
27	Ukraine	27
28	Norway	24

a Figure excludes specific industry/farm roads not maintained by government highways department.

Road accidents
No. of accidents

1	Germany	377,262	16	Hungary	19,665
2	United Kingdom	240,046	17	Netherlands	19,176
3	Italy	190,131	18	Sweden	15,514
4	Russia	156,515	19	Ireland	13,913
5	France	124,387	20	Bosnia	12,865
6	Spain	86,067	21	Croatia	12,846
7	Turkey	66,906	22	Slovakia	8,998
8	Poland	61,855	23	Norway	8,864
9	Portugal	51,229	24	Romania	8,457
10	Belgium	51,167	25	Denmark	7,447
11	Austria	39,225	26	Bulgaria	6,905
12	Ukraine	36,299	27	Finland	6,902
13	Czech Republic	27,207	28	Belarus	6,849
14	Greece	24,836	29	Lithuania	6,445
15	Switzerland	22,232	30	Slovenia	5,864

Injuries in road accidents
No. of injuries

1	Germany	497,339	16	Hungary	25,006
2	United Kingdom	323,945	17	Sweden	21,536
3	Italy	270,962	18	Netherlands	20,190
4	Russia	205,589	19	Croatia	18,118
5	France	168,535	20	Slovakia	12,902
6	Spain	130,851	21	Ireland	12,528
7	Turkey	115,489	22	Norway	12,121
8	Poland	77,560	23	Finland	9,097
9	Belgium	70,760	24	Lithuania	7,667
10	Portugal	68,942	25	Slovenia	7,358
11	Austria	52,040	26	Romania	7,221
12	Ukraine	40,174	27	Belarus	6,899
13	Czech Republic	35,227	28	Latvia	5,414
14	Greece	33,417	29	Cyprus	3,916
15	Switzerland	27,790	30	Macedonia	3,397

Deaths in road accidents
No. of deaths

1	Russia	27,665	16	Czech Republic	1,360
2	France	8,437	17	Netherlands	1,163
3	Germany	7,776	18	Bulgaria	1,003
4	Poland	7,080	19	Austria	963
5	Italy	6,226	20	Lithuania	829
6	Spain	5,604	21	Slovakia	819
7	Ukraine	5,522	22	Croatia	646
8	Turkey	4,352	23	Latvia	627
9	United Kingdom	3,599	24	Switzerland	597
10	Romania	2,778	25	Azerbaijan	594
11	Greece	2,226	26	Moldova	544
12	Portugal	1,909	27	Sweden	529
13	Belarus	1,843	28	Georgia	494
14	Belgium	1,500	29	Ireland	466
15	Hungary	1,478	30	Denmark	454

Rail transport

Railway networks
'000 km

1	Russia	86.2		20	Slovakia	3.7
2	Germany	38.1		21	Belgium	3.4
3	France	31.7		22	Switzerland	3.1
4	Poland	23.2		23	Netherlands	2.8
5	Ukraine	22.5			Portugal	2.8
6	United Kingdom	17.2		25	Croatia	2.7
7	Italy	16.1		26	Latvia	2.4
8	Spain	13.7		27	Denmark	2.3
9	Romania	11.4			Greece	2.3
10	Sweden	11.1		29	Lithuania	2.0
11	Czech Republic	9.4		30	Ireland	1.9
12	Turkey	8.6		31	Georgia	1.6
13	Hungary	7.8		32	Moldova	1.2
14	Finland	5.9			Slovenia	1.2
15	Austria	5.6		34	Estonia	1.0
16	Belarus	5.5		35	Armenia	0.8
17	Serbia & Montenegro	4.3		36	Bosnia	0.6
18	Bulgaria	4.1		37	Albania	0.4
19	Norway	4.0		38	Luxembourg	0.3

Passenger travel
m km

1	Russia	97,429		20	Bulgaria	4,740
2	France	64,186		21	Portugal	4,602
3	Germany	59,185		22	Finland	3,377
4	Ukraine	49,938		23	Slovakia	3,116
5	Italy	41,475		24	Norway	2,590
6	United Kingdom	36,128		25	Greece	1,552
7	Poland	20,553		26	Ireland	1,421
8	Spain	18,281		27	Latvia	1,059
9	Netherlands	14,879		28	Croatia	921
10	Romania	13,422		29	Lithuania	715
11	Belarus	13,268		30	Moldova	656
12	Switzerland	12,903		31	Slovenia	645
13	Austria	7,971		32	Georgia	397
14	Belgium	7,097		33	Luxembourg	300
15	Sweden	7,010		34	Estonia	236
16	Czech Republic	7,001		35	Macedonia	150
17	Hungary	6,794		36	Albania	90
18	Turkey	6,160		37	Armenia	84
19	Denmark	5,369		38	Bosnia	4

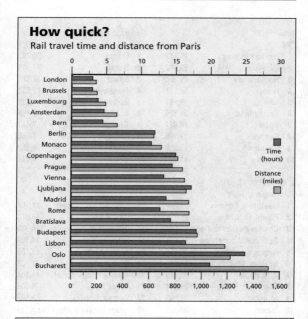

How quick?
Rail travel time and distance from Paris

Time (hours)

Distance (miles)

London
Brussels
Luxembourg
Amsterdam
Bern
Berlin
Monaco
Copenhagen
Prague
Vienna
Ljubljana
Madrid
Rome
Bratislava
Budapest
Lisbon
Oslo
Bucharest

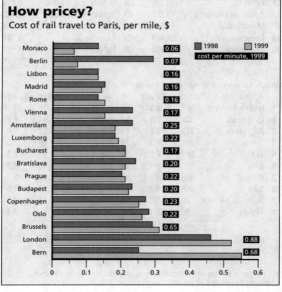

How pricey?
Cost of rail travel to Paris, per mile, $

1998   1999
cost per minute, 1999

City	cost per minute, 1999
Monaco	0.06
Berlin	0.07
Lisbon	0.16
Madrid	0.16
Rome	0.16
Vienna	0.17
Amsterdam	0.25
Luxemborg	0.22
Bucharest	0.17
Bratislava	0.20
Prague	0.22
Budapest	0.20
Copenhagen	0.23
Oslo	0.22
Brussels	0.65
London	0.88
Bern	0.68

Air transport

Who flies most[a]

Total travel '000			Domestic travel '000		
1	United Kingdom	145,173	1	France	30,793
2	Germany	83,012	2	Russia	27,348
3	Netherlands	69,058	3	Spain	14,015
4	France	58,513	4	Norway	12,531
5	Italy	28,867	5	Turkey	10,201
6	Switzerland	28,579	6	Italy	8,756
7	Spain	26,027	7	Germany	7,412
8	Russia	17,108	8	Sweden	7,035
9	Belgium	15,338	9	United Kingdom	6,953
10	Austria	11,833	10	Greece	4,078

Busiest airports[a]

Passengers, '000s

1	Heathrow, London	62,264	16	Arlanda, Stockholm	17,364
2	Rhiem, Frankfurt	45,858	17	Linate, Milan	16,914
3	Charles de Gaulle, Paris	43,597	18	Dusseldorf	15,926
4	Schiphol, Amsterdam	36,781	19	Fornebu, Oslo	14,109
5	Gatwick, London	30,559	20	Ataturk, Istanbul	13,159
6	Barajas, Madrid	27,532	21	Dublin	12,802
7	Orly, Paris	25,349	22	Vienna International	11,204
8	Fiumicino, Rome	24,024	23	Tegel, Berlin	9,606
9	Munich	21,283	24	Vantaa, Helsinki	9,563
10	Zurich	20,900	25	Sheremetyevo, Moscow	9,556
11	Brussels	20,025	26	Fühlsbuttel, Hamburg	9,459
12	Palma de Mallorca	19,227	27	Stansted, London	9,453
13	Manchester	17,760	28	Gran Canaria	9,220
14	Copenhagen	17,404	29	Tenerife Sur	8,731
15	Barcelona	17,368	30	Lisbon	8,668

Biggest airlines

Number and average age of aeroplanes

	Airline	Fleet size	Av. age		Airline	Fleet size	Av. age
1	British Airways	357	8.0	11	Olympic	56	12.8
2	Lufthansa	298	7.5	12	British Midlands	54	6.8
3	Air France	223	9.3	13	Sabena	52	8.0
4	Iberia	215	11.3	14	Aer Lingus	50	7.9
5	KLM	202	8.3	15	TAP	33	4.3
6	SAS	190	9.3	16	Virgin Atlantic	30	10.2
7	Alitalia	155	9.1	17	Ryanair	26	15.1
8	SAir	155	4.7	18	Virgin Express	23	6.3
9	Austrian Airlines	88	5.3	19	EasyJet	18	3.9
10	Finnair	56	10.7		**Average age[b]**		**8.4**

a Passengers arriving and departing from airports participating in ACI survey.
b Weighted by number of aircraft.

Sea transport

Largest merchant fleets
No. of vessels over 100 GRT[a]

1	Russia	4,694	19	Iceland	308
2	Norway	2,350	20	Azerbaijan	286
3	Malta	1,574	21	Finland	279
4	Spain	1,562	22	Croatia	257
5	Cyprus	1,556	23	Estonia	219
6	Greece	1,491	24	Lithuania	192
7	United Kingdom	1,391	25	Belgium	184
8	Italy	1,389	26	Latvia	174
9	Netherlands	1,276	27	Bulgaria	173
10	Turkey	1,152	28	Ireland	153
11	Denmark	1,057	29	Georgia	104
12	Germany	1,028	30	Luxembourg	55
13	Ukraine	936	31	Albania	33
14	France	713	32	Austria	22
15	Sweden	570	33	Switzerland	21
16	Poland	439	34	Slovakia	3
17	Portugal	325	35	Czech Republic	1
	Romania	325		Hungary	1

Largest ports
Total cargo, '000 tonnes

1	Malta	28,205	20	Romania	1,221
2	Greece	24,833	21	Bulgaria	1,036
3	Cyprus	23,641	22	Croatia	869
4	Norway	23,446	23	Azerbaijan	654
5	Russia	10,649	24	Estonia	453
6	Italy	8,048	25	Switzerland	439
7	Germany	6,514	26	Lithuania	424
8	Turkey	6,325	27	Portugal	295
9	Denmark	5,913	28	Ireland	219
10	Netherlands	4,814	29	Iceland	192
11	United Kingdom	4,331	30	Georgia	132
12	Sweden	2,947		Belgium	132
13	Canada	2,496	32	Latvia	118
14	France	1,813	33	Austria	71
15	Ukraine	1,775	34	Albania	21
16	Finland	1,658	35	Slovakia	15
17	Luxembourg	1,343	36	Hungary	12
18	Poland	1,319	37	Czech Republic	2
19	Spain	1,269		Slovenia	2

a GRT = gross tonnage, which is the total volume within the hull and above deck.
   1 GRT = 100 cubic feet.

Freight

Road importance
% inland freight carried by road, 1998 or latest

1	Greece	98.12	17	Serbia & Montenegro	68.16
2	Turkey	91.41	18	Albania	65.88
3	Ireland	91.33	19	Poland	53.35
4	Denmark	90.08	20	Switzerland	52.63
5	Italy	89.93	21	Netherlands	50.32
6	United Kingdom	89.89	22	Austria	49.07
7	Spain	89.33	23	Russia	46.24
8	Norway	85.97	24	Romania	41.63
9	Portugal	85.73	25	Croatia	38.57
10	France	79.86	26	Lithuania	34.07
11	Macedonia	79.39	27	Estonia	28.15
12	Belgium	72.60	28	Moldova	27.71
13	Finland	71.04	29	Slovakia	27.53
14	Sweden	70.01	30	Belarus	27.11
15	Germany	69.12			
16	Luxembourg	68.20		**EU15**	**77.40**

Rail importance
% inland freight carried by rail, 1997 or latest

1	Bulgaria	89.99	17	Sweden	29.99
2	Latvia	86.55	18	Finland	27.56
3	Ukraine	85.30	19	Serbia & Montenegro	25.00
4	Hungary	76.75	20	Macedonia	20.61
5	Belarus	72.51	21	Luxembourg	20.32
6	Estonia	71.85	22	France	18.13
7	Moldova	71.13	23	Germany	16.65
8	Lithuania	65.88	24	Belgium	15.05
9	Slovakia	63.97	25	Portugal	14.27
10	Romania	51.66	26	Norway	14.03
11	Croatia	49.41	27	Slovenia	11.38
12	Russia	47.98	28	Spain	10.67
13	Switzerland	46.51	29	United Kingdom	9.99
14	Poland	46.07	30	Italy	9.98
15	Austria	44.37			
16	Azerbaijan	39.80		**EU15**	**14.96**

Water importance
% inland freight carried by water, 1997 or latest

1	Georgia	95.79	12	Austria	6.56
2	Slovenia	81.00	13	Latvia	5.82
3	Azerbaijan	56.06	14	Russia	5.78
4	Netherlands	45.87	15	Ukraine	3.10
5	Germany	14.23	16	France	2.01
6	Belgium	12.34	17	Albania	1.93
7	Croatia	12.02	18	Finland	1.40
8	Luxembourg	11.49	19	Hungary	0.78
9	Slovakia	8.51	20	Poland	0.58
10	Serbia & Montenegro	6.84			
11	Romania	6.71		**EU15**	**7.63**

Part VIII

HEALTH
AND
EDUCATION

Life and death

Life expectancy
At birth, years

1998			2025–30		
1	Iceland	79	1	Sweden	82.0
	Sweden	79	2	Iceland	81.9
	Switzerland	79		Italy	81.9
4	Cyprus	78	4	France	81.6
	France	78	5	Switzerland	81.2
	Greece	78	6	Greece	80.9
	Italy	78		Spain	80.9
	Netherlands	78	8	Netherlands	80.8
	Norway	78	9	Cyprus	80.7
	Spain	78	10	Austria	80.4
11	Austria	77		Belgium	80.4
	Belgium	77		Finland	80.4
	Finland	77		United Kingdom	80.4
	Germany	77	14	Ireland	80.2
	Luxembourg	77		Malta	80.2
	Malta	77	16	Germany	80.0
	United Kingdom	77		Luxembourg	80.0
18	Denmark	76	18	Norway	79.7
	Ireland	76	19	Portugal	79.5
20	Portugal	75	20	Denmark	78.6
21	Czech Republic	74	21	Slovenia	77.6
	Slovenia	74	22	Macedonia	77.3
23	Albania	73	23	Bosnia	76.9
	Bosnia	73		Czech Republic	76.9
	Croatia	73		Georgia	76.9
	Georgia	73	26	Croatia	76.7
	Macedonia	73	27	Slovakia	76.5
	Poland	73	28	Bulgaria	76.3
	Serbia & Montenegro	73		Serbia	76.3
	Slovakia	73	30	Poland	76.2
31	Armenia	71	31	Armenia	75.9
	Bulgaria	71		Azerbaijan	75.9
	Hungary	71	33	Turkey	75.8
			34	Estonia	75.6

Infant mortality
Rates per 1,000 live births, 1998

1	Turkey	37	12	Estonia	18
2	Azerbaijan	36		Latvia	18
3	Albania	30		Serbia & Montenegro	18
4	Moldova	28		Ukraine	18
5	Armenia	25	16	Bosnia	16
6	Macedonia	23	17	Bulgaria	14
7	Belarus	22	18	Hungary	10
8	Romania	21		Liechtenstein	10
	Russia	21		Poland	10
10	Georgia	19	21	Slovakia	9
	Lithuania	19	22	Croatia	8

Death rate
Crude death rates per 1,000 population

1998			2025–30		
1	Bulgaria	14	**1**	Hungary	15.0
	Estonia	14		Russia	15.0
	Hungary	14	**3**	Bulgaria	14.5
	Latvia	14		Estonia	14.5
	Russia	14		Latvia	14.5
	Ukraine	14		Slovenia	14.5
7	Belarus	13	**7**	Ukraine	14.2
8	Denmark	12	**8**	Czech Republic	14.0
	Lithuania	12	**9**	Croatia	13.9
10	Croatia	11	**10**	Italy	13.8
	Czech Republic	11	**11**	Belarus	13.4
	Germany	11	**12**	Lithuania	13.2
	Moldova	11		Romania	13.2
	Portugal	11	**14**	Denmark	13.0
	Romania	11		Germany	13.0
	Sweden	11		Greece	13.0
	United Kingdom	11	**17**	Bosnia	12.7
18	Austria	10	**18**	Finland	12.6
	Belgium	10		Spain	12.6
	Finland	10	**20**	Portugal	12.5
	Greece	10	**21**	Belgium	12.4
	Italy	10		Netherlands	12.4
	Norway	10	**23**	Switzerland	12.3
	Poland	10	**24**	Serbia	12.2
	Serbia & Montenegro	10	**25**	Austria	12.1
	Slovakia	10		Poland	12.1
	Slovenia	10	**27**	Slovakia	11.8
28	France	9		United Kingdom	11.8
	Georgia	9	**29**	France	11.6
	Luxembourg	9		Norway	11.6
	Netherlands	9	**31**	Luxembourg	11.5
	Spain	9		Sweden	11.5
	Switzerland	9	**33**	Malta	10.8
				Moldova	10.8

	Cyprus	8		Austria	5
	Portugal	8		Czech Republic	5
25	Belgium	6		Denmark	5
	Euro-11	6		EU15	5
	Greece	6		France	5
	Ireland	6		Germany	5
	Italy	6		Iceland	5
	Malta	6		Luxembourg	5
	San Marino	6		Monaco	5
	Spain	6		Netherlands	5
	United Kingdom	6		Slovenia	5
34	Andorra	5		Switzerland	5

Causes of death

Heart disease
Deaths per 100,000 population

1	Moldova	521.7	14	Bulgaria	232.9
2	Ukraine	460.4	15	Ireland[b]	217.2
3	Belarus	417.0	16	Croatia	207.9
4	Azerbaijan	407.6	17	Czech Republic	198.5
5	Georgia[a]	399.7	18	Finland[c]	192.9
6	Estonia	366.4	19	Malta	169.8
7	Latvia	357.4	20	United Kingdom[d]	162.6
8	Russia	338.1	21	Iceland[b]	154.1
9	Lithuania	328.7	22	Norway[b]	150.7
10	Armenia	321.9	23	Sweden[c]	148.8
11	Slovakia	276.1	24	Austria	147.2
12	Hungary	255.9	25	Germany[d]	142.6
13	Romania	248.4	26	Denmark[c]	142.0

Cancer
Deaths per 100,000 population

1	Hungary	284.1	14	Lithuania	194.1
2	Croatia	239.6	15	Russia	193.1
3	Czech Republic	238.6	16	Luxembourg[d]	193.0
4	Slovakia	238.4	17	Germany[d]	189.4
5	Denmark[c]	226.5	18	France[d]	187.8
6	Ireland[b]	214.9	19	Italy[c]	187.7
7	Poland[c]	213.8	20	Iceland[b]	184.9
8	Belgium[a]	213.0	21	Belarus	182.5
9	Slovenia	211.3	22	Switzerland[a]	182.1
10	Netherlands[d]	204.6	23	Norway[b]	180.8
11	Estonia	204.4	24	Malta	180.4
12	United Kingdom[d]	198.1	25	Austria	178.1
13	Latvia	196.7	26	Spain[c]	176.0

Injuries and poisons
Deaths per 100,000 population

1	Russia	186.0	14	Slovakia	63.0
2	Belarus	168.1	15	Czech Republic	62.5
3	Estonia	159.7	16	Belgium[a]	60.2
4	Latvia	158.7	17	France[d]	59.9
5	Lithuania	146.2	18	Iceland[b]	58.8
6	Ukraine	138.2	19	Switzerland[a]	57.8
7	Moldova	110.0	20	Bulgaria	56.7
8	Hungary	92.5	21	Denmark[c]	52.3
9	Slovenia	77.5	22	Georgia[a]	50.1
10	Finland[c]	73.5	23	Luxembourg[d]	48.8
11	Romania	72.6	24	Portugal	48.2
12	Poland[c]	72.4	25	Austria	45.7
13	Croatia	69.9	26	Norway[b]	42.9

a 1994   b 1995   c 1996   d 1997
e To December 1998.
f To November 1998.

Infectious and parasitic diseases
Deaths per 100,000 population

1	Azerbaijan	25.1	14	Belgium[a]	10.2
2	Latvia	19.7	15	Armenia	10.1
	Russia	19.7	16	Belarus	10.0
	Ukraine	19.7	17	Bulgaria	9.3
5	Moldova	17.6	18	Croatia	9.1
6	Lithuania	14.7	19	Spain[c]	8.8
7	Romania	14.4	20	Denmark[c]	8.2
8	Switzerland[a]	13.9	21	Netherlands[d]	7.7
9	Estonia	12.6	22	Finland[c]	6.8
10	Portugal	11.3	23	Poland[c]	6.5
11	Macedonia[d]	11.0	24	Hungary	6.4
12	Georgia[a]	10.6	25	Malta	6.3
13	France[d]	10.3		Norway[b]	6.3

Motor vehicle traffic accidents
Deaths per 100,000 population

1	Latvia	27.0		Hungary	13.8
2	Lithuania	23.5	15	Luxembourg[d]	13.5
3	Estonia	20.8	16	Spain[c]	13.2
4	Greece[d]	20.5	17	France[d]	12.3
5	Russia	19.7	18	Italy[c]	11.8
6	Belarus	18.1	19	Ireland[b]	11.4
7	Portugal	17.8	20	Ukraine	11.2
8	Belgium[a]	17.2	21	Austria	9.8
	Poland[c]	17.2		Germany[d]	9.8
	Slovakia	17.2		Iceland[b]	9.8
11	Moldova	15.5	24	Bulgaria	9.4
12	Slovenia	14.9	25	Denmark[c]	9.1
13	Croatia	13.8	26	Switzerland[a]	8.4

AIDS

Cumulative cases to June 1999

1	Spain	54,964
2	France[e]	49,421
3	Italy	44,516
4	Germany	18,239
5	United Kingdom	16,437
6	Switzerland	6,641
7	Portugal	6,020
8	Romania	5,928
9	Netherlands	5,054
10	Belgium	2,599
11	Denmark	2,216
12	Greece	1,964
13	Austria	1,915
14	Sweden	1,663
15	Ukraine	1,022
16	Serbia & Montenegro	806
17	Poland	794

Cumulative deaths to Dec. 1998

1	Italy	30,527
2	France[f]	30,190
3	Spain	29,527
4	Germany	11,658
5	United Kingdom	11,526
6	Switzerland	4,839
7	Portugal	3,517
8	Romania	2,317
9	Denmark	1,742
10	Belgium	1,535
11	Austria	1,199
12	Sweden	1,149
13	Greece	1,134
14	Serbia & Montenegro	583
15	Norway	508
16	Poland	431
17	Ireland	342

Drinking and smoking

Pure alcohol

Litres per head per year, 1998

1	Luxembourg	13.3
2	Portugal	11.2
3	France	10.8
	Ireland	10.8
5	Germany	10.6
6	Czech Republic	10.2
7	Spain	10.1
8	Denmark	9.5
	Romania	9.5
10	Hungary	9.4
11	Austria	9.2
	Switzerland	9.2
13	Greece	9.1
14	Belgium	8.9
15	Slovakia	8.3
16	Netherlands	8.1
17	Russia	7.9
18	Italy	7.7
19	United Kingdom	7.5
20	Finland	7.1
	Latvia	7.1
22	Bulgaria	6.8
	Cyprus	6.8
24	Poland	6.2
25	Malta	5.1
26	Sweden	4.9
27	Iceland	4.3
	Norway	4.3
29	Estonia	2.4

% change consumed per head, 1970–98

1	Turkey	140.0
2	Cyprus	107.3
3	Ireland	83.7
4	Greece	72.7
5	Finland	65.1
6	Romania	52.0
7	Netherlands	41.6
8	United Kingdom	40.7
9	Denmark	39.7
10	Iceland	36.1
11	Luxembourg	33.3
12	Russia	21.7
13	Czech Republic	21.4
14	Norway	19.4
15	Poland	14.0
16	Portugal	13.5
17	Germany	3.4
18	Hungary	3.2
19	Bulgaria	1.2
20	Belgium	-0.2
21	Slovakia	-0.8
22	Austria	-12.3
23	Spain	-13.0
24	Switzerland	-14.1
25	Sweden	-14.9
26	France	-33.5
27	Italy	-44.0

Wine

Litres consumed per head per year, 1998

1	Luxembourg	70.0	16	Netherlands	18.4
2	France	58.1	17	Czech Republic	16.9
3	Portugal	53.2	18	Malta	16.5
4	Italy	52.0	19	Finland	15.2
5	Switzerland	43.2	20	Sweden	14.6
6	Greece	35.9	21	United Kingdom	14.4
7	Spain	35.6	22	Slovakia	13.3
8	Austria	30.1	23	Cyprus	12.2
9	Denmark	29.1	24	Norway	8.5
10	Hungary	29.0	25	Iceland	7.2
11	Ireland	25.6	26	Latvia	6.4
12	Romania	25.2	27	Russia	6.0
13	Belgium	25.0	28	Poland	5.9
14	Germany	22.8	29	Estonia	2.2
15	Bulgaria	22.1	30	Ukraine	1.0

Beer

Litres consumed per head per year, 1998

1	Czech Republic	161.8	16	Sweden	57.3
2	Ireland	150.5	17	Cyprus	55.0
3	Germany	127.4	18	Norway	52.6
4	Luxembourg	110.9	19	Greece	42.0
5	Austria	108.6	20	Poland	41.0
6	Denmark	105.0	21	Iceland	40.1
7	United Kingdom	99.4	22	France	38.6
8	Belgium	98.0	23	Romania	35.0
9	Slovakia	91.8	24	Bulgaria	33.2
10	Netherlands	84.2	25	Latvia	32.0
11	Finland	80.1	26	Italy	26.9
12	Spain	66.4	27	Russia	26.0
13	Portugal	64.6	28	Turkey	14.4
14	Switzerland	59.7	29	Estonia	6.3
15	Hungary	59.3	30	Ukraine	5.2

Heaviest smokers

Cigarettes smoked per head per day, 1998

1	Greece	7.8	16	Slovakia	4.4
2	Bulgaria	6.6	17	Italy	4.3
	Poland	6.6	18	Romania	4.2
4	Estonia	6.1	19	France	3.9
	Hungary	6.1		Lithuania	3.9
6	Spain	6.0		Ukraine	3.9
7	Switzerland	5.9	22	Latvia	3.8
8	Czech Republic	5.3	23	Denmark	3.6
9	Russia	5.2	24	Moldova	3.2
10	Austria	5.1		United Kingdom	3.2
11	Ireland	4.8	26	Belarus	2.9
12	Germany	4.6		Netherlands	2.9
	Turkey	4.6	28	Finland	2.6
14	Belgium	4.5	29	Georgia	2.2
	Portugal	4.5	30	Sweden	1.8

Cutting back

% decrease of cigarettes smoked, 1993–98

1	Estonia	52.9	14	Denmark	4.9
2	Russia	51.9	15	Moldova	2.6
3	Ukraine	25.6	16	Belgium	2.5
4	Slovakia	21.3	17	Italy	2.1
5	Bulgaria	20.8	18	Portugal	0.8
6	Czech Republic	20.4	19	Netherlands	0.5
7	Romania	17.1	20	Hungary	-4.5
8	Spain	15.9	21	Switzerland	-7.6
9	Lithuania	13.3	22	Poland	-8.9
10	Latvia	9.1	23	Belarus	-10.1
11	Austria	7.8	24	France	-12.3
12	Germany	6.8	25	Norway	-12.8
13	Ireland	5.6	26	Finland	-18.5

Health matters

Population per doctor

1	Italy	182	16	Switzerland	313
2	Russia	217	17	Estonia	323
3	Ukraine	222		Sweden	323
4	Belarus	233	19	Armenia	333
5	Spain	238		Portugal	333
6	Greece	256		Slovakia	333
	Lithuania	256	22	Czech Republic	345
8	Azerbaijan	263		Denmark	345
	Georgia	263		France	345
10	Moldova	278	25	Austria	357
11	Bulgaria	286		Finland	357
12	Belgium	294	27	Netherlands	385
	Germany	294	28	Norway	400
	Hungary	294	29	Macedonia	435
	Latvia	294		Poland	435

Population per nurse

1	Finland	46	16	Switzerland	130
2	Monaco	67	17	Ireland	139
3	Ukraine	83	18	Slovenia	146
4	Malta	84	19	Russia	152
5	Belarus	86	20	Bulgaria	153
6	Azerbaijan	93	21	Estonia	157
7	Sweden	95	22	Latvia	159
8	Moldova	98	23	Netherlands	167
9	Lithuania	102	24	Hungary	172
10	Slovakia	105	25	Austria	189
11	Czech Republic	106		Poland	189
12	Belgium	108	27	Croatia	213
13	Georgia	116	28	Romania	233
14	Armenia	120	29	Cyprus	235
	United Kingdom	120	30	Albania	236

Population per hospital bed

1	Switzerland	48	16	France	115
2	Norway	67	17	Armenia	132
3	Belarus	82		Romania	132
4	Moldova	83	19	Slovakia	133
	Russia	83	20	Estonia	135
6	Ukraine	85	21	Belgium	139
7	Netherlands	88	22	Italy	154
8	Bulgaria	94	23	Croatia	169
9	Latvia	97	24	Slovenia	175
10	Germany	104	25	Sweden	179
	Lithuania	104	26	Poland	185
12	Austria	109	27	Serbia & Montenegro	189
	Czech Republic	109	28	Macedonia	192
	Finland	109	29	Greece	200
15	Hungary	110	30	Georgia	208

Fighting measles
% of one-year-olds fully immunised against measles

1	Hungary	100			Ukraine	96
2	Moldova	99		**20**	Bulgaria	95
	Slovakia	99			Czech Republic	95
4	Azerbaijan	98			United Kingdom	95
	Belarus	98		**23**	Armenia	94
	Finland	98		**24**	Norway	93
	Iceland	98			Slovenia	93
	Macedonia	98		**26**	Croatia	91
	Monaco	98		**27**	Luxembourg	91
	Russia	98		**28**	Poland	91
11	France	97		**29**	Andorra	90
	Latvia	97			Austria	90
	Lithuania	97			Cyprus	90
	Romania	97			Georgia	90
15	Netherlands	96			Greece	90
	Portugal	96			Switzerland	90
	San Marino	96		**35**	Estonia	89
	Sweden	96		**36**	Germany	88

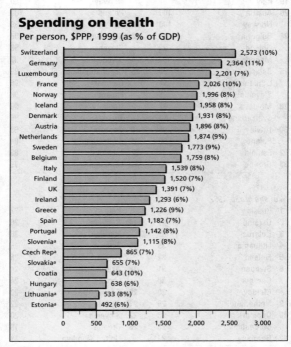

Spending on health
Per person, $PPP, 1999 (as % of GDP)

Switzerland	2,573 (10%)
Germany	2,364 (11%)
Luxembourg	2,201 (7%)
France	2,026 (10%)
Norway	1,996 (8%)
Iceland	1,958 (8%)
Denmark	1,931 (8%)
Austria	1,896 (8%)
Netherlands	1,874 (9%)
Sweden	1,773 (9%)
Belgium	1,759 (8%)
Italy	1,539 (8%)
Finland	1,520 (7%)
UK	1,391 (7%)
Ireland	1,293 (6%)
Greece	1,226 (9%)
Spain	1,182 (7%)
Portugal	1,142 (8%)
Slovenia[a]	1,115 (8%)
Czech Rep[a]	865 (7%)
Slovakia[a]	655 (7%)
Croatia	643 (10%)
Hungary	638 (6%)
Lithuania[a]	533 (8%)
Estonia[a]	492 (6%)

0   500   1,000   1,500   2,000   2,500   3,000

a 1998

Education enrolment ratios

Primary

% of age group, 1997			*1980*		
1	Portugal	128	1	Portugal	123
2	United Kingdom	116	2	Azerbaijan	115
3	Netherlands	108	3	Albania	113
4	Albania	107	4	France	111
	Russia	107	5	Spain	109
	Spain	107	6	Belarus	104
	Sweden	107		Belgium	104
	Turkey	107		Romania	104
9	Azerbaijan	106	9	Estonia	103
10	France	105		Greece	103
	Ireland	105		United Kingdom	103
12	Czech Republic	104	12	Latvia	102
	Germany	104		Russia	102
	Romania	104		Ukraine	102
15	Belgium	103	15	Ireland	100
	Hungary	103		Italy	100
17	Denmark	102		Macedonia	100
	Slovakia	102		Netherlands	100
19	Italy	101		Norway	100
20	Austria	100		Poland	100
	Norway	100	21	Austria	99
22	Bulgaria	99	22	Bulgaria	98
	Finland	99		Slovenia	98
	Macedonia	99	24	Sweden	97
25	Belarus	98	25	Czech Republic	96
	Lithuania	98		Denmark	96
	Slovenia	98		Finland	96
28	Moldova	97		Hungary	96
	Switzerland	97		Turkey	96
30	Latvia	96	30	Georgia	93
	Poland	96	31	Switzerland	84
32	Estonia	94	32	Moldova	83
33	Greece	93	33	Lithuania	79

Tertiary

% of age group, 1997					
1	Russia	46		Italy	27
2	Ukraine	42	14	Belgium	26
3	Belarus	39		Norway	26
4	Lithuania	35	16	Estonia	25
5	Finland	32		France	25
6	Sweden	31	18	Azerbaijan	24
7	Georgia	30		Latvia	24
	Moldova	30	20	Spain	23
9	Netherlands	29	21	Austria	22
10	Denmark	28	22	Slovenia	20
	Macedonia	28	23	Croatia	19
12	Germany	27		United Kingdom	19

Secondary

% of age group, 1997			*1980*		
1	Belgium	146	**1**	Estonia	127
2	Sweden	140	**2**	Lithuania	114
3	Netherlands	132	**3**	Georgia	109
4	United Kingdom	129	**4**	Denmark	105
5	Denmark	121	**5**	Finland	100
6	Spain	120	**6**	Czech Republic	99
7	Norway	119		Latvia	99
8	Finland	118	**8**	Belarus	98
	Ireland	118	**9**	Russia	96
10	France	111	**10**	Azerbaijan	95
	Portugal	111	**11**	Norway	94
12	Estonia	104		Romania	94
	Germany	104		Switzerland	94
14	Austria	103		Ukraine	94
15	Switzerland	100	**15**	Austria	93
16	Czech Republic	99		Netherlands	93
17	Hungary	98	**17**	Belgium	91
	Poland	98	**18**	Ireland	90
19	Greece	95	**19**	Sweden	88
	Italy	95	**20**	Spain	87
21	Slovakia	94	**21**	Bulgaria	85
22	Belarus	93		France	85
23	Slovenia	92	**23**	United Kingdom	84
24	Armenia	90	**24**	Greece	81
25	Lithuania	86	**25**	Moldova	78
26	Latvia	84	**26**	Croatia	77
27	Croatia	82		Poland	77
28	Moldova	81	**28**	Italy	72
29	Romania	78	**29**	Hungary	70
30	Azerbaijan	77	**30**	Albania	67
	Bulgaria	77	**31**	Macedonia	61
	Georgia	77	**32**	Portugal	37
33	Macedonia	63	**33**	Turkey	35

1980					
1	Finland	74	**13**	Denmark	45
2	Norway	62		Estonia	45
3	Belgium	57	**15**	Belarus	44
4	Spain	53	**16**	Ukraine	42
5	United Kingdom	52	**17**	Bulgaria	41
6	France	51		Georgia	41
7	Sweden	50		Ireland	41
8	Austria	48		Russia	41
9	Germany	47	**21**	Portugal	38
	Greece	47	**22**	Slovenia	36
	Italy	47	**23**	Switzerland	34
	Netherlands	47	**24**	Latvia	33

Education spending

Spending on education

As % GDP, 1996

1	Moldova	10.9
2	Sweden	8.3
3	Denmark	8.2
4	Poland	7.5
5	Finland	7.5
	Norway	7.5
7	Ukraine[a]	7.3
8	Estonia[b]	7.2
9	Latvia	6.3
10	France	6.0
	Ireland	6.0
12	Belarus	5.9
13	Portugal	5.8
14	Slovenia[a]	5.7
15	Austria	5.5
16	Lithuania	5.5
17	Iceland	5.4
	Switzerland	5.4
19	United Kingdom[a]	5.3
20	Croatia	5.3
21	Czech Republic	5.1
	Malta	5.1
	Macedonia	5.1
	Netherlands	5.1
25	Spain	5.0

As % of general govt. exp., 1995–96

1	Moldova	28.1
2	Lithuania	22.8
3	Estonia	22.3
4	Macedonia	20.0
5	Belarus	17.8
6	Norway	16.7
7	Poland	15.7
	Ukraine[a]	15.7
8	Luxembourg	15.1
10	Switzerland	14.7
11	Latvia	14.1
12	Czech Republic	13.6
12	Ireland	13.5
14	Denmark	13.1
15	Spain	12.8
16	Slovenia	12.6
17	Iceland	12.3
18	Finland	12.2
19	Sweden	11.6
20	Malta	11.4
	United Kingdom[b]	11.4
21	France	11.1
23	Austria	10.6
24	Romania	10.5
25	Russia[b]	9.6

Spending per student

EU15 countries[c], $PPP, 1996

Primary

1	Denmark	6,318	6	Netherlands	3,392
2	Austria	5,678	7	France	3,361
3	Sweden	5,206	8	Germany	3,200
4	Italy	4,664	9	Luxembourg	3,192
5	Finland	4,247	10	United Kingdom	3,167

Secondary

1	Luxembourg	9,570	6	Sweden	5,396
2	Austria	7,589	7	Netherlands	5,198
3	Denmark	6,360	8	Finland	4,695
4	France	6,314	9	United Kingdom	4,661
5	Italy	5,701	10	Germany	4,106

Tertiary

1	Sweden	12,156	6	Ireland	7,738
2	Austria	9,969	7	Denmark	7,494
3	Netherlands	8,907	8	Finland	7,024
4	Germany	8,887	9	France	6,246
5	United Kingdom	7,851	10	Portugal	5,878

a 1995 b 1997 c Belgium unavailable.

Current spending
% of total spending on education allocated to current spending

Primary, 1996

1	Belarus	72.5
2	Germany[a]	72.2
3	Albania[b]	57.2
4	Ukraine[a]	54.7
5	Macedonia	54.4
6	Bulgaria	52.4
7	Luxembourg[a]	51.9
8	Turkey[a]	43.0
9	Poland	42.8
10	Romania[c]	36.5
11	Greece	35.3
12	Portugal	35.2
13	Malta[b]	32.0
14	Sweden	31.1
15	San Marino	30.9
16	Iceland	30.8
17	Slovakia	30.6
18	Norway	30.5
19	United Kingdom[a]	29.7
20	Switzerland[a]	26.8
21	Finland[a]	24.5
	Ireland	24.5
23	Spain	24.1
24	Italy[a]	23.4
25	Netherlands[a]	23.2
26	Denmark[a]	21.5
	Hungary	21.5
28	Austria	21.1
	Belgium[b]	21.1
30	France[a]	19.8
31	Czech Republic	19.7
32	Slovenia[a]	19.3

Secondary, 1996

1	Latvia	58.9
2	Moldova	52.9
3	Lithuania	50.9
4	Estonia	50.7
	Spain	50.7
6	France[a]	50.0
7	Czech Republic	49.7
8	Slovenia[a]	48.4
9	Austria	47.7
10	Italy[a]	47.5
	Switzerland[a]	47.5
12	Belgium[b]	46.9
13	Hungary	46.3
14	Monaco	44.9
15	United Kingdom[a]	44.0
16	Luxembourg[a]	43.3
17	Portugal	42.7
18	Iceland	41.9
19	Ireland	41.5
20	Denmark[a]	39.7
	Netherlands[a]	39.7
22	Greece	38.0
23	Finland[a]	36.1
24	Sweden	35.9
25	San Marino	32.5
26	Slovakia	28.0
27	Malta[b]	24.0
28	Romania[c]	23.8
29	Macedonia	23.6
30	Norway	23.0
31	Turkey[a]	22.0
32	Albania[b]	20.6

Tertiary, 1996

1	Turkey[a]	34.7	13	Belgium[b]	20.3
2	Netherlands[a]	29.9	14	Switzerland[a]	19.7
3	Finland[a]	28.8	15	Lithuania	18.3
4	Norway	27.9	16	Bulgaria	18.0
5	Sweden	25.5	17	Estonia	17.9
6	Greece	25.0	18	Iceland	17.7
7	Ireland	23.8	19	France[a]	17.0
8	United Kingdom[a]	23.7	20	Slovenia[a]	16.9
9	Denmark[a]	22.8	21	Portugal	16.4
10	Germany[a]	22.6	22	Romania[c]	15.9
11	Macedonia	22.0	23	Hungary	15.6
12	Austria	21.6	24	Czech Republic	15.1

a 1995 b 1994 c 1993

School time

Pupil:teacher ratio

Primary, 1996 or latest			Secondary, 1996 or latest		
1	Turkey	28	**1**	Turkey	22
2	Liechtenstein	25	**2**	Netherlands	21
3	Moldova	23	**3**	Poland	21
4	Bosnia	22	**4**	Macedonia	16
	Ireland	22	**5**	Germany	15
6	Azerbaijan	20	**6**	Ireland	14
	Belarus	20		United Kingdom	14
	Romania	20	**8**	Romania	13
	Russia	20	**9**	Cyprus	12
	Ukraine	20		France	12
11	Armenia	19		Greece	12
	Croatia	19	**12**	Bulgaria	11
	Czech Republic	19		Malta	11
	France	19		Sweden	11
	Macedonia	19			
	Malta	19			
	Monaco	19			
	Netherlands	19			
	Slovakia	19			
	United Kingdom	19			

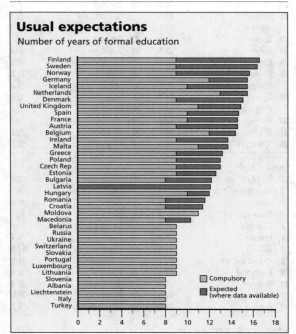

Usual expectations

Number of years of formal education

☐ Compulsory
■ Expected (where data available)

Part IX

SOCIETY

Family matters

Tying the knot
Marriages per 1,000 population

1	Liechtenstein	13.2	23	Slovakia	5.2
2	United Kingdom	10.8	24	Germany	5.1
3	Cyprus	7.8		Spain	5.1
	Turkey	7.8	26	Lithuania	5.0
5	Belarus	7.5	27	Austria	4.8
6	Monaco	7.3		France	4.8
7	Albania	6.8		Italy	4.8
8	Malta	6.7		Norway	4.8
	Portugal	6.7	31	Finland	4.7
10	Denmark	6.5	32	Hungary	4.5
	Macedonia	6.5		Ireland	4.5
	Russia	6.5	34	Belgium	4.4
13	Romania	6.4	35	Bulgaria	4.1
14	Ukraine	6.1	36	Latvia	3.9
15	Moldova	6.0	37	Luxembourg	3.9
16	Czech Republic	5.7	38	Estonia	3.7
17	Netherlands	5.5		Slovenia	3.7
18	Greece	5.4	40	Georgia	3.6
	Iceland	5.4		Sweden	3.6
	Poland	5.4	42	Armenia	3.3
	Switzerland	5.4	43	Andorra	2.2
22	Croatia	5.3			

Breaking up
Divorces per 1,000 population

1	Belarus	5.0	22	Luxembourg	1.8
2	Russia	3.9	23	Slovakia	1.7
3	Ukraine	3.9	24	Portugal	1.5
4	Estonia	3.7		Romania	1.5
5	Moldova	3.4	26	San Marino	1.3
6	United Kingdom	3.3	27	Liechtenstein	1.2
7	Lithuania	3.2		Poland	1.2
8	Czech Republic	3.1	29	Slovenia	1.1
9	Finland	2.7	30	Bulgaria	1.0
	Norway	2.7		Cyprus	1.0
11	Belgium	2.6	32	Croatia	0.9
	Latvia	2.6		Greece	0.9
13	Denmark	2.5		Spain	0.9
	Hungary	2.5	35	Albania	0.8
	Switzerland	2.5		Azerbaijan	0.8
16	Germany	2.3	37	Armenia	0.6
	Sweden	2.3		Italy	0.6
18	Austria	2.1	39	Turkey	0.5
	Netherlands	2.1	40	Georgia	0.4
20	France	2.0	41	Bosnia	0.3
21	Iceland	1.9		Macedonia	0.3

Births outside marriage
Per 100 births, 1996

1	Iceland	60.1	22	Belgium[c]	15.9
2	Sweden	53.9	23	Luxembourg	15.0
3	Norway	48.3	24	Moldova	14.6
4	Estonia	48.1	25	Slovakia	14.0
5	Denmark[a]	46.5	26	Ukraine[b]	12.8
6	France[b]	36.1	27	Lithuania[a]	12.6
7	Finland	35.4	28	Belarus[b]	12.1
8	United Kingdom[a]	33.6	29	Spain[b]	10.8
9	Latvia	33.1	30	Poland	10.2
10	Slovenia	31.8	31	Armenia[a]	9.3
11	Bulgaria	28.2	32	Macedonia[a]	8.1
12	Austria	28.0	33	Italy[a]	7.7
13	Ireland[a]	22.7	34	Croatia[b]	7.6
14	Hungary	22.6	35	Bosnia[d]	7.4
15	Georgia[c]	21.8	36	Switzerland	7.3
16	Russia[a]	21.1	37	Liechtenstein[d]	6.9
17	Romania	20.7	38	Azerbaijan[c]	4.4
18	Portugal	18.3		Turkey[d]	4.4
19	Czech Republic	16.9	40	Malta	3.2
	Netherlands	16.9	41	Greece	3.0
21	Germany[a]	16.1	42	Cyprus	1.5

Abortion
No. per 1,000 women of child-bearing age, 1995

1	Romania	78.0	19	Slovakia	19.7
2	Russia[a]	68.4	20	Sweden	18.7
3	Belarus	67.5	21	Denmark[a]	16.1
4	Ukraine	57.2	22	Azerbaijan	16.0
5	Estonia	53.8	23	England and Wales	15.6
6	Bulgaria	51.3	24	Norway	15.6
7	Latvia	44.1	25	Croatia	12.9
8	Moldova	38.8	26	France[a]	12.4
9	Liechtenstein[b]	37.0	27	Italy	11.4
10	Armenia	35.4	28	Scotland	11.2
11	Hungary	34.7	29	Finland	10.0
12	Lithuania	34.4	30	Switzerland	8.4
13	Macedonia	28.5	31	Germany	7.6
14	Albania	27.2	32	Belgium	6.8
15	Turkey[e]	25.0	33	Netherlands	6.5
16	Slovenia	23.2	34	Ireland	5.9
17	Georgia	21.9	35	Spain	5.7
18	Czech Republic	20.7			

a 1995
b 1994
c 1992
d 1990
e 1993

Age factors

Legal sex
Age of consent

	Heterosexuals	Lesbians	Gay men
Albania	14	14	14
Andorra	16	16	16
Austria	14	14	14/18
Belgium	16/18	16/18	16/18
Bulgaria	14	14	14
Croatia	14	18	18
Cyprus	16	16	banned
Czech Republic	15	15	15
Denmark	15/18	15/18	15/18
Estonia	14	14	16
Finland	16	18	18
France	15/18	15/18	15/18
Germany	14/16	14/16	14/16
Greece	15	15	15
Hungary	14	18	18
Iceland	14	14	14
Ireland[a]	17	15	17
Italy	14/16	14/16	14/16
Liechtenstein	14	14	18
Luxembourg	16	16	16
Malta	12/18	12/18	12/18
Netherlands	12/16	12/16	12/16
Norway	16	16	16
Poland	15	15	15
Portugal	14/16	14/16	14/16
Romania	14	banned	banned
San Marino	14/16	14/16	14/16
Serbia	14	14	18
Slovakia	15	15	15
Spain	12/16	12/16	12/16
Sweden	15	15	15
Switzerland	16	16	16
Turkey[b]	15/18	15/18	15/18
United Kingdom[c]	16	16	18

a Ireland: the age of consent shown is the age for intercourse, including anal intercourse, which is 17, except in the case of heterosexual couples who marry at 16 with their parents' consent. The age of consent for other sexual acts is 15 for heterosexuals and lesbians, and 17 for gay men.

b Turkey: the age of consent is 18 for vaginal intercourse and for anal intercourse, and 15 for all other sexual acts.

c United Kingdom: the age of consent for heterosexual sex is 17 in Northern Ireland, except in the case of couples who marry at 16 with their parents' consent.

Notes
Male homosexuality is banned in Armenia, Azerbaijan, Bosnia, Georgia, Macedonia and Romania. Female homosexuality is also banned in Romania.
When two ages are shown this is either because a higher age applies where the older person is in a position of authority or influence over the younger, or because sexual activity is legal at the lower age unless the younger person subsequently complains.

Voting age

Monaco	21	Lithuania	18
Liechtenstein	20	Luxembourg	18
Albania	18	Macedonia FYR	18
Andorra	18	Malta	18
Armenia	18	Moldova	18
Austria	18	Netherlands	18
Azerbaijan	18	Norway	18
Belarus	18	Poland	18
Belgium	18	Portugal	18
Bulgaria	18	Romania	18
Cyprus	18	Russia	18
Czech Republic	18	San Marino	18
Denmark	18	Slovakia	18
Estonia	18	Spain	18
Finland	18	Sweden	18
France	18	Switzerland	18
Georgia	18	Turkey	18
Germany	18	Ukraine	18
Greece	18	United Kingdom	18
Hungary	18	Bosnia[b]	16
Iceland	18	Croatia[b]	16
Ireland	18	Serbia[b]	16
Italy[a]	18	Slovenia[b]	16
Latvia	18		

Retirement age
EU15

	Men	Women
Austria	65	60
Belgium	65	61
Denmark	67	67
Finland	65	65
France	60	60
Germany	65	65
Greece	65	65
Ireland	65	65
Italy	64	59
Luxembourg	65	65
Netherlands	65	65
Portugal	65	63
Spain	65	65
Sweden	65	65
United Kingdom	65	60

a Senatorial elections, minimun age 25.
b If employed, otherwise 18.

Religion

Who belongs to which faith
% of total population

Albania

Muslim 70	Orthodox 20	Other 10

Andorra

Roman Catholic 99		Other 1

Armenia

Orthodox 94		Other 6

Austria

Roman Catholic 85	Protestant 6	Other 9

Azerbaijan

Muslim 93	Orthodox 5	Other 2

Belarus

Orthodox 80		Other 20

Belgium

Roman Catholic 75	Protestant 20	Other 5

Bosnia

Muslim 40	Orthodox 31	Other 29

Bulgaria

Orthodox 85	Muslim 13	Other 2

Croatia

Roman Catholic 77	Orthodox 11	Other 12

Cyprus

Orthodox 78	Muslim 18	Other 4

Czech Republic

Atheist 40	Roman Catholic 39	Other 21

Denmark

Evangelical Lutheran 91	Protestant 2	Other 7

Estonia

Evangelical Lutheran 65	Orthodox 30	Other 5

Finland

Evangelical Lutheran 89	Orthodox 1	Other 10

France

Roman Catholic 90	Protestant 3	Other 7

Georgia

Orthodox 65	Muslim 11	Other 24

Germany

Protestant 38	Roman Catholic 34	Other 28

Greece

Orthodox 98	Muslim 1	Other 1

Hungary

Roman Catholic 68	Calvinist 20	Other 12

Iceland

Evangelical Lutheran 96	Protestant 3	Other 1

Ireland

Roman Catholic 93	Anglican 3	Other 4

Italy

Roman Catholic 98		Other 2

Latvia

| Evangelical Lutheran 70 | Orthodox 28 | Other 2 |

Liechtenstein

| Roman Catholic 80 | Protestant 17 | Other 3 |

Lithuania

| Roman Catholic 56 | Orthodox 26 | Other 18 |

Luxembourg

| Roman Catholic 97 | Jewish 2 | Other 1 |

Macedonia

| Orthodox 67 | Muslim 30 | Other 3 |

Malta

| Roman Catholic 98 | | Other 2 |

Moldova

| Orthodox 98 | Jewish 2 |

Monaco

| Roman Catholic 95 | | Other 5 |

Netherlands

| Roman Catholic 34 | Protestant 25 | Other 41 |

Norway

| Evangelical Lutheran 88 | Roman Catholic 4 | Other 8 |

Poland

| Roman Catholic 95 | Orthodox 2 | Other 3 |

Portugal

| Roman Catholic 97 | Protestant 2 | Other 1 |

Romania

| Orthodox 70 | Roman Catholic 6 | Other 24 |

Russia

| Orthodox 56 | Muslim 23 | Other 21 |

Serbia and Montenegro

| Orthodox 65 | Muslim 19 | Other 16 |

Slovakia

| Roman Catholic 60 | Protestant 8 | Other 32 |

Slovenia

| Roman Catholic 71 | Orthodox 11 | Other 1 |

Spain

| Roman Catholic 99 | | Other 1 |

Sweden

| Evangelical Lutheran 94 | Roman Catholic 2 | Other 4 |

Switzerland

| Roman Catholic 47 | Protestant 40 | Other 13 |

Turkey

| Muslim 99 | | Other 1 |

Ukraine

| Orthodox 45 | Roman Catholic 36 | Other 19 |

United Kingdom

| Anglican 47 | Roman Catholic 16 | Other 37 |

Vatican

| Roman Catholic 100 | |

Income and savings

Poor shares[a]
% of income

Lowest 20% share, 1998		*Lowest 10% share, 1998*	
Russia[b]	4.4	Russia[b]	1.7
Turkey[bc]	5.8	Estonia[d]	2.2
Estonia[d]	6.2	Turkey	2.3
United Kingdom[e]	6.6	Ireland[f]	2.5
Ireland[f]	6.7	Switzerland[g]	2.6
Moldova[g]	6.9	United Kingdom[e]	2.6
Switzerland[g]	6.9	Moldova[g]	2.7
France[d]	7.2	France[d]	2.8
Netherlands[c]	7.3	Netherlands[c]	2.8
Portugal[d]	7.3	Spain[i]	2.8
Greece[h]	7.5	Latvia	2.9
Spain[i]	7.5	Greece[h]	3.0
Latvia	7.6	Poland[i]	3.0
Poland[i]	7.7	Lithuania[bi]	3.1
Lithuania[bi]	7.8	Portugal[d]	3.1
Germany[cd]	8.2	Slovenia[d]	3.2
Slovenia[d]	8.4	Germany[c]	3.3
Bulgaria[bd]	8.5	Bulgaria[bd]	3.4
Ukraine[i]	8.6	Italy[bd]	3.5
Italy[bd]	8.7	Denmark[bg]	3.6
Hungary[bi]	8.8	Belgium[bg]	3.7
Romania[c]	8.9	Romania[c]	3.7
Croatia[b]	9.3	Sweden[bg]	3.7
Luxembourg[bc]	9.4	Hungary[bi]	3.9
Belgium[bg]	9.5	Ukraine	3.9
Denmark[bg]	9.6	Croatia[b]	4.0
Sweden[bg]	9.6	Luxembourg[bc]	4.0
Norway[bd]	9.7	Norway[bd]	4.1
Finland[be]	10.0	Finland[be]	4.2

Rich shares[a]
% of income, highest 10% share, 1998

Russia[b]	38.7	Spain[i]	25.2
Turkey[bc]	32.3	Netherlands[c]	25.1
Portugal[d]	28.4	France[d]	25.1
Ireland[f]	27.4	Hungary[bi]	24.8
United Kingdom[e]	27.3	Germany[c]	23.7
Ukraine[i]	26.4	Romania[c]	22.7
Poland[i]	26.3	Bulgaria[bd]	22.5
Estonia[d]	26.2	Czech Republic[bi]	22.4
Latvia	25.9	Luxembourg[bc]	22.0
Moldova[g]	25.8	Norway[bd]	21.8
Lithuania[bi]	25.6	Italy[bd]	21.8
Greece[h]	25.3	Finland[be]	21.6
Switzerland[g]	25.2	Croatia[b]	21.6

a Income shares by percentiles of population and ranked by income per person.
b Spending shares by percentiles of population and ranked by spending per person.
c 1994 d 1995 e 1991 f 1987 g 1992 h 1993 i 1990 j 1996

Distribution of income[a]
Gini index[k], 1998

Russia[b]	48.7	Latvia	32.4
Turkey[bc]	41.5	Hungary[bj]	30.8
United Kingdom[e]	36.1	Germany[c]	30.0
Ireland[f]	35.9	Bulgaria[bd]	28.3
Portugal[d]	35.6	Romania[c]	28.2
Estonia[d]	35.4	Italy[bd]	27.3
Moldova[g]	34.4	Luxembourg[bc]	26.9
Switzerland[g]	33.1	Slovenia[d]	26.8
Poland[j]	32.9	Croatia[b]	26.8
Greece[h]	32.7	Norway[bd]	25.8
France[d]	32.7	Finland[be]	25.6
Netherlands[c]	32.6	Czech Republic[bj]	25.4
Ukraine[j]	32.5	Sweden[bg]	25.0
Spain[i]	32.5	Belgium[bg]	25.0
Lithuania[bj]	32.4	Denmark[bg]	24.7

Household savings rates
% of disposable income

	1980			1990	
1	Portugal	24.3	1	Italy[l]	17.0
2	Italy[l]	23.4	2	Portugal	16.4
3	Belgium	19.3	3	Belgium	13.9
4	France[l]	17.6		France[l]	13.9
5	Ireland	15.8	5	Austria[l]	12.2
6	United Kingdom[l]	13.4	6	Germany[l]	12.0
7	Germany[l]	12.8	7	Netherlands[m]	11.9
8	Austria[l]	11.5	8	Spain[l]	11.8
9	Spain[l]	11.3	9	Denmark	11.4
10	Sweden	6.7	10	Switzerland	10.3
11	Finland	5.4	11	Ireland	9.8
12	Norway	2.7	12	United Kingdom[l]	7.7

	1995			1998	
1	France[l]	16.0	1	Hungary	19.3
2	Belgium	15.1	2	France[l]	15.5
3	Italy[l]	14.5	3	Belgium	12.9
4	Spain[l]	13.4	4	Ireland	11.7
5	Hungary	12.7	5	Italy[l]	11.2
6	Germany[l]	11.4	6	Germany[l]	11.0
7	United Kingdom[l]	10.5		Spain[l]	11.0
8	Portugal	10.3	8	Portugal	9.2
9	Ireland	9.9	9	Austria[l]	8.8
10	Austria[l]	9.8	10	Switzerland	8.7
11	Switzerland	9.5	11	United Kingdom[l]	6.6
12	Denmark	7.1	12	Norway	6.5

k The Gini index is a measure of income inequality. 0 means all households have the same income, 100 means one household has all the income.
l Gross savings.
m Excludes mandatory savings through occupational pension schemes.

Consumer spending

Who spends how much on what
1998, % of household budget spent on

All food

1	Albania	62
2	Armenia	52
3	Azerbaijan	51
4	Estonia	41
5	Belarus	36
	Romania	36
7	Ukraine	34
8	Georgia	33
	Lithuania	33
	Macedonia	33
	Spain	33
12	Greece	32
13	Moldova	31
14	Bulgaria	30
	Latvia	30

Clothing and footwear

1	Spain	12
2	Greece	11
	Italy	11
	Russia	11
5	Austria	10
6	Ireland	9
7	Luxembourg	8
	Portugal	8
	Slovenia	8
10	Belarus	7
	Estonia	7
	France	7
	Netherlands	7
	Norway	7
	Romania	7
	Slovakia	7
	Turkey	7
	United Kingdom	7

Fuel and power

1	Estonia	24
2	Poland	19
3	Armenia	18
	Turkey	18
5	Bulgaria	17
	Hungary	17
7	Azerbaijan	16
	Latvia	16
	Russia	16
	Slovakia	16
	Ukraine	16
12	Belarus	15
	Macedonia	15

Education

1	Lithuania	27
2	Latvia	23
3	Hungary	20
	Romania	20
5	Portugal	19
6	Switzerland	18
7	Denmark	17
	Italy	17
9	Slovenia	16
10	Armenia	15
	Finland	15
	Moldova	15
	Russia	15

Health care

1	Azerbaijan	9
2	Bulgaria	8
	Estonia	8
4	Belarus	7
	Russia	7
6	Hungary	6
	Latvia	6
	Macedonia	6
	Poland	6
	Turkey	6
	Ukraine	6

Transport and communications

1	Czech Republic	16
2	Ukraine	14
3	France	12
	Hungary	12
	Moldova	12
6	Belarus	11
	Latvia	11
	Slovenia	11
9	Ireland	10
	Slovakia	10

Growth in consumer spending
Average annual growth, volume, %
1990–98

1	Moldova	9.0	16	Austria	2.0
2	Georgia	6.2		United Kingdom	2.0
3	Albania	6.1	18	Greece	1.8
4	Azerbaijan	5.8	19	Germany	1.3
5	Macedonia	5.5		Romania	1.3
6	Poland	5.0	21	Belgium	1.2
7	Ireland	4.6		France	1.2
8	Russia	4.3	23	Spain	1.1
9	Turkey	4.1	24	Italy	0.6
10	Slovenia	3.7	25	Switzerland	0.5
11	Denmark	3.4	26	Finland	0.4
12	Norway	3.1	27	Sweden	0.1
13	Czech Republic	2.7	28	Slovakia	-0.7
14	Portugal	2.5	29	Estonia	-1.1
15	Netherlands	2.2	30	Hungary	-1.3

Working time to buy

All manufacturing industries
1 kilo bread, minutes

1	Lithuania	27
2	Hungary	25
3	Romania	19
4	Croatia	18
	Slovakia	18
6	Finland	17
7	Czech Republic	16
8	Austria	14
	Macedonia	14
10	France	13
	Greece	13
	Norway	13
	Sweden	13
14	Poland	10
	Spain	10
16	Luxembourg	9
17	Belgium	8
	Italy	8
	Switzerland	8
20	Germany	7
21	United Kingdom	6
22	Denmark	4

All manufacturing industries
Colour TV (hours)

1	Romania	564.1
2	Slovakia	310.4
3	Lithuania	296.4
4	Croatia	251.3
5	Hungary	247.8
6	Czech Republic	193.6
7	Poland	162.0
8	Macedonia	150.0
9	Greece	124.6
10	Austria	113.9
11	Belgium	53.9
12	Sweden	52.5
13	Luxembourg	51.8
14	Finland	48.9
15	Germany	42.4
16	France	41.2
17	United Kingdom	36.7
18	Norway	35.5
19	Spain	34.3
20	Italy	30.5
21	Denmark	12.5

Wired world

Televisions
Colour TVs, % of households, 1998

1	Ireland	99.0	15	Italy	94.2
2	United Kingdom	98.3	16	Austria	92.5
3	Netherlands	98.1	17	Slovakia	92.0
4	Czech Republic	98.0	18	Slovenia	91.0
5	Norway	98.0	19	Estonia	90.0
6	Belgium	97.8		Hungary	90.0
7	Denmark	97.0	21	Greece	89.4
	Germany	97.0	22	Malaysia	89.2
	Poland	97.0	23	Azerbaijan	89.0
	Sweden	97.0	24	Spain	87.0
11	Switzerland	96.7	25	Croatia	84.0
12	Portugal	96.4	26	Lithuania	82.0
13	Finland	96.0	27	Latvia	79.0
14	France	95.8		Russia	79.0

Video cassette recorders
% of households, 1998

1	Denmark	83	15	Poland	57
2	United Kingdom	82	16	Austria	55
3	Germany	81	17	Croatia	53
4	Ireland	78	18	Portugal	46
5	Netherlands	77	19	Hungary	42
6	Sweden	75	20	Czech Republic	38
7	Norway	73	21	Greece	36
8	Switzerland	71		Slovakia	36
9	Finland	66	23	Turkey	30
10	Belgium	64	24	Estonia	21
11	France	60		Lithuania	21
	Italy	60	26	Latvia	13
13	Slovenia	58	27	Russia	12
	Spain	58			

Internet
Hosts by country

1	United Kingdom	1,901,812	16	Hungary	113,659
2	Germany	1,702,486	17	Czech Republic	112,748
3	Netherlands	820,944	18	Turkey	90,929
4	France	779,879	19	Portugal	90,757
5	Italy	658,307	20	Greece	77,954
6	Finland	631,248	21	Ireland	59,681
7	Sweden	594,627	22	Iceland	29,958
8	Spain	415,641	23	Estonia	29,682
9	Norway	401,889	24	Ukraine	26,713
10	Denmark	336,928	25	Slovakia	25,906
11	Belgium	320,840	26	Romania	24,689
12	Switzerland	306,073	27	Slovenia	20,535
13	Austria	274,173	28	Croatia	14,147
14	Russia	214,704	29	Lithuania	12,701
15	Poland	183,057	30	Bulgaria	11,854

Cable
% of households
1998

1	Belgium	98.4	15	Russia	31.7
2	Netherlands	89.7	16	Iceland	31.6
3	Switzerland	83.4	17	Slovakia	23.9
4	Luxembourg	81.9	18	Czech Republic	21.6
5	Denmark	54.9	19	France	10.1
6	Hungary	52.6	20	United Kingdom	9.9
7	Germany	51.2	21	Portugal	7.2
8	Sweden	50.9	22	Turkey	5.8
9	Ireland	48.9	23	Croatia	5.3
10	Norway	40.0	24	Spain	3.2
11	Slovenia	39.9	25	Moldova	2.7
12	Finland	39.8	26	Greece	0.4
13	Poland	35.9	27	Italy	0.1
14	Austria	34.9			

Satellite dishes
% of households
1998

1	Austria	49.8	15	Portugal	12.3
2	Croatia	40.3	16	Finland	11.9
3	Denmark	39.7	17	France	11.2
4	Slovakia	37.0	18	Romania	10.7
5	Estonia	33.4	19	Ireland	9.9
6	Germany	30.2	20	Spain	9.4
7	Slovenia	22.3	21	Greece	6.0
8	Poland	21.0	22	Italy	4.0
9	Hungary	20.7		Netherlands	4.0
10	Sweden	18.7	24	Lithuania	3.5
11	United Kingdom	17.9	25	Moldova	2.9
12	Norway	17.8	26	Belgium	2.8
13	Czech Republic	15.6	27	Turkey	2.7
14	Switzerland	13.0	28	Russia	0.8

Cellular mobile subscribers
Per 100 inhabitants, 1998

1	Finland	57.1	12	Switzerland	23.5
2	Norway	47.4	13	Netherlands	21.3
3	Sweden	46.4	14	Greece	19.4
4	Denmark	36.4	15	France	18.8
5	Italy	35.7	16	Spain	17.9
6	Iceland	33.1	17	Belgium	17.3
7	Portugal	30.9	18	Estonia	17.0
8	Luxembourg	30.8		Germany	17.0
9	Ireland	25.7	20	Cyprus	15.7
10	United Kingdom	25.2	21	Hungary	10.5
11	Austria	24.9	22	Czech Republic	9.4

Books and newspapers

Books sales: by value

Total, $m, 1998			Per head, $, 1998		
1	Germany	8,928	1	Norway	130
2	United Kingdom	4,636	2	Germany	109
3	France	2,903	3	Finland	98
4	Italy	2,648	4	Belgium	97
5	Spain	2,617	5	Switzerland	93
6	Netherlands	1,014	6	United Kingdom	78
7	Belgium	983	7	Denmark	71
8	Switzerland	682		Sweden	71
9	Sweden	633	9	Spain	66
10	Norway	573	10	Netherlands	65
11	Poland	517	11	Ireland	57
12	Finland	505	12	Austria	54
13	Austria	436	13	France	49
14	Denmark	373	14	Italy	46
15	Portugal	352	15	Portugal	36
16	Greece	228	16	Greece	21
17	Russia	213	17	Bulgaria	15
18	Ireland	210	18	Hungary	13
19	Hungary	130		Poland	13
20	Bulgaria	122	20	Czech Republic	9
21	Czech Republic	95	21	Slovakia	4
22	Turkey	31	22	Russia	1
23	Slovakia	20	23	Turkey	<1

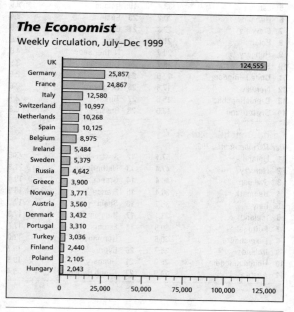

The Economist
Weekly circulation, July–Dec 1999

UK	124,555
Germany	25,857
France	24,867
Italy	12,580
Switzerland	10,997
Netherlands	10,268
Spain	10,125
Belgium	8,975
Ireland	5,484
Sweden	5,379
Russia	4,642
Greece	3,900
Norway	3,771
Austria	3,560
Denmark	3,432
Portugal	3,310
Turkey	3,036
Finland	2,440
Poland	2,105
Hungary	2,043

Daily newspapers
Number of titles, 1996

1	Germany	375	25	Serbia		18
2	Russia	285	26	Austria		17
3	Greece	156		Bulgaria		17
4	France	117	28	Estonia		15
5	Romania	106	29	Armenia		11
6	United Kingdom	99	30	Croatia		10
7	Sweden	94	31	Cyprus		9
8	Switzerland	88	32	Belarus		8
9	Spain	87	33	Slovenia		7
10	Norway	83	34	Azerbaijan		6
11	Italy	78		Ireland		6
12	Turkey	57	36	Albania		5
13	Finland	56		Iceland		5
14	Poland	55		Luxembourg		5
15	Ukraine	44	39	Moldova		4
16	Hungary	40	40	Andorra		3
17	Netherlands	38		Bosnia		3
18	Denmark	37		Macedonia		3
19	Belgium	30		San Marino		3
20	Portugal	27	44	Liechtenstein		2
21	Latvia	24		Malta		2
22	Czech Republic	21	46	Georgia		1
23	Lithuania	19		Monaco		1
	Slovakia	19		Vatican		1

Circulation, per 1,000 population per day, 1996

1	Liechtenstein	606	22	Belarus[b]	174
2	Norway	593	23	Estonia	173
3	Iceland	535	24	Belgium	160
4	Finland	455	25	Greece[b]	153
5	Sweden	446		Ireland	153
6	United Kingdom	332	27	Bosnia[b]	146
7	Switzerland	330	28	Malta	130
8	Luxembourg	327	29	Croatia	114
9	Romania[a]	324	30	Poland	113
10	Denmark	311	31	Cyprus	111
	Germany	311		Turkey	111
12	Netherlands	305	33	Serbia	110
13	Austria	294	34	Russia	105
14	Czech Republic	256	35	Italy	104
15	Bulgaria	253	36	Spain	99
16	Monaco[b]	250	37	Lithuania	92
17	Latvia	246	38	Portugal	75
18	France	218	39	San Marino	72
19	Slovenia	206	40	Moldova	59
20	Hungary	189	41	Andorra	58
21	Slovakia	185	42	Ukraine	54

a 1992 b 1995

Crime and punishment

Offensive records
Total criminal offences per 100,000 population, 1998

1	Iceland	14,727	18	Estonia	3,145
2	Finland	14,405	19	Slovenia	2,822
3	Norway	10,048	20	Poland	2,775
4	United Kingdom	9,823	21	Andorra	2,606
5	Denmark	9,428	22	Spain	2,312
6	Belgium	8,478	23	Ireland	2,279
7	Germany	7,869	24	Lithuania	2,057
8	Netherlands	7,808	25	Bulgaria	1,992
9	Luxembourg	6,409	26	Russia	1,760
10	France	6,096	27	Slovakia	1,740
11	Austria	5,940	28	Romania	1,723
12	Hungary	5,926	29	Latvia	1,492
13	Switzerland	5,406	30	Belarus	1,204
14	Italy	4,214	31	Croatia	1,173
15	Czech Republic	4,126	32	Ukraine	1,141
16	Greece	3,759	33	Macedonia	1,102
17	Monaco	3,337	34	Moldova	957

Juvenile crime
% of total crime committed by people under age 21 yrs, 1998

1	Belarus	59.5		Poland	14.7
2	Norway	37.0	17	Austria	14.4
3	Macedonia	29.8	18	Germany	13.0
4	United Kingdom	23.9	19	Ireland	13.0
5	Andorra	23.3	20	Albania	12.6
6	France	21.8	21	Slovakia	11.4
7	Estonia	17.9	22	Russia	11.1
	Switzerland	17.9	23	Romania	10.4
9	Latvia	17.3	24	Monaco	10.3
10	Netherlands	17.0	25	Croatia	9.7
11	Slovenia	15.8	26	Hungary	9.2
12	Czech Republic	15.0	27	Bulgaria	8.8
13	Finland	14.8	28	Ukraine	8.6
14	Lithuania	14.7	29	Luxembourg	8.5
	Moldova	14.7	30	Turkey	6.8

Murder most foul
Murder per 100,000 population, 1998

1	Albania	30.0	12	Macedonia	5.4
2	Russia	20.1	13	Belgium	5.3
3	Estonia	17.1	14	Azerbaijan	5.1
4	Netherlands	10.9	15	Georgia	4.7
5	Belarus	10.2	16	Italy	4.4
6	Moldova	9.9	17	Hungary	4.3
7	Latvia	9.8	18	Germany	4.0
8	Lithuania	9.4	19	Denmark	3.9
9	Ukraine	9.1	20	France	3.7
10	Bulgaria	7.5	21	Greece	3.4
11	Croatia	6.1		Slovenia	3.4

Note: comparable data not available for some countries.

Prisoners en masse
Total prison population, 1998

1	Russia	998,627	13	Lithuania	13,813
2	Germany	78,584	14	Netherlands	13,333
3	England and Wales	65,298	15	Bulgaria	11,773
4	Turkey	64,907	16	Moldova	10,250
5	Poland	54,864	17	Latvia	9,520
6	France	53,607	18	Georgia	9,350
7	Romania	51,418	19	Belgium	8,271
8	Italy	49,050	20	Armenia	7,689
9	Spain	44,763	21	Greece	7,129
10	Czech Republic	22,067	22	Austria	6,962
11	Portugal	14,598	23	Slovakia	6,628
12	Hungary	14,218	24	Switzerland	6,041

Prisoners in proportion
Prisoners per 100,000 population, 1998

1	Russia	679	16	France	88
2	Latvia	389	17	Austria	86
3	Lithuania	373	18	Italy	85
4	Estonia	332		Netherlands	85
5	Moldova	275		Switzerland	85
6	Romania	233	21	Belgium	81
7	Czech Republic	214	22	Greece	75
8	Portugal	147	23	Malta	72
9	Hungary	142	24	Ireland	71
10	Bulgaria	138	25	Denmark	64
11	Slovakia	123	26	Sweden	60
12	England and Wales[a]	120	27	Macedonia	58
13	Spain	112	28	Norway	57
14	Turkey	98	29	Finland	54
15	Germany	96	30	Croatia	49

How crowded prisons are
Prison population per 100 places, 1998

1	Bulgaria	197		Germany	108
2	Estonia	173		Spain	108
3	Albania	165	17	Lithuania	100
4	Greece	157	18	Sweden	99
5	Romania	154	19	Latvia	97
6	Hungary	139	20	Malta	96
7	Portugal	132	21	Cyprus	94
8	Russia	125	22	Denmark	92
9	Italy	115	23	Netherlands	89
10	Czech Republic	114		Switzerland	89
11	Ireland	111	25	Austria	88
12	England and Wales[a]	109		Turkey	88
13	Belgium	108	27	Norway	87
	France	108	28	Moldova	83

a 1997

Music

Album sales
Sales of LPs, CDs and music cassettes per head, 1999

1	Denmark	3.4		Spain	1.6
	Norway	3.4	**16**	Cyprus	1.3
	United Kingdom	3.4	**17**	Poland	1.0
4	Iceland	3.3	**18**	Italy	0.8
5	Switzerland	3.0	**19**	Czech Republic	0.7
6	Germany	2.8		Greece	0.7
7	Sweden	2.6		Hungary	0.7
8	Austria	2.3		Russia	0.7
9	Belgium	2.2	**23**	Estonia	0.5
	Netherlands	2.2		Latvia	0.5
11	Finland	2.1	**25**	Slovakia	0.4
12	Ireland	2.0	**26**	Croatia	0.3
13	France	1.9		Slovenia	0.3
14	Portugal	1.6			

CD popularity
Penetration of CDs as % of total album sales of LPs, CDs and music cassettes, 1999

1	Belgium	99	**17**	Cyprus	80
	Denmark	99	**18**	Italy	73
	France	99	**19**	Slovenia	67
	Netherlands	99	**20**	Czech Republic	59
5	Norway	98	**21**	Slovakia	53
	Iceland	98	**22**	Croatia	50
7	Sweden	97	**23**	Hungary	48
8	Austria	96	**24**	Poland	45
9	Switzerland	95	**25**	Estonia	43
10	Greece	93	**26**	Lithuania	28
11	Finland	92	**27**	Latvia	15
12	Germany	90	**28**	Ukraine	10
13	United Kingdom	89	**29**	Russia	8
14	Ireland	85	**30**	Bulgaria	6
15	Spain	83	**31**	Romania	5
16	Portugal	82			

Classical business
Sale of classical records as % of market value, 1998

1	Austria	12	**12**	Romania	7
2	Poland	11		Spain	7
3	Czech Republic	10		United Kingdom	7
	Finland	10	**15**	Russia	6
	France	10		Slovakia	6
	Germany	10	**17**	Ireland	5
	Switzerland	10	**18**	Greece	4
8	Belgium	9		Norway	4
	Hungary	9		Portugal	4
	Netherlands	9		Sweden	4
11	Denmark	8	**22**	Ukraine	2

Recorded music sales

$, 1999			$ per head, 1999		
1	United Kingdom	2908.9	1	Iceland	64.5
2	Germany	2832.5	2	Norway	59.0
3	France	1983.4	3	Denmark	50.1
4	Spain	639.5	4	United Kingdom	49.6
5	Italy	607.3	5	Sweden	40.2
6	Netherlands	522.1	6	Austria	39.7
7	Sweden	356.6	7	Switzerland	38.0
8	Belgium	342.3	8	Germany	34.5
9	Austria	322.9	9	France	33.8
10	Switzerland	277.1	10	Belgium	33.8
11	Denmark	263.9	11	Netherlands	33.3
12	Norway	260.9	12	Ireland	30.8
13	Portugal	176.8	13	Finland	25.0
14	Poland	154.9	14	Cyprus	23.1
15	Russia	153.1	15	Portugal	17.9
16	Finland	128.6	16	Spain	16.1
17	Turkey	127.0	17	Italy	10.6
18	Ireland	113.3	18	Slovenia	10.2
19	Greece	98.8	19	Greece	9.3
20	Hungary	58.7	20	Hungary	5.8
21	Czech Republic	51.1	21	Czech Republic	5.0
22	Slovenia	20.3	22	Estonia	4.5
23	Cyprus	17.8	23	Poland	4.0
24	Iceland	17.8	24	Croatia	2.9
25	Ukraine	15.1	25	Slovakia	2.4
26	Croatia	12.9	26	Turkey	2.0
27	Slovakia	12.7	27	Latvia	1.7
28	Romania	11.9	28	Russia	1.0

Pirates

Piracy level as % of units, 1998

<10%	10–25%	25–50%	50%>
Austria	Greece	Cyprus	Bulgaria
Belgium	Hungary	Latvia	Lithuania
Czech Republic	Italy	Poland	Romania
Denmark		Slovenia	Russia
Finland		Turkey	
France			
Germany			
Iceland			
Ireland			
Netherlands			
Norway			
Portugal			
Slovakia			
Spain			
Sweden			
Switzerland			
United Kingdom			

Pets

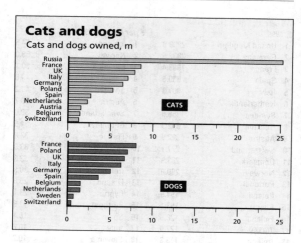

Cats and dogs
Cats and dogs owned, m

CATS

Russia
France
UK
Italy
Germany
Poland
Spain
Netherlands
Austria
Belgium
Switzerland

DOGS

France
Poland
UK
Italy
Germany
Spain
Belgium
Netherlands
Sweden
Switzerland

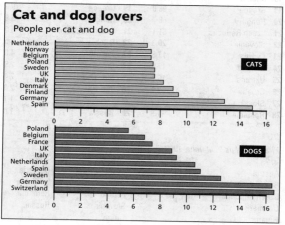

Cat and dog lovers
People per cat and dog

CATS

Netherlands
Norway
Belgium
Poland
Sweden
UK
Italy
Denmark
Finland
Germany
Spain

DOGS

Poland
Belgium
France
UK
Italy
Netherlands
Spain
Sweden
Germany
Switzerland

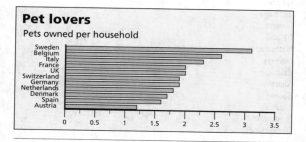

Pet lovers
Pets owned per household

Sweden
Belgium
Italy
France
UK
Switzerland
Germany
Netherlands
Denmark
Spain
Austria

=== Part X ===

GOVERNMENT
AND
DEFENCE

Europe's national governments

Albania

Parliamentary republic with an interim constitution adopted in 1991. Legislative power is vested in the People's Assembly, a single chamber of 155 deputies with elections held every four years. Forty deputies are elected by proportional representation. The People's Assembly elects a president of the republic as head of state whose term of office is five years. Executive power is the responsibility of a council of ministers, the chairman of which is the head of government. The chairman is appointed by the president, as are ministers, after recommendation by the chairman and subject to approval by the People's Assembly.

Andorra

Parliamentary monarchy with a constitution adopted in 1993. Andorra is uniquely a co-principality. Its joint heads of state are the bishop of Urgel and the president of France, though since 1993 the positions have been almost entirely honorary. The legislature is the General Council (*Conseil General*) whose 28 councillors are elected for four-year terms. Executive authority resides with a head of government (*Cap du Govern*) elected by a majority of the General Council. Government ministers are nominated by the head of government.

Armenia

Parliamentary republic with a constitution adopted in 1995. Legislative authority resides with the National Assembly, made up of 131 deputies, elected for terms of four years. A president, directly elected for five years, is head of state and exercises executive power. In addition the president appoints a prime minister and, subject to the prime minister's recommendation, members of the government.

Austria

Federal parliamentary republic with a constitution adopted in 1920. The bicameral legislature, the Federal Assembly, consists of the National Council (*Nationalrat*) and the Federal Council (*Bundesrat*). The former has 183 members, elected for four-year terms by a system of proportional representation. The latter has 64 members, allocated according to the strengths of the parties in the provincial assemblies, with terms corresponding to those of the provincial government represented. A president is elected directly every six years as head of state and appoints a chancellor as head of the federal executive branch, and other ministers on the chancellor's advice.

The provincial assemblies (*landtage*) of the nine states elect state governments of a provincial governor and councillors.

Azerbaijan

Presidential republic with a constitution adopted in 1995. The national assembly (*Milli Majlis*) is the supreme legislative body and has 125 members elected directly for terms of five years, one-fifth by proportional representation from a party list and the remainder in single-member constituencies. Executive power is held by the head of state, a president, who is also elected for five years. The president appoints and exercises executive power through a cabinet of ministers headed by a prime minister. The president retains the right to call legislative elections.

Belarus

Presidential republic with a constitution adopted in 1994 and amended in 1996. The bicameral national assembly exercises legislative power. It comprises the 110-member House of Representatives elected directly and the House of the Republic with 64 members, 56 members elected by local councils (eight per region) and eight appointed by the president. The terms for all members of the National Assembly are four years.

The president, elected directly every five years, is head of state. Executive power resides with a cabinet of ministers under a chairman appointed by the president, subject to ratification by the House of Representatives.

Belgium

Parliamentary monarchy with a constitution adopted in 1831 but subsequently considerably revised. Legislative power is exercised by a bicameral parliament and the monarch who is head of state. Parliament comprises the Chamber of Representatives with 150 members, elected by proportional representation, and a Senate with 71 members, of whom 40 are elected directly by proportional representation and 10 are appointed by the elected senators, 21 appointed by the assemblies of the three linguistic communities. Children of the monarch are also entitled to honorary membership of the Senate. Members of both houses are elected for terms of up to four years. Supreme executive power is nominally held by the monarch but is exercised by a cabinet headed by a prime minister. Considerable autonomy is exercised by assemblies representing the three regions of Flanders, Wallonia and Brussels, and the three linguistic communities.

Bosnia

Presidential republic with a constitution adopted in 1994 and amended to incorporate the terms of the Dayton peace agreement and the division of the country into a Serb republic and a Croat-Muslim federation. A president is head of state and is one of three members of a rotating presidency representing Croats, Muslims and Serbs, elected directly for terms of four years. A bicameral parliament comprises the 42-member, directly elected Chamber of Representatives (made up one-third of Serbs and two-thirds of Croats and Muslims) and the 15-member Chamber of Peoples, comprises five members representing each community, elected by sub-national self-governing ethnic assemblies. Both houses are elected for two-year terms by a system of proportional representation. The central government is responsible for defence, commerce and foreign affairs.

At sub-national level the Croat-Muslim federation has a president (alternately Croat and Muslim) and a bicameral legislative assembly, comprising the 140-member Chamber of Representatives and the 42-member Chamber of Peoples, both elected for terms of two years by a system of proportional representation.

The Serb Republic has a unicameral 83-member legislature and a president elected for two-year terms by a system of proportional representation.

Bulgaria

Parliamentary republic with a constitution adopted in 1991. The single chamber National Assembly holds legislative power. It has 240 members elected for four-year terms. Executive power is exercised by a council of ministers headed by a chairman who is also prime minister. A president, who is directly elected as head of state for five years, appoints the prime minister, usually from one of the two largest parties.

Croatia

Presidential republic with a constitution adopted in 1990. The assembly (*Sabor*) exercises legislative power through the Chamber of Representatives (*Zastupnicki dom*) and the Chamber of Counties (*Zupanijski dom*), both of which are directly elected for four-year terms. The former comprises 80 members; the latter has 68 members, five appointed by the president. The president, prime minister and ministers have executive authority. The prime minister and members of the government are appointed by the president and are responsible both to the president and the Chamber of Representatives. The president is elected directly for five-year terms and is head of state.

Cyprus

The island of Cyprus is divided between two administrations. The southern (Greek-Cypriot) presidential republic has an executive president who exercises power through a council of ministers. The legislative House of Representatives nominally contains 80 members according to the 1960 power-sharing constitution but in 1963 the 24 members elected by the Turkish-Cypriot minority stopped attending. Members are elected for five-year terms by proportional representation.

The Turkish Republic of Northern Cyprus, which is not recognised internationally, has a 50-seat Legislative Assembly and an executive president as head of state who exercises power through a council of ministers.

Czech Republic

Parliamentary republic with a constitution adopted in 1992. A bicameral legislature consists of the 200-member Chamber of Deputies, elected for four-year terms, and an 81-member Senate directly elected for six-year terms. The president is head of state and is elected by a joint session of both chambers for five years. Executive power is vested in a council of ministers under a prime minister appointed by the president.

Denmark

Parliamentary monarchy with a constitution adopted in 1849 and last revised in 1953. A unicameral parliament (*Folketing*) holds legislative power jointly with the monarch though the latter's powers are nominal.

100-member upper chamber (*Senat*) and a 460-member lower chamber (*Sejm*).Both are elected for terms of four years, the latter by a system of proportional representation. A president is head of state and is elected directly for terms of five years.

Portugal

Parliamentary republic with a constitution adopted in 1976 and revised fundamentally in 1982. Legislative authority is vested in a unicameral assembly comprising between 230 and 235 members elected for four-year terms by a system of proportional representation. Executive authority resides with a prime minister appointed by a president, and a council of ministers appointed by the president on the recommendation of the prime minister. The president, who is elected directly for five years, is head of state.

Romania

Presidential republic with a constitution adopted in 1991. Legislative authority is the responsibility of a bicameral parliament comprising the 343-member Chamber of Deputies and the 143-member Senate. Members of both houses are elected for terms of four years by a system of proportional representation. A president has executive authority and is directly elected for four-year terms. As head of state the president appoints a prime minister who in turn appoints a council of ministers.

Russia

Presidential republic with a constitution adopted in 1993. A bicameral federal assembly is the supreme legislative body comprising a 178-member upper chamber, the Federation Council, and a 450-member lower chamber (*Duma*). The Federation Council is appointed by regional assemblies: two members from each territorial unit. The lower chamber is elected directly for terms of four years. A president, directly elected for four-year terms, is head of state and holds executive authority in tandem with a prime minister and ministers. The prime minister and ministers have competence in budgetary matters and law and order. The president appoints the prime minister with the approval of the lower chamber.

San Marino

Parliamentary republic with a constitution which has evolved from San Marino's 12th century origins. Legislative authority is vested in the Great and General Council, comprising 60 members, elected for five-year terms by a system of proportional representation. Two Captains-Regent are elected by the council every six months to serve as joint heads of state. The council also elects a ten-member Congress of State with concurrent terms which has executive authority.

Serbia

Federal republic with a constitution adopted in 1992 to cover Serbia and Montenegro – the rump of the Federal Republic of Yugoslavia. Legislative authority resides with a bicameral federal assembly. The Chamber of Citizens contains 138 members directly elected for terms of four years; the Chamber of the Republics has 40 members, 20 each from Serbia and Montenegro. A federal president is head of state and is elected for a four-year term by a joint session of the federal assembly. The president is responsible for appointing a federal prime minister. Legislative authority is shared with the directly elected assemblies of Serbia and Montenegro. The republics also have their own elected executive presidents.

Slovakia

Parliamentary republic with a constitution adopted in 1992. The National Council for the Slovak Republic has supreme legislative authority, comprising a single chamber of 150 members elected directly for terms of four years. Executive power is vested in a prime minister and ministers responsible to the National Council. A president is elected by the National Council for five years and is head of state.

Slovenia

Parliamentary republic with a constitution adopted in 1991. Legislative authority resides with a unicameral national assembly (*Drzavni Zbor*) comprising 90 members serving terms of four years. Of these 88 are elected by simple majority. The remaining two represent the minority ethnic Italian and Hungarian communities. Some legislative powers are shared with a national council (*Drzavni Svet*) comprising 18 members appointed by an electoral college representing social, economic and local interest-groups and 22 members directly elected for five-year terms. Executive authority is vested in a prime minister, elected by a majority vote of the national assembly, and ministers appointed by the national assembly on the prime minister's recommendation. The head of state is a president who is directly elected for five years but whose powers are largely nominal.

Spain

Parliamentary monarchy with a constitution adopted in 1978. A bicameral parliament (*Cortes Generales*) is the legislative authority with both chambers elected for four-year terms. The senate contains 256 members, 208 directly elected, the remainder elected by the regional assemblies. The Congress of Deputies has 350 members elected by proportional representation. Executive power is in the hands of a prime minister and a council of ministers appointed by the monarch, who is head of state.

Sweden

Parliamentary monarchy with a constitution adopted in 1975 formalising and revising former basic laws which previously served as a constitution. A unicameral parliament (*Riksdag*) holds legislative power, comprising 349 members elected for four-year terms by a system of proportional representation. Executive authority rests with a cabinet (*Regeringen*) headed by a prime minister nominated by the speaker and subject to the approval of parliament. The monarch is head of state but has only a limited ceremonial role.

Switzerland
Federal republic with a constitution adopted in 1874. The legislature, a bicameral federal assembly, comprises the Council of States and the National Council. The former contains 46 members elected for three- to four-year terms, two members from each of the 23 Cantons (three cantons are divided, so each half Canton sends one member). The latter contains 200 members elected for terms of four years by proportional representation. Executive authority resides with a federal council of 7 members elected for four years by the federal assembly. One member of the federal council is then elected president of the confederation by the federal assembly for a one-year term and is head of state. Each Canton has its own legislature and executive power is devolved further by the relative ease with which referendums can be called to propose or mandate legislation.

Turkey
Presidential republic with a constitution adopted in 1982. The unicameral Turkish Grand National Assembly holds legislative authority; its 550 members are directly elected for five-year terms. A president, who holds executive power and is head of state, is elected for a seven-year term by the assembly.

Ukraine
Presidential republic with a constitution adopted in 1996. Legislative authority is vested in the 450-member Supreme Council elected directly for four-year terms. Executive authority is jointly held by a prime minister and a president, who is directly elected for five years and appoints the prime minister and cabinet. The president is head of state.

United Kingdom
Parliamentary monarchy without a formal written constitution. The system of government is defined by convention, the common law, acts of parliament and tradition. Legislative authority is vested in a bicameral parliament. The pre-eminent chamber, the House of Commons, contains 659 members elected directly for five years, though elections can be held more frequently. The upper chamber, the House of Lords, has power to delay or modify legislation. Executive power is vested in a prime minister, usually the leader of the largest party in the House of Commons, who appoints a cabinet. The monarch is head of state. Scotland and Wales now have their own elected parliaments. Scotland's has 129 members with some legislative and tax-raising autonomy, Wales's 60-member assembly has not and the extent of its powers remains unclear. An assembly was re-established for Northern Ireland in 1999.

Vatican City
The Vatican city state was established in 1929 by the Lateran Treaty. The Pope, who is head of state and head of the Roman Catholic church, is appointed for life by a college of cardinals appointed by his predecessors. Cardinals appointed to the Vatican (*in curia*) administer the church while a pontifical commission under a president administers the state itself.

Defence

Spending on defence

	\$bn (1995 prices)		% of GDP	
	1985	*1998*	*1985*	*1998*
NATO Europe				
Belgium	5.6	3.7	3.0	1.5
Denmark	2.9	2.8	2.2	1.6
France	44.6	39.8	4.0	2.8
Germany	48.1	32.4	3.2	1.5
Greece	3.2	5.7	7.0	4.8
Italy	23.5	22.6	2.3	2.0
Luxembourg	0.1	0.1	0.9	0.9
Netherlands	8.1	6.6	3.1	1.8
Norway	2.8	3.1	3.1	2.2
Portugal	1.7	2.3	3.1	2.3
Spain	10.3	7.3	2.4	1.3
Turkey	3.1	8.2	4.5	4.4
United Kingdom	43.5	36.6	5.2	2.8
Total	**197.5**	**176.5**	**3.1**	**2.2**
Non-NATO Europe				
Albania	0.3	0.1	5.3	6.6
Armenia	…	0.1	…	8.4
Austria	1.8	1.8	1.2	0.8
Azerbaijan	…	0.2	…	4.6
Belarus	…	0.5	…	3.2
Bosnia	…	0.4	…	8.1
Bulgaria	7.9	0.4	6.6	3.7
Croatia	…	1.4	…	8.3
Cyprus	0.1	0.5	3.6	5.5
Czech Republic[a]	…	1.1	…	2.1
Estonia	…	0.1	…	1.3
Finland	2.1	1.9	2.8	1.5
Macedonia	…	0.1	…	9.9
Georgia	…	0.1	…	2.5
Hungary[a]	3.2	0.6	7.2	1.4
Ireland	0.4	0.8	1.8	1.0
Latvia	…	0.2	…	2.5
Lithuania	…	0.1	…	1.3
Malta		0.0		0.9
Moldova		0.1		4.3
Poland[a]	7.9	3.4	8.1	2.2
Romania	1.9	0.9	4.5	2.3
Slovakia	…	0.4	…	2.0
Slovenia	…	0.4	…	1.7
Sweden	4.4	5.5	3.3	2.5
Switzerland	2.6	3.6	2.1	1.4
Ukraine	…	1.4	…	2.9
Russia	…	53.9	…	5.2
Serbia & Montenegro	…	1.5	…	9.1

Armed forces
'000s

	1985	1998		1985	1998
NATO Europe					
Belgium	91.6	43.7	Netherlands	105.5	57.2
Denmark	29.6	32.1	Norway	37	28.9
France	464.3	358.8	Portugal	73	53.6
Germany	478	333.5	Spain	320	194.0
Greece	201.5	168.5	Turkey	630	639.0
Italy	385.1	298.4	United Kingdom	327.1	210.9
Luxembourg	0.7	0.8	**Total**	**3,143.40**	**2,419.4**

	1985	1998		1985	1998
Non-NATO Europe					
Albania	40.4	54.0	Ireland	13.7	11.5
Armenia	...	53.4	Latvia	...	5.0
Austria	54.7	45.5	Lithuania	...	11.1
Azerbaijan	...	72.2	Malta	0.8	1.9
Belarus	...	83.0	Moldova	...	11.1
Bosnia	...	40.0	Poland	319	240.7
Bulgaria	148.5	101.5	Romania	189.5	219.7
Croatia	...	56.2	Russia	...	1,159.0
Cyprus	10	10.0	Serbia & Mont	...	114.2
Czech Republic	...	59.1	Slovakia	...	45.5
Estonia	36.5	4.3	Slovenia	...	9.6
Finland	...	31.7	Sweden	65.7	53.1
Hungary	106	43.3	Switzerland	20	26.3
Macedonia	...	20.0	Ukraine	...	346.4
Georgia	...	33.2			

Conscripts
1998

1	Turkey	528,000	18	Czech Republic	25,000
2	Russia	330,000	19	Finland	23,100
3	Ukraine	301,000	20	Hungary	22,900
4	Germany	142,000	21	Austria	16,600
5	Poland	141,600	22	Norway	16,500
6	Italy	126,100	23	Georgia	16,000
7	Romania	108,600	24	Slovakia	13,600
8	Greece	105,820	25	Cyprus	8,700
9	France	103,500	26	Macedonia	8,000
10	Spain	102,700	27	Denmark	7,880
11	Azerbaijan	57,000	28	Portugal	6,470
12	Bulgaria	49,800	29	Moldova	5,200
13	Armenia	45,000	30	Slovenia	4,200
14	Serbia	43,000	31	Lithuania	3,560
15	Belarus	40,000	32	Estonia	2,870
16	Sweden	35,600	33	Latvia	2,120
17	Croatia	30,000			

a Joined NATO in 1999.

Military equipment

1998	Tanks	Combat aircraft
Armenia	102	6
Austria	285	24
Azerbaijan	262	48
Belarus	1,778	252
Belgium	155	137
Bulgaria	1,475	233
Croatia	301	44
Cyprus	145	3
Czech Republic	938	114
Denmark	337	76
Estonia	0	3
Finland	230	85
France	1,207	596
Georgia	79	7
Germany	3,096	534
Greece	1,735	522
Hungary	807	136
Ireland	14	7
Italy	1,256	535
Latvia	0	3
Lithuania	0	0
Macedonia	4	14
Malta	0	0
Moldova	0	0
Netherlands	359	164
Norway	170	73
Poland	1,675	298
Portugal	187	101
Romania	1,373	360
Russia	5,510	2,870
Serbia & Montenegro	1,310	238
Slovakia	478	94
Slovenia	96	0
Spain	676	201
Sweden	748	253
Switzerland	769	171
Turkey	2,554	346
Ukraine	4,014	964
United Kingdom	542	533

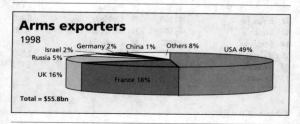

Arms exporters

1998

Israel 2% Germany 2% China 1% Others 8% USA 49%
Russia 5%
UK 16%
France 18%

Total = $55.8bn

Part XI
THE EUROPEAN UNION

Members and votes

Who joined what when

ECSC 1951	EEC Treaty of Rome 1957	EC 1973
Belgium	Belgium	Denmark
W. Germany	W. Germany	Ireland
France	France	United Kingdom
Italy	Italy	
Luxembourg	Luxembourg	
Netherlands	Netherlands	

EC 1981	EC 1986	EC 1990	EU 1995
Greece	Spain	E. Germany	Austria
	Portugal		Finland
			Sweden

Other applicants: Morocco and Turkey (1987), Malta and Cyprus* (1990), Norway (1961, 1967, 1992), Switzerland (1992), Hungary* and Poland* (1994), Bulgaria, Estonia*, Latvia, Lithuania, Romania and Slovakia (1995), Czech Republic* and Slovenia* (1996). (*Negotiations for accession opened.)

Presidency of the Council
Held for 6 months

	Jan–Jun	Jul–Dec
2000	Portugal	France
2001	Sweden	Belgium
2002	Spain	Denmark
2003	Greece	

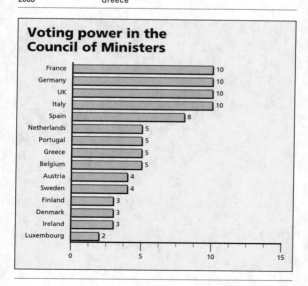

Voting power in the Council of Ministers

Country	Votes
France	10
Germany	10
UK	10
Italy	10
Spain	8
Netherlands	5
Portugal	5
Greece	5
Belgium	5
Austria	4
Sweden	4
Finland	3
Denmark	3
Ireland	3
Luxembourg	2

A question of identity

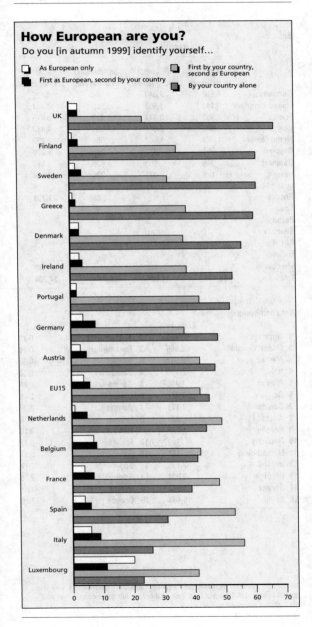

How European are you?
Do you [in autumn 1999] identify yourself...

- ☐ As European only
- ■ First as European, second by your country
- ☐ First by your country, second as European
- ☐ By your country alone

Budget contributions

Who pays what and receives what
Ecus, m

	1980		1985	
	Contributions to Brussels	Receipts from Brussels	Contributions to Brussels	Receipts from Brussels
Germany	4,610	2,940	7,504	4,185
United Kingdom	3,168	1,803	5,090	3,107
France	2,992	3,372	5,319	5,416
Italy	1,929	2,611	3,630	4,480
Netherlands	1,273	1,667	1,889	2,232
Belgium	951	677	1,293	1,070
Denmark	346	680	620	913
Ireland	139	827	296	1,549
Luxembourg	20	15	51	9
Greece	...	...	388	1,703
Spain	...	...	...	...
Portugal	...	...	...	...
Sweden	...	...	...	...
Austria	...	...	...	...
Finland	...	...	...	...
Miscellaneous	...	12	...	40
Total	**15,428**	**14,604**	**26,080**	**24,704**

Accounting budgetary balances, 1997
Net contributions

		Ecus, m			% of GDP
1	Germany	10,466	1	Netherlands	0.78
2	United Kingdom	5,659	2	Luxembourg	0.70
3	Netherlands	3,047	3	Belgium	0.55
4	Italy	2,110	4	Sweden	0.50
5	France	1,718	5	Germany	0.48
6	Belgium	1,427	6	United Kingdom	0.45
7	Sweden	1,123	7	Austria	0.38
8	Austria	823	8	Finland	0.18
9	Finland	229		Italy	0.18
10	Denmark	193	10	France	0.12
11	Luxembourg	134	11	Denmark	0.11
12	Ireland	-2,135	12	Spain	-1.17
13	Portugal	-2,824	13	Portugal	-2.65
14	Greece	-4,567	14	Ireland	-3.08
15	Spain	-6,483	15	Greece	-3.70

Note: Presentational changes in the EU budget mean that different years are not strictly comparable. On top of contributions there are other revenue sources and carried-over annual surpluses.

1990		1998	
Contributions to Brussels	Receipts from Brussels	Contributions to Brussels	Receipts from Brussels
10,358	4,807	20,633	10,167
6,534	3,147	12,537	6,878
8,090	6,285	13,584	11,866
6,098	5,681	10,581	8,471
2,615	2,984	5,105	2,058
1,764	990	3,131	1,704
775	1,198	1,695	1,502
368	2,261	985	3,120
75	14	217	83
564	3,034	1,310	5,877
3,671	5,383	5,752	12,235
502	1,103	1,105	3,929
...	...	2,383	1,260
...	...	2,086	1,263
...	...	1,146	917
...	391		5,164
41,413	**37,278**	**82,249**	**76,494**

% shares of

		Financing			GDP
1	Germany	25.1	1 Germany		26.0
2	France	16.5	2 France		17.5
3	United Kingdom	15.2	3 United Kingdom		15.1
4	Italy	12.9	4 Italy		13.8
5	Spain	7.0	5 Spain		6.6
6	Netherlands	6.2	6 Netherlands		4.6
7	Belgium	3.8	7 Belgium		3.1
8	Sweden	2.9	8 Sweden		2.7
9	Austria	2.5	9 Austria		2.6
10	Denmark	2.1	10 Denmark		2.1
11	Greece	1.6	11 Finland		1.5
12	Finland	1.4		Greece	1.5
13	Portugal	1.3	13 Portugal		1.3
14	Ireland	1.2	14 Ireland		0.8
15	Luxembourg	0.3	15 Luxembourg		0.2

Budget breakdown

Payments to member states by sector

	ecus, m	% of total
1998		
EAGGF-Guarantee	39,148	44.2
Structural operations	33,377	37.6
Administration	4,425	5.0
External actions	5,643	6.4
Internal policies	5,702	6.4
Repayment, guarantees, reserves	371	0.4
Total	**88,665**	**100.0**
1990		
EAGGF-Guarantee	24,980	57.7
Structural operations	10,368	23.9
Repayment, guarantees, reserves	2,381	5.5
Administration	2,298	5.3
Research and technological development	1,429	3.3
Co-operation	1,225	2.8
Training, youth and social operations	334	0.8
Energy, environment, internal market	309	0.7
Total	**43,325**	**100.0**
1985		
EAGGF-Guarantee	19,726	70.2
Regional policy and transport	1,726	6.2
Social policy	1,491	5.3
Administration	1,296	4.6
Repayments	1,248	4.4
Co-operation with developing countries	1,085	3.9
Agricultural structures, fisheries	820	2.9
Research, energy etc	708	2.5
Total	**28,099**	**100.0**
1980		
EAGGF-Guarantee	11,283	69.3
Regional policy and transport	1,103	6.8
Repayments	846	5.2
Administration	820	5.0
Social policy	772	4.7
Agricultural structures, fisheries	646	4.0
Co-operation with developing countries	509	3.1
Research, energy etc	312	1.9
Total	**16,290**	**100.0**

EAGGF is the European Agricultural Guidance and Guarantee Fund.

Where the money comes from
Ecus, m

1998	
Agricultural levies	1,102
Sugar and isoglucose levies	1,070
Customs duties	13,506
VAT own resources	33,086
GNP resources	35,052
Costs incurred in collection	-1,568
Total	**82,249**

1990	
Agricultural levies	1,173
Sugar and isoglucose levies	911
Customs duties	11,428
VAT own resources	28,968
GNP resources	285
Costs incurred in collection	-1,351
Total	**41,413**

1985	
Agricultural levies	1,122
Sugar and isoglucose levies	1,057
Customs duties	8,310
VAT own resources	15,592
Total	**26,080**

1980	
Agricultural levies	1,535
Sugar and isoglucose levies	467
Customs duties	5,906
VAT own resources	7,520
Total	**15,428**

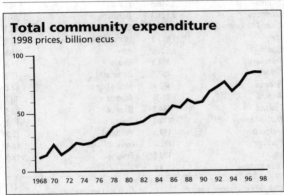

Total community expenditure
1998 prices, billion ecus

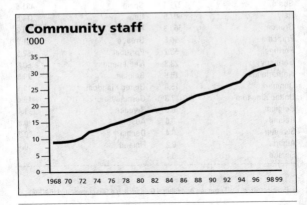

Community staff
'000

Agricultural and regional aid

Agricultural aid by product[a]
Ecus, m

	1980	1985	1990	1998
Cereals and oilseeds	1,719	2,360	3,881	17,945
Sugar	575	1,804	1,388	1,777
Fats and protein	748	2,174	5,482	2,644
Fruit and vegetables	687	1,231	1,253	1,510
Wine	300	921	745	700
Tobacco	309	863	1,232	870
Milk products	4,752	5,933	4,895	2,597
Meat, eggs, poultry	1,618	3,477	4,711	7,023
Other	576	963	2,356	3,682
Total	**11,284**	**19,726**	**24,980**	**38,748**

Who got what for what
Ecus, m, 1998

Cereals and oilseeds		Sugar	
France	5,416.5	France	578.6
Germany	3,927.7	Germany	257.1
United Kingdom	1,953.6	Belgium	218.1
Italy	1,951.2	United Kingdom	208.0
Spain	1,681.6	Italy	185.9
Denmark	684.9	Spain	74.9
Sweden	490.8	Denmark	73.3
Greece	462.4	Netherlands	64.6
Austria	387.8	Austria	30.7
Finland	264.3	Greece	23.1
Netherlands	218.4	Sweden	19.1
Belgium	182.8	Portugal	15.2
Portugal	182.7	Ireland	14.4
Ireland	130.8	Finland	13.6
Luxembourg	9.8		

Oils, fats and protein plants		Fruit and vegetables	
Spain	1,271.4	Spain	491.5
Italy	607.5	Italy	314.5
Greece	550.3	France	294.2
France	96.8	Greece	251.2
Portugal	53.2	Portugal	52.5
Germany	23.3	Netherlands	50.8
Netherlands	15.9	Belgium	20.8
Denmark	15.8	United Kingdom	16.1
United Kingdom	7.3	Germany	15.4
Belgium	0.5	Sweden	1.4
Ireland	0.5	Austria	0.8
Sweden	0.4	Denmark	0.2
Austria	0.2	Finland	0.1
Finland	0.1		

a Payments from the European Agricultural Guidance and Guarantee Fund (EAGGF).

Wine		Tobacco	
Spain	238.2	Greece	365.8
Italy	225.7	Italy	260.0
France	195.7	Spain	107.4
Portugal	26.7	France	79.8
Greece	11.5	Germany	29.5
United Kingdom	0.8	Portugal	19.8
Germany	0.7	Belgium	3.2
Austria	0.3	Austria	0.7
Netherlands	0.2		
Luxembourg	0.1		
Sweden	0.1		

Milk products		Meat, eggs, poultry	
France	692.4	United Kingdom	1,664.1
Netherlands	619.4	France	1,377.5
Germany	261.5	Ireland	979.2
United Kingdom	225.0	Spain	881.5
Denmark	198.8	Germany	617.4
Belgium	194.7	Italy	377.2
Ireland	191.6	Netherlands	276.7
Italy	95.2	Greece	195.7
Finland	78.3	Belgium	163.0
Sweden	26.5	Portugal	136.3
Spain	14.4	Austria	121.8
Portugal	2.1	Denmark	105.9
Luxembourg	-0.9	Sweden	78.9
Greece	-1.1	Finland	41.8
Austria	-1.1	Luxembourg	6.3

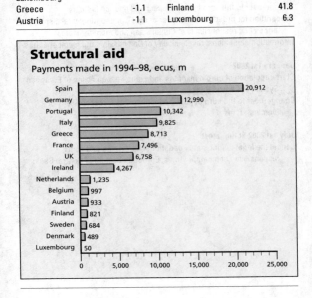

Structural aid

Payments made in 1994–98, ecus, m

Spain	20,912
Germany	12,990
Portugal	10,342
Italy	9,825
Greece	8,713
France	7,496
UK	6,758
Ireland	4,267
Netherlands	1,235
Belgium	997
Austria	933
Finland	821
Sweden	684
Denmark	489
Luxembourg	50

The euro

Fixed conversion rates for participants
Dec 31st 1998
1 euro =

Belgian franc	40.3399	Luxembourg franc	40.3399
D-mark	1.95583	Guilder	2.20371
Peseta	166.386	Schilling	13.7603
French franc	6.55957	Escudo	200.482
Punt	0.787564	Markka	5.94573
Italian lira	1936.27		

What's to happen when

In place or under way since January 1st 1999
Conversion rates irrevocably fixed; responsibility of Council (based on Commission proposal)

Single monetary policy in euro; responsibility of European System of Central Banks

Foreign exchange operations in euro; responsibility of European System of Central Banks

Public debt issues in euro, some outstanding debt redenominated in euro; responsibility of member states, European Investment Bank, Commission and other issuers

Many large companies begin issuing invoices and making payments in euro; responsibility of member states, European Investment Bank, Commission and other issuers

Banks begin converting payments in national currency units into euro for euro accounts; responsibility of member states, European Investment Bank, Commission and other issuers

Change-over to the euro by the banking and finance industry

Preparation for orderly change-over of eg, IT, accounting, dual display of prices etc; responsibility of Commission and member states

Information campaigns; responsibility of Commission and member states

January 1st 2002
Start circulation of euro banknotes and coins; responsibility of European System of Central Banks

Change-over to the euro of public administrations; responsibility of member states

July 1st 2002 at the latest
Cancel the legal tender status of national banknotes and coins; responsibility of member states, European System of Central Banks

A bumpy start

1 euro =	Sterling	Swedish krone	Danish krone	Greek drachma	US dollar
1999					
Jan 1st	0.71	9.52	7.47	329	1.17
Feb 1st	0.69	8.84	7.44	321	1.13
Mar 1st	0.68	9.00	7.43	322	1.09
Apr 1st	0.67	8.89	7.43	326	1.08
May 1st	0.66	8.95	7.43	325	1.06
Jun 1st	0.65	8.98	7.43	324	1.05
Jul 1st	0.65	8.74	7.44	325	1.02
Aug 1st	0.66	8.75	7.44	326	1.07
Sept 1st	0.66	8.70	7.43	326	1.06
Oct 1st	0.65	8.74	7.43	329	1.07
Nov 1st	0.64	8.67	7.43	329	1.05
Dec 1st	0.63	8.62	7.44	329	1.01
2000					
Jan 1st	0.63	8.57	7.44	330	1.02
Feb 1st	0.60	8.55	7.44	332	0.97
Mar 1st	0.61	8.43	7.45	334	0.97
Apr 1st	0.60	8.30	7.45	335	0.96
May 1st	0.58	8.14	7.46	336	0.91
June 1st	0.62	8.34	7.47	337	0.93

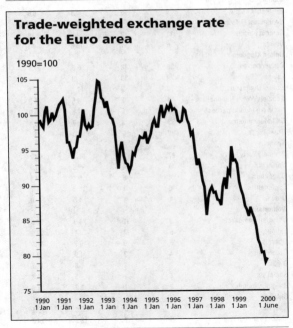

Trade-weighted exchange rate for the Euro area

1990=100

The European Parliament

The 1999 election results

Party	Seats	Gain/loss	% vote 1999	% vote in previous Euro-election
Germany				
Christian Democrats/CSU	53	6	48.7	38.8
Social Democrats	33	-7	30.7	32.2
Greens	7	-5	6.4	10.1
ex-Communists	6	6	5.8	4.7
France				
Socialists/Radicals	22	-6	22	26.5
Anti-EU Gaullists	13	0	13	12.3
Gaullists/Liberal Democrats	12	} -8[a]	12.7	} 25.5[a]
UDF (centrists)	9		9.3	
Greens	9	9	9.7	2.9
Communists	6	0	6.8	6.9
Hunters' party	6	6	6.8	3.9
National Front	5	-5	5.7	10.5
Workers Struggle	5	5	5.2	0
Italy				
Forza Italia	22	-5	25.2	30.6
Left Democrats	15	-1	17.4	19.1
National Alliance	9	-2	10.3	12.5
Emma Bonino List	7	5	8.5	2.1
Democrats	7	7	7.7	0
Northern League	4	-2	4.5	6.6
Communist Refoundation	6	1	4.3	6.1
Centrist parties	11	3	4.3	10
Others	6	-7	15.8	13
United Kingdom				
Conservatives	36	18	35.8	27.8
Labour	29	-33	28	44.2
Liberal Democrats	10	8	12.7	16.7
Scottish/Welsh Nationalists	4	2	4.5	4.5
Northern Ireland parties	3	0	1.8	0.9
UK Independence	3	3	7	0.4
Greens	2	2	6.3	3.2
Spain				
People's Party	27	-1	39.7	40.2
Socialists	26	4	35.3	30.6
Communists	4	-5	5.8	13.4
Regionalists	6	1	15.3	11.1
Greens	1	1	4.5	0
Netherlands				
Christian Democrats	9	-1	26.9	30.8
Labour	6	-2	20.1	22.9
Liberals	6	0	19.7	17.9
Green Left	4	3	11.9	3.7
D-66	2	-2	5.8	11.7
Socialists	1	1	5	1.3
Religious parties	3	1	8.7	7.8
Belgium				
Liberals	6	0	23.5	20.5
Christian Democrats	5	-2	18.9	24.3

Socialists	5	-1	18.8	22.3
Greens	5	3	15.8	11.5
Flemish nationalist parties	4	0	16.4	15.1
Greece				
New Democracy	9	0	36	32.7
Socialists	9	-1	32.9	37.6
Communists	3	1	8.7	6.3
Other left parties	5	3	12	6.2
Portugal				
Socialists	12	2	43.1	34.7
Social Democrats (centre-right)	9	0	31.1	34.3
Communist coalition	2	-1	10.3	11.2
Popular Party/CDS	2	-1	8.2	12.4
Sweden				
Social Democrats	6	-1	26.1	28.1
Moderates	5	0	20.6	23.2
Liberals	3	2	13.8	4.8
Left	3	0	15.8	12.9
Greens	2	-2	9.4	17.2
Others	3	1	13.8	14.2
Austria				
Social Democrats	7	1	31.7	29.1
People's Party	7	0	30.7	29.6
Freedom Party	5	-1	23.5	27.6
Greens	2	1	9.3	6.7
Denmark				
Liberals	5	1	23.3	18.9
Social Democrats	3	0	16.5	15.8
Anti-EU parties	4	0	23.4	25.5
Conservatives	1	-2	8.5	17.7
Radicals	1	0	9.1	8.5
Socialists	1	0	7.1	8.6
Far-right	1	1	5.8	2.9
Finland				
Conservatives	4	0	25.3	20.2
Centre	4	0	21.3	24.4
Social Democrats	3	-1	17.8	21.5
Greens	2	1	13.4	7.6
Ex-Communists	1	-1	9.1	10.5
Others	2	1	9.2	8.6
Ireland				
Fianna Fail	6	-1	38.7	35
Fine Gael	4	0	24.6	24.3
Greens	2	0	6.7	3.7
Progressive Democrats	1	0	4.6	6.5
Labour	1	0	8.8	11
Independent	1	1	3.7	NA
Luxembourg				
Christian Democrats	2	0	31.9	31.5
Socialists	2	0	23.2	24.8
Liberals	1	0	20.8	18.8
Greens	1	0	10.7	10.9

a Run as joint list.

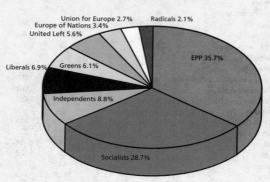

Parliamentary divisions

% of seats held by political groups, June 1999

- Union for Europe 2.7%
- Radicals 2.1%
- Europe of Nations 3.4%
- United Left 5.6%
- Liberals 6.9%
- Greens 6.1%
- Independents 8.8%
- EPP 35.7%
- Socialists 28.7%

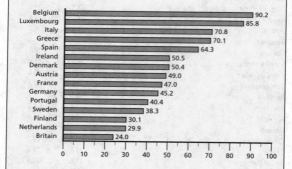

VOTER TURNOUT, %

Country	%
Belgium	90.2
Luxembourg	85.8
Italy	70.8
Greece	70.1
Spain	64.3
Ireland	50.5
Denmark	50.4
Austria	49.0
France	47.0
Germany	45.2
Portugal	40.4
Sweden	38.3
Finland	30.1
Netherlands	29.9
Britain	24.0

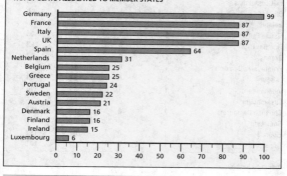

NO. OF SEATS ALLOCATED TO MEMBER STATES

Germany	99
France	87
Italy	87
UK	87
Spain	64
Netherlands	31
Belgium	25
Greece	25
Portugal	24
Sweden	22
Austria	21
Denmark	16
Finland	16
Ireland	15
Luxembourg	6

Sources

Land and the environment
Cassell, *What's what and who's who in Europe*
Europa Publications, *Europa World Yearbook*
Eurostat, *Yearbook*
John Wiley & Sons, *World Facts & Figures*
OECD, *Environmental Data, 1999*
Helicon, *The World Weather Guide* by E.A. Pearce and C.G. Smith
World Bank, *World Development Indicators*
World Resources Institute, *World Resources 1998–99*

Population
Central Intelligence Agency, *World Factbook*
Europa Publications, *Europa World Yearbook*
European Commission
Eurostat, *Social Portrait of Europe*
National statistics
Statesman's Yearbook
Summer Institute of Linguistics, *Ethnologue*
United Nations, *World Population Prospects; World Urbanization Prospects*
World Bank, *World Development Indicators*

The economy
BP, *Statistical Review of World Energy*
Central Intelligence Agency, *World Factbook*
Economist Intelligence Unit, *Country Reports; Country Forecasts*
European Bank for Reconstruction and Development, *Transition Report*
Eurostat, *External and Intra-EU Trade; Statistics in Focus*
International Monetary Fund, *International Financial Statistics; Direction of Trade Statistics*
OECD, *National Accounts; Monthly Statistics of Foreign Trade*
Primark Datastream
Taiwan Statistical Data Book
United Nations, *Energy Statistics Yearbook*
World Bank, *Monitoring Environmental Progress; World Development Indicators*
World Trade Organisation, *International Trade Statistics*

Government finance
International Monetary Fund, *International Financial Statistics*
OECD, *Development Co-operation Revenue Statistics; Tax/Benefit Position of Production Workers*
World Bank, *World Development Report; Global Development Finance; World Development Indicators*

Labour
Economist Intelligence Unit, *Country Reports*
International Labour Organisation, *Yearbook of Labour Statistics; World Labour Report*
International Metalworkers' Federation
KPMG, www.tax.kpmg.net
OECD, *Employment Outlook; Labour Force Statistics; Tax Database; Tax/Benefit Position of Production Workers; Taxing Wages*
UK National Statistics, *Labour Market Trends*
Union Bank of Switzerland, *Prices and Earnings around the World*
World Bank, *World Development Report*

Business and finance
Economist Intelligence Unit, *World Car Forecasts; Motor Business Europe; ebusinessforum.com*
Euromonitor, *European Marketing Data and Statistics*
European Commission, *European Economy*
Financial Times Business Information, *The Banker*
Food and Agriculture Organisation, www.fao.org
IMD, *World Competitive Yearbook; Competitiveness Yearbook*
International Finance Corporation, *Emerging Markets Factbook*
International Iron and Steel Institute
International Labour Organisation, *Yearbook of Labour Statistics*
Legalease, *The European Legal 500*
Lloyd's Register, *World Shipbuilding Statistics; World Fleet Statistics*
Privatisation International, London
Swiss Re
Time Inc Magazines, *Fortune*
UNCTAD, *World Investment Report*
United Nations, *Monthly Bulletin of Statistics*

World Tourism Organisation,
www.world-tourism.org

Tourism and transport
Airports Council International
International Civil Aviation Organisation
(ICAO)
International Road Federation, *Road
Transport Statistics*
Lloyd's Register, *World Fleet Statistics*
Rail Europe, *European Rail Fares &
Schedule Information*
World Tourist Organisation, *Yearbook
of Tourism Statistics*

Health and education
ERC, *World Cigarettes: The 1997 Survey*
European Centre for the
Epidemiological Monitoring of AIDS,
HIV/AIDS Surveillance in Europe
NTC Publications in association with
Produktschap voor Gedistilleerde
Dranken, *World Drink Trends*
The State of the World's Children 2000
UNESCO, *World Education Report;
Statistical Yearbook*
Unicef, The State of the World's
Children, 2000
United Nations, *World Population
Prospects; Demographic Yearbook;
Statistical Yearbook*
World Health Organisation, Europe,
Health For All Database

Society
The Economist
Eurolink Age
Euromonitor, *World Consumer Markets;
The World Market for Petfood*
Eurosecretariat of the national Danish
organisation for gays and lesbians
(LBL), *Euroletter*

International Planned Parenthood
Federation
International Federation of
Phonographic Industry, *The
Recording Industry in Numbers*
International Telecommunication
Union, website www.itu.int/ri/
industryoverview/index.htm
Interpol, *International Crime
Statistics*
Network Wizards, www.nw.com
OECD, *Employment Outlook*
Penal Reform International
Reader's Digest
Screen International
Stonewall
UNESCO, www.unesco.org; *Yearbook*
World Bank, *World Development
Report*

Government and defence
Embassies
Europa Publications, *Europa World
Yearbook*
International Institute for Strategic
Studies, *The Military Balance*

The European Union
DBS, *The European Companion*
The Economist, June 12th, 19th, 1999
European Commission, *Annual
Economic Report; The Community
Budget; Eurobarometer; Infeuro
newsletter; europa.eu.int*
European Parliament, *Session News*
Official Journals of the European
Communities, *Court of Auditors
Reports*
Primark Datastream